Educational Records

Educational Records

A Practical Guide for Legal Compliance

Daniel R. Murphy and
Mike L. Dishman

ROWMAN & LITTLEFIELD EDUCATION

A division of

ROWMAN & LITTLEFIELD PUBLISHERS, INC.
Lanham • New York • Toronto • Plymouth, UK

Published by Rowman & Littlefield Education
A division of Rowman & Littlefield Publishers, Inc.
A wholly owned subsidiary of The Rowman & Littlefield Publishing Group, Inc.
4501 Forbes Boulevard, Suite 200, Lanham, Maryland 20706
http://www.rowmaneducation.com

Estover Road,
Plymouth PL6 7PY
United Kingdom

British Library Cataloguing in Publication Information Available

Library of Congress Cataloging-in-Publication Data

Murphy, Daniel R., 1967–
Educational records : a practical guide for legal compliance / Daniel R. Murphy and Mike L. Dishman.
p. cm.
Includes index.
ISBN 978-1-60709-571-2 (cloth : alk. paper) — ISBN 978-1-60709-572-9 (pbk. : alk. paper) — ISBN 978-1-60709-573-6 (electronic)
1. Student records—Law and legislation—United States. 2. Schools—Records and correspondence—Law and legislation—United States. I. Dishman, Mike L. II. Title.
KF4156.5.M87 2010
344.73'079—dc22 2009031960

Printed in the United States of America

∞™ The paper used in this publication meets the minimum requirements of American National Standard for Information Sciences—Permanence of Paper for Printed Library Materials, ANSI/NISO Z39.48-1992.

Table of Contents

Acknowledgments

The authors wish to thank Ms. Ellen Campbell and Ms. Ingrid Brault of the Family Policy Compliance Office for their assistance in tracking down various opinion letters of that Office that were most helpful in identifying and understanding the Department of Education's position on various questions arising under FERPA and/or the PPRA. Their timely and comprehensive responses to our frequent inquiries were a challenge to our own endeavors to continue our work and research. Of course, the opinions and conclusions expressed herein are entirely those of the authors, and in no way reflect the official or unofficial conclusions of Ms. Campbell, Ms. Brault, the Family Policy Compliance Office, or the Department of Education.

The authors also wish to thank Dr. Jeffery C. Welch for his thoughtful review of Chapter II, and Ms. Deborah Collier for her careful analysis of Chapter IX. In both cases, their notes, observations, and further questions contributed greatly to the clarity and accessibility of the final publication. We also express our appreciation to Ms. Deborah Golymbieski for her contributions to the examination of a host of the legal issues addressed in Chapter VIII. And this publication benefitted greatly from Dr. Alice Murphy's review of Chapter VIII, and her practical expertise in this most challenging of areas. In regards to all of these chapters, of course, all remaining shortcomings are entirely the responsibility of the authors.

As always, we so thoroughly appreciate the support, encouragement, and efforts of the editorial team at Rowman & Littlefield Publishing Group—Dr. Tom Koerner, Maera Stratton, and Melissa McNitt. We have no doubt that without their assistance this publication would never have evolved beyond several dozen power point slides and many pages of lecture notes. Finally and most importantly, the authors express their deepest appreciation to Alice and Traci, whose patience and understanding ultimately made this work possible.

Chapter 1

Introduction

On Thursday, January 15, 2009, U.S. Airways Pilot Chesley B. "Sully" Sullenberger III saved the lives of 155 passengers and crew by landing his crippled jet in the Hudson River. After the incident, Sullenberger went into seclusion in his home, while the national media scrambled to find information on Sullenberger. The following day, Fox News ran a story entitled, "Hero Pilot's Records, IQ Scores Released by School District in 'Accident.'"[2] In attempting to locate information on Sullenberger, a Fox News producer contacted Denison High School—Sullenberger's alma mater—requesting a copy of his school photographs. Unfortunately, a copy of Sullenberger's transcript—to which the photograph was attached—was also released to the press. As Fox—now detailing the "illegal"[3] release of school records as an independent story—observed, "[Sullenberger's] official records were never meant to be released, and the Denison School District is now scrambling to recover the confidential documents that brought the private pilot even more into the public eye." The school's principal, Mr. Cavin Boettger, promised to investigate the matter; however, as he quickly learned, it is as equally difficult to retrieve confidential information inadvertently released to the national media as it is to proverbially un-ring a bell. . . .[1]

The story of Denison High School's inadvertent release of Sullenberger's student records—and subsequent violation of federal laws designed to protect the privacy of student records—is hardly unique. Many current and former school principals reading this may shudder at the probable result of a national news channel contacting their school's secretary and asking for records on one of their former students who has been catapulted into the national spotlight because of a heroic act. Violations of the Family Educational Rights and Privacy Act of 1974 (commonly known as "FERPA)—the omnibus federal law governing the privacy of student records—are a regular and ongoing occurrence in schools. While these routine violations seldom make the national news, they frequently do result in complaints to both the United States Department of Education and state agencies governing educator certification, creating tremendous political headaches for school administrators and policy-makers.

Yet, it is difficult for schools not to violate FERPA. Perhaps no federal laws so touch the lives of all students as those protecting the privacy of their educational records. Approximately 77 million students are enrolled in America's public and private schools. These students represent arguably the largest and most diverse group of learners in the history of the human race and are educated in schools geographically spanning a third of the globe. However, they are all—from pre-kindergarten to post-doctoral students—covered by federal laws protecting the privacy of educational records and the student information contained therein.

While most educators reading this book will be familiar with FERPA, numerous other federal and state education laws directly and indirectly protect the privacy of students' records. As these laws can be violated by something as simple as two (2) teachers carrying on an inappropriate conversation in a public place regarding information contained in a student's educational record, complying with these laws is a daily and ongoing challenge for schools.

The purpose of this Introduction is to provide an overview of FERPA and other federal laws addressing student records, giving the reader a "forest" overview before looking at the individual "trees" in each chapter. Virtually all of the questions posed and answered in very summary form in this Introduction will be explored in significant detail in the following chapters.

What is the Family Educational Rights and Privacy Act?

The Family Educational Rights and Privacy Act ("FERPA") is a federal law enacted in 1974, governing the retention and dissemination of educational records. FERPA has three primary purposes:

- To provide parents or eligible students with the right to inspect and review educational records;
- To permit parents or eligible students to amend educational records; and
- To ensure that personally identifiable information about students will not be disclosed from educational records except as permitted by law.

While other federal laws also address educational records, FERPA is, was, and remains the primary federal law governing educational records and, as such, is the focus of this book. However, other federal laws governing educational records (and discussed in less detail) include:

- The Protection of Pupil Rights Amendment ("PPRA")
- The National School Lunch Act
- The Americans with Disabilities Act
- The Individuals with Disabilities Education Act.

Which Federal Laws Most Directly Affect Student Educational Records?

FERPA and PPRA are the two (2) primary federal laws governing the retention, inspection, and dissemination of educational records. Collectively, FERPA and PPRA regulate:

- The rights of parents or eligible students to review and seek to amend educational records retained by local educational agencies or those acting on their behalf;
- Procedures under which records are stored, communicated, released, and retained; and,
- The rights of parents to review, and in some cases, consent for their child's participation in certain surveys, analyses, or evaluations administered by or on behalf of a school or school district.

What About the Educational Records of Students with Disabilities?

The Individuals with Disabilities Education Act ("IDEA") contains its own regulations relating to the preservation and dissemination of educational records; however, in many cases, these protections overlap with FERPA. There are some differences (such as the amount of time the school district has to provide records after a parental request). These distinctions are detailed more thoroughly in Chapter VIII, which specifically addresses the educational records rights of students with disabilities.

To What Schools Does FERPA Apply?

FERPA applies to all public primary, secondary, and post-secondary institutions, as well as private schools that directly or indirectly receive federal funds. The scope of FERPA is so broad that it is very difficult to picture a school to which FERPA does not apply.

To What Records Does FERPA Apply?

FERPA protects "educational records," which have an extremely broad definition. Indeed, it would be easier to identify which records are not educational records under FERPA. FERPA defines an educational record as information:

- Directly related to a student that is recorded in any way, including handwriting, print, electronically, video or audio tape, film, microfilm, or microfiche; and is
- Maintained by an educational agency or institution, or parties acting for the agency or institution.

This sweeping definition seemingly incorporates everything from student transcripts to individual student tests retained by a teacher in anticipation of parent/teacher conferences. However, there are certain categories of student records that are expressly not included in FERPA. These include:

- Student work samples that are not graded or recorded;
- Personal notes of teachers and other school officials that are intended for personal use only, and are only made available to someone acting as a "substitute" for that educator (the "sole use" exception);
- Employment records of students who are employed at the school or college (this does not include employment records created or maintained as any part of a course for which the student receives credit);
- Records created by law enforcement units of a school or college that are intended solely for law enforcement purposes; and
- Certain information obtained about students after they are no longer enrolled.

For further information on each of these exceptions, please see Chapters IV and VI.

Why Should Educators Care About What Constitutes an Educational Record?

Schools generally—and educators specifically—should care a great deal whether student information constitutes an educational record. First, if information is not an educational record nor contained in an educational record, FERPA does not apply—for good or bad. In our experience, if FERPA does not apply to a record, it may be much more attainable by the press—or anyone else—under a state's open records laws as it is not a record that the federal government requires be kept confidential. Second, if information on a student is an educational record, FERPA is very specific about how that information must be kept and to whom it may be disclosed. Finally, if a record is an educational record under FERPA, parents have an absolute right to inspect it—and consider whether you have seen educators' communications that you (or they) would very much not want parents to see.

Would an Email Between Two Teachers be an Educational Record?

The answer to this is the book's first unequivocal "it depends." Under FERPA, it matters less what something is called than what it actually does. If an email contains personally identifiable information about an individual student AND is maintained by the school, it is probably an educational record. However, please see Chapter VII for a much more involved discussion of when an email may be an educational record.

Can Educators be Personally Sued for Violating FERPA?

Not under FERPA. FERPA generally prohibits institutions—which are the primary custodians for student records—from disclosing those records. Should an institution have a "pattern or practice" of disclosing student records in violation of FERPA, the institution may lose federal educational funds. Should an individual violate FERPA, the law leaves appropriate enforcement up to the individual's employer—or if he or she is a certificated educator, the state's educational ethics enforcement agency.

If I Already Know About FERPA, Why Do I Need to Read This Book?

First, very few people truly know everything there is to know about FERPA. The authors of this book are both practicing school attorneys with many years of experience, and in the process of writing this book, they discovered a great deal about FERPA! Second, in December 2008, the United States Department of Education enacted the most significant regulatory changes to FERPA since 1974, examining and effectively re-writing a number of the law's requirements, and "updating" the law to address the challenges of 21st century schools (such as maintaining and communicating records electronically, and addressing the challenges of an increasingly diverse and fractured family).

When Can a School Disclose an Educational Record?

FERPA generally prohibits schools from disclosing personally identifiable information from a student's educational record without the express authorization of the student's parent or guardian or, if the student is eighteen or in a post-secondary institution, the student himself or herself. Naturally, this is subject to numerous exceptions, including permitting school officials with a "legitimate educational interest" to access records without prior permission, and the "directory information" exception, which allows schools to print yearbooks and athletic programs.

What is Directory Information?

When FERPA was enacted in 1974, it included an exception permitting schools to designate certain types of information as "directory" and disclose this information without the express authorization of parents or eligible students. This information includes, but is not limited to, the student's name, class rank, address, telephone number, photograph, extracurricular activities, honors, and height and weight (if a member of an athletic team).

The designation of directory information by a school is entirely voluntary, and a school does not have to consider any information directory. However, if a school wishes to use the directory information exception, it must first notify parents or eligible students of its directory information policy and provide them an opportunity to "opt out," or notify the school that they do not want their student's directory information disclosed.

What is the "Legitimate Educational Interest" Exception?

The legitimate educational interest exception (or "LEI") permits school officials to access a student's personally identifiable information in an educational record without the advance permission of the student's parent or guardian (or an eligible student). LEI requires school officials wishing to inspect records have a legitimate educational interest in so doing—essentially, the official's examination of the record must be necessitated by some task he or she is required by his or her job to perform for the student or on his or her behalf (such as a school counselor examining a student's disciplinary history as part of providing counseling services). It does not include idle curiosity or examinations for the teacher's benefit (such as pulling a student's disciplinary record as part of a personnel hearing on whether a teacher's discipline of the student was excessive).

Do Other Exceptions Permit Disclosure or Inspection of a Student's Educational Records Without Parental Consent?

Absolutely. FERPA contains numerous exceptions permitting school officials to inspect and use student records without a parent or eligible student's prior permission. These may be found in Chapter IV (internal disclosures without prior permission) and Chapter VI (external disclosure without prior permission).

What Should Teachers and School Staff Know About Educational Records Laws?

It has been our experience that most FERPA, PPRA, and IDEA records violations stem purely from ignorance of the law and its requirements. FERPA, PPRA, and IDEA are federal laws, and educators violating them—whether intentionally or through ignorance—may face significant professional consequences. While teachers and other school staff cannot be held personally liable for violating FERPA or PPRA (and depending upon the federal circuit, IDEA), they can face significant sanction from their professional licensure body (their state office of teacher certification) and/or their employer. Additionally, many states have state laws relating to the privacy and/or dissemination of student records, and a violation of one of these laws may carry the consequence of personal liability (such as an educator being sued for violating a student's "right to privacy"). Regardless, it is important—at a minimum—that educators and other individuals working with educational records receive training on the requirements of federal law, any state laws relating to the same, and district and school policy and practice.

If a Child is in an Accident, Can We Release Records to Emergency Medical Services (EMS) Without the Parents' Consent?

Yes. In a "health or safety emergency" (another of FERPA's exceptions permitting disclosure without prior parental consent), a student's educational records may be released without prior authorization.

Was the "Health or Safety Emergency" Exception Substantially Amended Under the December 2008 Regulatory Changes?

Yes. The authority of school officials to determine the existence of a health or safety emergency necessitating the unauthorized release of a student's records was significantly expanded in the December 2008 regulatory changes. Previously, this standard was "strictly construed," with the Department of Education taking a very narrow interpretation of the exception; however, after December 2008, school officials were given much more discretion to determine whether a health or safety emergency requires the release of student records to an individual or agency without the prior approval of the student's parents (or an eligible student).

Does the United States Freedom of Information Act ("FOIA") Apply to Student Records?

Generally, no. FOIA applies to records collected by the United States government, whereas FERPA governs the dissemination of educational records typically created and maintained by the states. Regardless, many states have "state-FOIA" laws (often called "open records" or "sunshine" laws). These laws may be applicable to all records created or retained by state agencies (such as public school districts); however, many of these laws contain exceptions forbidding disclosure of records required to be kept confidential by federal law (such as FERPA). Prior to disclosing educational records pursuant to a "state FOIA" request, educators may wish to check with their school district's legal counsel as to the parameters of their state's open records law.

What Notice Must Schools Provide Parents or Eligible Students of Their FERPA Rights?

FERPA requires schools and colleges to annually provide parents and eligible students with effective notice of their rights under FERPA. These include:

- The right to inspect and review their student's record;
- The right to seek amendment of the record if they believe information to be inaccurate, misleading, or otherwise in violation of their child's rights;
- Their right to consent to disclosures of personally identifiable information, with certain exceptions authorized by FERPA; and
- Their right to file a complaint with the United States Department of Education if they believe their student's FERPA rights are being violated.

Schools must provide the annual FERPA notice in a manner that "effectively informs" parent or eligible students who have a disability (such as blindness) or whose home language is other than English.

What Rights do Parents or Eligible Students have to Inspect or Challenge Educational Records?

FERPA's inspection provisions primarily relate to ensuring the accuracy or completeness of a student's educational records. Parents or eligible students have a right to inspect educational records within forty-five (45) days of a request to do so. Save in exceptional circumstances, this is a right to inspect—parents have no right under FERPA to receive copies of their child's educational records (should a school choose to provide them, it can require a "reasonable fee" for their duplication—subject, naturally, to an exception detailed further in this book).

Importantly, FERPA does not give students or parents the right to challenge the substance of individual assignments or teacher grades—the "inspection" and "challenge" rights are limited primarily to grade accuracy or completeness. An excellent example of a FERPA challenge would be a school mis-recording the number of days a student was out in a particular year, or recording the incorrect semester grade on the student's transcript.

Does FERPA Address Record Access by Non-Custodial Parents?

Yes. FERPA allows either parent the right to review educational records. The only way this right can be revoked is through a court order specifically terminating the right to educational records—or a complete termination of parental rights. Schools can—and should—require parents to submit documentation verifying their relationship to a child prior to releasing records.

What About Step or Foster Parents?

FERPA contains a very expansive definition of a parent. Under FERPA, a parent can be an adoptive or natural parent, non-custodial or foster parent, a legal guardian, or an individual acting in the place of a parent. With the expansion of the traditional concept of the American family, schools are seeing many students living with grandparents or aunts and uncles, and treating these individuals' homes as the student's place of residence. In the absence of a natural parent, it would be difficult for a school to argue that it considers grandmother's home to be the student's place of residence and not treat the grandmother as standing in the place of the parent for the purposes of FERPA.

Can a Parent Waive a Student's FERPA Rights?

Yes—unless the student is eighteen years of age or older, or otherwise qualifies as an "eligible student" to whom FERPA rights have transferred. However, FERPA generally considers parents to be the repository of a student's rights, and parents can authorize the dissemination of a student's educational records to whomever they please.

CONCLUSION

As you can see from this summary, FERPA (and the accompanying other laws addressing educational records) is not simple, straightforward or clear—it is, however, a federal law with which educators and educational institutions are required to comply. Hopefully, the following pages will do a great deal to "de-mystify" FERPA and answer questions you may have about the law.

ENDNOTE

1. Fox News "Hero Pilot's Records, IQ Scores Released by School District in 'Accident.'" Downloaded from www.foxnews.com/printer_friendly_ story/0,3544,380250,00.html on January 16, 2009.

Chapter 2

Educational Records: Identification, Maintenance, and Disclosure

This Chapter discusses some of the most fundamental concepts under the Family Educational Rights and Privacy Act—including perhaps most significantly the very definition of an educational record itself. In addition to the language from the Act and the regulations defining those records subject to FERPA, this is also the area of the law where we see the most sweeping impact of the Supreme Court's monumental decision in *Owasso v. Falvo*, where the Court held that peer-graded student classroom work was not an educational record for purposes of FERPA. This Chapter also discusses those records which Congress and the Department specifically contemplated and excluded from the definition of educational records, as well as the current status of the rules relating to maintaining records (including retention, security, and record destruction issues), as well as the concept of disclosing information from such records—including the proper execution of the release in order to do so.

EDUCATIONAL RECORDS—WHAT ARE THEY?

What is the definition of a record under FERPA?

Under FERPA, the definition of a "record" is exceptionally broad, and essentially incorporates anything that an educational institution records in any way." FERPA specifically defines a record to include "any information" that is "recorded in any way," including, but not limited to, "handwriting, print, computer media, video or audio tape, film, microfilm, and microfiche." However, FERPA does not protect *all* records—just certain *educational* records (as will be explained further below).[1]

What is the definition of an educational record under FERPA?

An educational record is defined as "those records that are (1) directly related to a student; and (2) maintained by an educational agency or institution or by a party acting for the agency or institution."[2] Again, while this is an exceptionally broad definition that would seemingly encompass all information produced by or about a student, the Department has stated, for example, that this term "does not include student work that is created, used, or kept in the classroom and does not become a part of the student's institutional record."[3]

An Example—Tessie Teacher routinely posts examples of her second-grade students' work in the hallway outside her classroom door. The best examples may have grades or other evaluations of the student's work on them, such as, "Best in class!" Under the Department's definition and the United States Supreme Court's decision in *Owasso,* this student work would fall within that work "created, used, or kept in the classroom" which is not a part of the student's institutional record and therefore not confidential under FERPA.

Practice Pointer—The issue of whether and when student grades on individual pieces of academic work is an educational record is a problematic and may be influenced by a number of variables, including the district's use of technology to communicate with parents. For example, if the district establishes a parent portal where the student's grade on every piece of class work may be viewed by the parent, and even though the pieces of classroom work involved may be identical to the graded assignments in *Owasso*, it is arguable that the district has now established precisely the centralized database of information about the student which the Court referred to in the case.

Who is a student for purposes of FERPA?

Under FERPA, a student is defined as "any individual who is or has been in attendance at an educational agency or institution and regarding whom the agency or institution maintains education records."[4]

An Example—Doug the diligent has applied for admission to the university. In connection with his application, Doug solicits and has forwarded to the university several letters of recommendation. While waiting on his application, Doug also receives permission to audit a university class. Ultimately, however, Doug is denied admission to the university. When Doug asks to inspect his educational records, the university advises Doug that since he was never accepted for admission into the university, he does not have FERPA rights to access information related to his rejection.[5]

Does FERPA's definition of an educational record mean that any record which includes a student's name falls within FERPA?

No, but this is often a point of great difficulty and confusion. For example, in one case the college newspaper sought copies of the parking tickets of student-athletes, and the College argued that the tickets (which included the student's names) were educational records under FERPA and could not be disclosed. The court, however, rejected this argument, noting instead that FERPA is more properly concerned with records "relating to individual student academic performance, financial aid, or scholastic probation."[6]

What about video records, such as the tapes from school bus or school hallway surveillance cameras, and which include the images of students—are these educational records under FERPA?

This is a very controversial (and confusing) issue.[7] The current position of the Department appears to be that videotapes are educational records of individual students to the extent they capture or contain information used to make educational decisions about a student.[8] For example, a videotape of two students engaged in a fight and which is used in part to make disciplinary determinations about the students would be considered to be an educational record of each of these two students. However, as to other students who are captured in the "background" of such a tape, but who in no way have any educational decisions made about them based upon the tape, the tape would not constitute an educational record.

An Example—Roger and Willie, two eleventh graders, get into a fight on a school bus. The bus video camera captures the fight, and Principal Paul wants to use the video as evidence at both students' long-term suspension hearings. In making his decision to do so, Paul has "converted" the videotape into an educational record for Roger and Willie; however, as to the other fifty (50) students on the bus who are not facing disciplinary action, the videotape would not be an educational record.

Practice Pointer—The distinction that the Department makes as to when videotapes are "educational records" appears to be a compromise between protecting the educational privacy of students and permitting school officials necessary latitude to fulfill their daily disciplinary responsibilities. Educators know that the videotape is likely to contain information about the allegedly uninvolved students (it is doubtful that they were sitting there quietly watching the fight); however, if the videotape was an "educational record" for all students shown on the video, it would be challenging for Principal Paul to obtain a parental release from each and every parent prior to using the videotape in Roger and Willie's disciplinary hearings. Consequently, the Department's "compromise" position—the videotape is only an educational record if educational or disciplinary decisions are made based on it—is a workable solution to a challenging problem.

Bonus Practice Pointer—In disputed cases concerning whether video records are educational records subject to FERPA, it may well be relevant to consider how these records are treated under the district's record retention policy. For instance, historically many school video records have been recorded over and "recycled" within a matter of days in the absence of any compelling reason to retain the individual tape. In such instances, it may be possible to argue that while the tape was an educational record for a period of time, the record was no longer maintained and subsequently destroyed in accordance with the district's record retention policy.[9] The maintenance of this record, after all, is at the very heart of the definition of an educational record discussed above.

What about video tape records of a classroom—are these educational records, and if so, who may be permitted to inspect them?

In an interesting case from Kentucky, the court held that videotapes made of a teacher's classroom after students complained about her where in fact educational records, but that the teacher has a legitimate educational interest in reviewing these records over the objection of the school district.[10] In that case, the court seemed particularly impressed by the fact that the teacher was present during the creation of the tape itself, so it was difficult to comprehend that the information on the tape was somehow confidential as to the teacher. This may an important distinction when addressing requests to review video tapes by members of the public or press, and especially when the tape is not considered to be an educational record.

Are there specific records that are excluded from the definition of educational records under FERPA?

Yes. The regulations specifically exclude six (6) categories of records from the definition of an educational record. These categories are "sole possession records," records of a law enforcement unit, records relating to employees of an educational agency, professional treatment records of students 18 years old or older (or who are under eighteen, but attending a postsecondary institution), records that contain information about an individual after she or he is no longer a student—commonly known as the "alumni exception" and "grades on peer-graded paper before they are collected and recorded by a teacher."[11] Each of these is discussed further below.

THE SOLE POSSESSION EXCEPTION

What exactly is a sole possession record?

A sole possession record is defined as a record "kept in the sole possession of the maker . . . used only as a personal memory aid, and . . . not accessible or revealed to any other person except a temporary substitute for the maker of the record."[12]

What is the purpose of the sole possession record exception?

In the words of the Department, "the main purpose of this exception is to allow school officials to keep personal notes private. For example, a teacher or counselor who observes a student and takes a note to remind him or herself of the student's behavior has created a sole possession record, so long as he or she does not share the note with anyone else."[13]

Does this mean that any record about a student which is created and used by one person, and never shared with anyone else, automatically qualifies under this exception?

No. A sole possession record must satisfy both the purpose and usage aspects of this definition, which means they must be used "as a personal memory aid," as well as the physical custody element (creation and maintenance by one person). The classic example of such records are the notes of a school counselor who has an ongoing counseling relationship with a student and who consequently takes and maintains notes so that she or he may meet with the student on multiple occasions.

Do sole possession records lose their status if they are shared with anyone other than a "temporary substitute for the maker"?

Yes. The definition of a sole possession record requires the record satisfy each of three elements of this definition (kept in the sole possession of the maker, used only as a personal memory aid, and not accessible or revealed to anyone other than a temporary substitute). Records which may have at one time fallen within this definition (and thus outside the definition of an educational record under FERPA) lose their status as sole possession records if they are shared with "any other person." Notably, this can even include sharing the record with the parent of the child.[14]

An Example—Ms. Jones maintains an informal "behavior inventory" of students in her class, recording what she considers to be "minor" infractions unworthy of a trip to the office. If they reach a certain level of frequency, she calls parents in for a conference to discuss the behavior. Provided Ms. Jones does not share this information with anyone else, this "inventory" may initially constitute a "sole use" record. However, if Ms. Jones shows the records or discloses their contents to parents when they come in to discuss their student's behavior, the record ceases to be a "sole use" memory aid and is likely to be considered an educational record subject to FERPA.

Practice Pointer—The "sole use" exception is a bit of an enigma in FERPA. In *Owasso,* the United States Supreme Court implied that FERPA-protected records were kept in a "central repository," which of course would not be where the vast majority of teachers' notes are maintained—regardless of whether they were excluded under the "sole use" concept. However, the existence of the "sole use" exception—protecting teachers' "private" notes only if they remain private—implies that records that are not kept private might be open to access and inspection under FERPA, even if these records are not otherwise maintained in the central repository referred to by the Court. Given this seeming dichotomy, schools taking a conservative approach should instruct teachers that the best method to protect the privacy of their personal notes is to vigorously comply with the "sole use" exception's technical requirements.

May sole possession records be subpoenaed by parents or other parties involved in litigation?

Absolutely. The fact that a counselor's personal notes, for example, may not qualify as educational records only means that the parents and/or eligible student do not enjoy FERPA rights (including access rights) in connection with such records. However, these notes would be subject to subpoena by any party able to demonstrate that such records fell within the scope of discoverable evidence under the relevant state or federal law. (For a discussion of the district's obligations to notify parents and eligible students when the student's records are subpoenaed, please see Chapter VI).

An Example—Ms. Green maintains a "sole use" journal in which she records her reflections on meetings with parents. Some of the characterizations of parents are less than charitable. Prior to a due process hearing for one of her students, she receives a subpoena for "any and all records relating to" the student in question. She does not want to disclose her journal, justifiably afraid that it contains embarrassing information. While the school district's attorney might make a valiant effort to prevent it, it is likely that Ms. Green's journal—and certainly the parts of it relating to the student in question—will end up in the hands of the parents of that student.

LAW ENFORCEMENT UNIT RECORDS

What is a law enforcement unit (or "LEU")?

A law enforcement unit can be "any individual, office, department, division, or other component of an educational agency or institution, such as a unit of commissioned police officers or non-commissioned security guards," that is officially authorized or designated by that agency to either enforce local, state, or federal law, refer individuals or organizations to local, state, or federal authorities for the purpose of enforcing these laws, or which has been designated to maintain the "physical security and safety" of the district.[15]

What are law enforcement unit records, and are they excluded from the definition of educational records?

Yes. As noted above, law enforcement unit records are excluded from the definition of "educational records" *if* they are used for law enforcement purposes (the distinction between "educational records" and "law enforcement unit records" will be explained further below). "Law enforcement unit records" are "records, files, documents, and other materials that are (1) created by a law enforcement unit, (2) created for a law enforcement purpose and (3) maintained by a law enforcement unit."[16]

Does the definition of law enforcement unit apply only to commissioned or certified law enforcement officers?

No. The definition of a "law enforcement unit" was specifically expanded to include security guards in addition to commissioned officers, and also to make clear that such a department may qualify even if it also serves to enforce the student code of conduct.[17]

Can a law enforcement unit be a single officer or individual?

Yes. FERPA does not require the LEU to be a traditional department of several individuals in the sense that many districts traditionally view such departments. The regulatory language plainly allows for the designation of an "individual" as the LEU.[18]

Does FERPA allow an educational agency to designate a municipal or county police officer hired by the institution as the LEU?

Yes. In many counties, public school districts and universities contract with local police departments to provide school-site police as "school resource officers" or create "campus police precincts." While these officers are police officers, they are paid for by the educational institution—either directly (as employees) or indirectly (through grants and other school funds). The Department's interpretation of the term LEU includes these units, even though they may not be school district or university employees.[19]

Is the district required to designate the members of a LEU as "school officials" with "a legitimate educational interest" in their annual FERPA notice?

Yes, if the institution wants to take advantage of the "legitimate educational interest" exception (discussed further in Chapter IV). The Department has specifically stated that if an institution wishes to take advantage of this exception (permitting LEUs to access student records without prior parental permission), and then "the officials of that unit must be designated under the school's FERPA policy as school officials with a legitimate educational interest."[20]

Practice Pointer—The "other school officials with a legitimate educational interest" exception (or "LEI") is one of the broadest grants of authority given to educational institutions to access student records without prior parent or eligible student permission. As might be predicted from the name, it essentially requires the "school official" to have a "legitimate educational interest" necessitating access to a student's record without prior permission. However, to protect students, LEI requires institutions to provide parents and eligible students with the criteria on which it will base determinations as to who is an "other school official" and what constitutes a "legitimate educational interest." Assuming that an institution chooses to do so, this designation places a powerful tool in the hands of its LEU.

An Example—Sherry is a school resource officer ("SRO") employed by City County School District, a school that designates SROs as falling within the LEI exception. Pam Principal receives a report from a student that Tyler Trouble, a special education student with a history of anti-social behavior, is planning an "attack" on the school. While Pam needs to gather additional information permitting her to make a determination as to whether this is a "true" threat or simply hyperbole, she calls Sherry into her office and shares the information with her, along with portions of Tyler's educational records she deems appropriate. Had City County not included SROs in its definition of "other school officials," Pam would have had to find another exception under which she could share this information with Sherry—virtually all of which have much stricter requirements than LEI.

Do all records created or maintained by a law enforcement unit qualify for this exception?

No. This exception does not apply to records created by the LEU "exclusively for a non-law enforcement purpose," (such as a record created and maintained only for purposes of school disciplinary action), nor does this exception apply to records initially created for a law enforcement purpose, but which are maintained by some other component (other than the LEU) of the institution.[21]

An Example—City College's administration suspects Mark, a senior, of bringing intoxicating beverages into his dormitory. Dean Doug asks the CCPD to investigate the matter. CCPD notes that the possession of intoxicating beverages in a dormitory is not a crime (although it is a violation of the College's rules). At the conclusion of the investigation, CCPD turns over its findings to the College's judicial panel for possible prosecution for violating the College's conduct rules. Although these records were created by the College's LEU, they were intended for a "non-law enforcement purpose," and as they contain personally identifiable information about Mark and are maintained by the college, they are educational records under FERPA.

What if the law enforcement unit creates an incident report for a law enforcement purpose, but then shares a copy with educational administrators?

The copy maintained by the principal is an education record subject to FERPA, but the original document created and maintained by the law enforcement unit is not an education record.[22]

An Example—In our scenario above, assume that possession of intoxicating beverages in a dormitory is a crime as well as a rule violation. Further, assume that after CCPD turns over its initial evidence to the College's judicial panel, it conducts further investigations of the allegations. While the *copy* of the report given to the judicial panel would be an educational record, both the CCPD's initial and subsequent investigatory records would not constitute educational records under FERPA.

What about student witness statements—are they education records or law enforcement records?

This depends on the party who took the statement, the purpose for which they were created and who is maintaining the statements.[23] For example, assume an assistant principal takes the statements of several students in connection with her investigation of an act of vandalism in the school bathroom. As vandalizing school property is a violation of the code of conduct, the A.P. intends to use the statements to enforce discipline against the student in a school disciplinary proceeding, and until the time of the hearing, she maintains these statements in her office. In this scenario, the statements are educational records. However, if the school police officer takes these same statements in connection with his investigation into the possible crime of vandalizing public property, keeping the statements in his possession until he determines whether he has sufficient evidence to pursue criminal charges, these statements are law enforcement records and not educational records under FERPA.[24]

What if the school police officer is investigating both the school code of conduct violation and a criminal matter of (for example, vandalizing public property), and creates and uses these statements in connection with both this school purpose as well as the law enforcement purpose?

In this case, the records are created for the "dual purpose" of law enforcement and a non-law enforcement purpose, resulting in their classification as law enforcement records. Only records created by a law enforcement unit *exclusively* for a *non-law enforcement purpose* become educational records.

Does FERPA apply to records created by local police or outside agencies who interview students at school?

FERPA does not generally apply to the interview of students at school by local police or outside agencies; however, if records of these interviews, notes or copies of any of those records are maintained by school officials (or anyone acting for the educational agency), then these documents may constitute educational records under FERPA.[25]

Practice Pointer—A number of states and educational institutions have laws and policies governing law enforcement interview of students, or interviews for the "dual" purpose of law and disciplinary rule enforcement. Although not a FERPA issue, educational institutions are advised to research state and local policies or protocols which may govern the contact and interview of students at school by outside entities, such as local law enforcement or family and children services.

When student witness statements are taken and maintained by a school official, are they educational records of the students who gave them, the student(s) described or identified in the statements, or both?

These statements are an educational record of both the student who is described or identified in the record as well as the student who produced the statement. FPCO has taken the position that an educational institution must redact the name and/or signature of the student who produced the statement before disclosing the document to the parents or attorney for the student accused of misconduct.[26] However, to the extent a statement may describe the conduct of behavior of two more students together and cannot be redacted without destroying the meaning of the statement, the parents of both (or all) students involved would have the right to review the unredacted statement.

For example—Assistant principal Alan collects and maintains the following statement—"John grabbed Michael's backpack and hit him over the head with it." In this case, the parents of both John and Michael would have the right to inspect this statement. However, if the statement also included other information about Michael (for example, that Michael also kicked Sally in the stomach), then John's parents would not have the right to inspect this unrelated reference to Michael's misconduct contained in the same record.[27]

If the institution shares educational records and personally identifiable information with a law enforcement unit, do these records become law enforcement records?

No. These records were created by the educational institution, not the LEU, and they do not lose their status as educational records merely because (or while) they are in the possession of the LEU.[28] The LEU must treat the records as educational records (including limitations on non-disclosure or re-disclosure), and not "traditional" law enforcement unit records.

Are the records of disciplinary proceedings involving students considered educational records?

Yes. The Department and a number of courts have held that the records of disciplinary action taken against individual students are educational records, resulting in these records being protected by FERPA's confidentiality requirement.[29]

However, as noted below, FERPA contains several exceptions permitting for limited disclosure of these records without parent or eligible student consent.

Is there an exception for sharing the result of disciplinary hearings with the victims of an offense?

At the higher education level, there certainly is an exception which permits (but does not require) the disclosure of the result of the disciplinary proceeding to the *victim* of a crime of violence. There is no comparable statutory or regulatory exception in the K–12 area, even at the higher education level; disclosure is permissible *only* to the victim of the crime itself.[30] However, in at least one case, a federal court found that a "contemporaneous disclosure to the parents of a victimized child of the results of any investigation and resulting disciplinary action taken against an alleged child perpetrator does not constitute a release of an 'educational record' within the meaning of" FERPA.[31]

Are there any distinctions between the rules governing disclosures of disciplinary proceedings at the victims at the P-12 and higher education level?

Yes. Under one provision, an institution may disclose to an alleged victim the result of a disciplinary proceeding, including both cases where a violation was and was not found to have been committed. In these cases, the alleged victim is subject to the re-disclosure rules under FERPA (which means they may not re-disclose information without consent). However, a second provision allows for the disclosure of the final results of disciplinary proceedings whenever a student is an alleged perpetrator of a crime of violence or non-forcible sex offense, and the institution determines the student has actually committed a violation of its rules or policies. In this second instance, the disclosure is not limited to the victim of the offense—although neither the victim nor any witness may be identified without their consent—and the re-disclosure rules do not apply.[32] See Chapter VI for a further discussion of both of these provisions.

Practice Pointer—In contrast to individual student disciplinary proceedings, a number of courts have held that campus police department incident reports are not educational records subject to FERPA. In some cases, these reports may fall within the exception for law enforcement unit records (and thus outside of FERPA), while in others, the court has more broadly found that such records are not the type of records contemplated by FERPA in the first instance.[33]

What about evidence from a P-12 student's disciplinary proceeding—is this considered an educational record under FERPA?

In one case involving a student charged with creating a "hit list," the court found no merit to the student's subsequent complaint that FERPA was violated when students who were on the list were notified by school officials. In addition to the fact that the list was written on the cover of a textbook "open for public inspection" (such that the student had no expectation of privacy in the hit list), the court further found that a student-created "hit list" is simply not an education record at all.[34]

Does the law enforcement unit exception allow an institution to share any information from a student's educational records with local police or prosecutors?

Generally, no. Typically, in order to permit the disclosure of educational records, an institution must be responding to a court order or subpoena.[35] However, if the disclosure is necessary to prevent a "health or safety emergency" (further defined in Chapter VI), the disclosure may occur without consent. Of course, if the records concerned are not educational records (such as the "hit list" noted above), then the LEU may share these records with local police as FERPA confidentiality requirements do not apply to non-educational records.

EMPLOYEE-STUDENT RECORDS

What records are covered by the exception for employees of an educational agency?

In order for a record to fall within this exclusion, the records must relate to the individual "exclusively" in his or her capacity as an employee, be unavailable to use for any other purpose, and must be created and maintained during the normal course of business.[36]

An Example—Todd is an assistant registrar employed by City County College ("CCC"). After six months in his position, he is eligible for tuition waivers, and he begins to take classes toward a bachelor's degree in political science. City County receives a request under its State open records act for the employment records of all City County's two thousand (2,000) employees. While the College must exclude Todd's transcripts and other educational records from this request, FERPA does not shield employment records, and CCC must disclose his employment records to the extent permitted by State law.

Are records relating to tuition waivers provided to employees and children of employees considered educational records or employment records?

Under FERPA's definition of "employment records," the record must both relate exclusively to the employee in his or her status as an employee, and be "unavailable" for any other purpose. It is unlikely that the method by which a student—whether an employee/student or the child of an employee—pays for his or her education "exclusively" relates to that individual's status as an employee. This is particularly true if the institution maintains this information for all other students, implying that the institution views it as information relating to student enrollment, not an employee benefit.

When does the employee records exception apply to the records of students employed by the educational agency?

FERPA considers that "records relating to an individual in attendance at the agency or institution who is employed as a result of his or her status as a student are education records."[37] For example, the records of a graduate student employed as a graduate assistant at a college would not fall within this exception, and therefore would be treated as education records, since in general one must first maintain the status of a being a graduate student in attendance in order to obtain the result of employment as a graduate assistant.[38]

An Example—Trena is a graduate student employed by City County College. City County receives a request under its State open records act for the employment records of all two thousand (2,000) City County College employees. Unlike Todd (above), Trena's employment is contingent upon her maintaining graduate student status, and therefore FERPA and FPCO would consider her employment records as relating to her education, and thereby protected under FERPA.

Does this mean that all of the records of an individual employed as a result of their status as a student are considered educational records?

Yes. All records (including employment records) of an individual who is employed as a result of their status as a student (i.e. a high school student enrolled in a work-study program) are considered educational records.[39] However, an employee who incidentally takes a class at an institution does not therefore convert their employment records into educational records under FERPA.[40]

Does that mean the college or university may not publish a graduate student's status or teaching assignments?

No. FPCO has advised that this information should and may be designated as directory information, since it is "of a nature of being common knowledge to those who are in the individual's class or who pass by the class."[41]

Does FERPA apply to the employee-student records even after the individual is no longer a student?

Yes. FERPA continues to apply after the employee or graduate student terminates enrollment.[42]

PROFESSIONAL TREATMENT RECORDS

What is the professional treatment records exception?

The professional treatment records exception applies to records created in connection with the "treatment" of an "eligible" student (eighteen years of age or older, or enrolled in a post-secondary institution) by a physician, psychiatrist, psychologist or other recognized, related professional or paraprofessional. Sometimes referred to as the "treatment" exception, records must satisfy three conditions in order to qualify under this definition—first, the records must be created by a proper party (discussed further below); second, the records must be used for purpose of treating the student; and third, the records may not be disclosed to anyone other than those providing the covered treatment.[43]

An Example—Camille is a twenty year old student at City County College. As a benefit of being a student, she is entitled to use the student health center. She receives treatment for depression from a college-employed psychologist, and subsequently attempts suicide. After recovering, she considers bringing a lawsuit against the College, and demands copies of the psychologist's treatment notes under FERPA, contending these are "educational records" to which she is now entitled access as an eligible student. However, as treatment records, the College psychologist's records are not subject to FERPA's access provisions and Camille is not entitled to inspect the psychologist's treatment notes.[44]

Since treatment records are not considered education records under FERPA, does that mean that the institution may disclose them without regard or reliance upon consent of an eligible student, or any specific nonconsensual disclosure provision under FERPA?

Not in the view of the Department. Even though treatment records are excluded from the FERPA definition of an educational record, the Department stated in 2008 that if treatment records are used or disclosed for any purpose other than treatment of the student, 'they may only be disclosed as education records subject to FERPA requirements."[45] In reference to the confidentiality of these records, it is notable that state confidentiality and/or privacy rules may also apply to these records even if FERPA does not.[46] For example, educator ethics rules almost always impose confidentiality requirements upon the individual educator (but not typically access rights to parents and students) which cover much more records (as well as information obtained from sources outside of educational records, such as the students themselves) than are covered under FERPA.

If the district discloses treatment records to anyone other than individuals providing treatment to the student, do these records lose their status as treatment records?

Yes. In the same way that sole possession records can become educational records subject to the requirements of FERPA as a result of the district or school employee's actions in sharing them with other individuals, treatment records can become educational records when so disclosed.[47]

Which students are potentially covered by the professional treatment records exception?

The treatment records exception applies to student 18 years of age or older, OR, students who are attending any postsecondary institution. By definition, therefore, treatment records only apply to eligible students for purposes of FERPA. Furthermore, the treatment records provision specifically EXCLUDES students in K–12 education who are under eighteen (18) years of age.

An Example—Consider Camille's younger sister, Katrina, is a sixteen (16) year old student receiving treatment by the school nurse at her high school. As Katrina is neither eighteen (18) nor enrolled in post-secondary education, the "treatment records" exception would not apply to her. Assuming the nurse's notes do not qualify for the "sole possession" exception, the treatment notes would become part of Katrina's educational record.

Practice Pointer—While these records would be part of Katrina's educational records and thereby subject to disclosure under FERPA, State laws may prevent the disclosure of certain records related to treatment without a subpoena. Before disclosing treatment records of a student less than eighteen (18) years old in an elementary, middle or secondary institution, we strongly suggest the reader check with an attorney familiar with the State's records laws.

Is it possible for an 18-year-old high student to be covered by the professional treatment records provision?

Yes. If a recognized physician, psychiatrist, psychologist or other recognized professional or paraprofessional has either created or maintained records in connection with the student's treatment, and the records have been used solely for the purpose of treating the student, the "treatment records" exception may apply.[48] However, note that these very same kinds of records created or maintained before the student reaches eighteen (18) *would not* fall within this exception, and therefore would in all likelihood be considered educational records under FERPA.

Who is a recognized professional or paraprofessional for purposes of the professional treatment exception?

FERPA does not define these individuals and the regulations are silent in this regard. However, the clear language of the regulation—which includes "related professions and paraprofessionals"—notes that the "treatment" exception is not limited to "physicians, psychiatrists, or psychologists [.]"[49]

If a school psychologist provides "treatment" to an eighteen (18) year old student enrolled in a secondary institution, can the psychologist invoke the medical treatment records exception to prevent disclosure of the records under FERPA?

In most instances, the actual involvement or work of a school psychologist is more accurately described as an evaluation, rather than actual or ongoing treatment of the individual student. Nevertheless, it is possible for a district to provide mental health services to individual students.

What kinds of records does the treatment exception cover?

The treatment exception only applies to records "made or maintained by a physician, psychiatrist, psychologist, or other recognized professional or paraprofessional acting in his or her professional capacity or assisting in a paraprofessional capacity," when such records are "made, maintained, or used only in connection with treatment of the student" and "disclosed only to individuals providing the treatment."[50] This part of the definition specifically excludes from the concept of "treatment" any "remedial educational activities or activities that are part of the program of instruction at the agency or institution."[51]

What about medical records submitted in support of a request for an accommodation of a student's disability—are these covered by the treatment records exception to FERPA?

No. FPCO has stated that "in order to qualify as treatment records, the record or information may not be made, maintained, or used for any purpose other than treatment . . . the regulations clearly . . . exclude educational and other non-medical activities from this concept . . . we conclude that "treatment" does not include determining appropriate accommodations for a disability."[52] As a result, medical records submitted in connection with a request for an accommodation do not qualify under the treatment records exclusion and therefore are covered by FERPA.

Does the "treatment records" exception (and exclusion from FERPA) apply to records created or maintained by "related service" providers who serve a student with disabilities over the age of eighteen (18)?

As noted previously, the treatment records provision does not apply to "activities that are part of the program of instruction." In the vast majority of cases, we believe this language renders the treatment records provision inapplicable to the record of related services provided to disabled students, even those over the age of eighteen (18), so that any such records probably are education records under FERPA.

An example—Phyllis the physical therapists works with a twenty year old autistic student twice a week for 30 minutes each session as specified within the student's I.E.P. Of course, Phyllis sees many students each week, and in addition to the data she records and submits to the student's I.E.P. team regarding his progress and performance, Phyllis keep her own notes as to how the student did each day, what worked well (as well as what did not), and any other bits of information she thinks may be helpful to remember and review as she serves this student in the future. Phyllis does not share these notes with any other person, including the I.E.P. team. While the professional treatment exception will not apply to these notes, it is distinctly possible that the sole possession exception will apply to Phyllis' notes.

What is the relationship between HIPAA, treatment records excluded from FERPA, and educational records covered by FERPA?

HIPAA is the Health Insurance Portability and Accountability Act of 1996, and is a major federal law governing the confidentiality of medical information. Both HIPAA and FERPA exclude student medical records from HIPAA protection—including education records subject FERPA as well as those which fall within the "treatment record" exception.[53]

What about student immunization or other health records maintained by the school?

FPCO has stated that "a K–12 student's health records, including immunization records, maintained by an educational agency or institution subject to FERPA, including records maintained by a school nurse, would generally be 'education records' subject to FERPA."[54] Consequently, student immunization records do not fall within the exclusion from FERPA for medical treatment records.

Does HIPAA either authorize or prohibit the disclosure of student immunization or other student health records to a State Department of Public Health?

HIPAA is generally inapplicable to the disclosure of such records as they are instead education records subject to FERPA. Generally, FERPA would not permit the disclosure (without consent) of these records for public health activities such as surveillance, investigations, or interventions. However, in limited circumstances the health or safety emergencies provisions of FERPA may apply.[55]

Does this mean that treatment records involving students with communicable diseases may only be reported to state authorities after parents or eligible student have provided their consent, even when state law requires such reports to be filed?

No. As will be further explained in Chapter VI, FERPA contains an exception permitting non-consensual disclosure in response or to prevent a "health or safety emergency"—an exception developed specifically with communicable diseases in mind. While FPCO has determined that such treatment records would be considered education records under FERPA, FPCO has further stated that "this office will not substitute its judgment for what constitutes a true threat or emergency unless the determination appears manifestly unreasonable or irrational . . . state reporting requirement(s) for communicable diseases satisfies the FERPA requirement for a case-by-case determination that a specific situation, i.e. an identified communicable disease, presents and imminent danger or threat to students or other members of the community."[56] In other words, FPCO has taken the position that while FERPA does apply to treatment records in this instance, the health or safety emergency will be interpreted to permit such reporting unless the state reporting requirement were found to be "manifestly unreasonable or irrational."[57]

What about other medical conditions which may be subject to state reporting requirements, but which do not involve communicable diseases, such as HIV/AIDS, cancer and sexually transmitted diseases?

FPCO declined to extend its reasoning concerning state communicable disease reporting rules to other, 'routine' or non-emergency reporting requirements. In reference to all such conditions, FPCO has stated that the school could only report such information if it has made "a specific, case-by-case determination that a health or safety emergency exists," or if the student/parent provides their consent.[58]

An example—The State maintains a cancer registry and requires by regulation that all health care professionals (including school nurses) report cancer cases to the registry. While subject to State rule, FPCO has advised that these reporting requirements in such non-emergency cases do not fall within the health and safety emergency (at least not categorically). In these later cases, the district must either make an individualized determination that a qualifying emergency exists, or obtain consent of the parent or eligible student.[59]

If treatment records are not education records under FERPA, do parents have any FERPA right to access or inspect these records?

Remember that since treatment records may only exist when dealing with eligible students, parents may only be permitted to inspect these records with the consent of the eligible student, or when one of the non-consensual exceptions under FERPA applies. For instance, the health or safety emergency or tax dependent student exceptions (discussed in Chapter VI) may in a given case allow the institution to share treatment records with the parent of an eligible student.[60]

What about eligible students—do they have FERPA access rights to these treatment records?

Not exactly. In regard to access of those records, FERPA does specifically provide that a student "may have those records reviewed by a physician or other appropriate professional of the student's choice."[61] This appears to be a distinct right of the student—if elected; the Institution must make the records available. However, once an eligible student's treatment records have been disclosed to any party for a purpose other than the treatment of the student (for instance, in the case of a health or safety emergency), these treatment records are no longer excluded from the FERPA definition of education records, and would now be subject to the eligible student's FERPA access and inspection rights.

ALUMNI RECORDS

What is the "alumni records exception," and what is the purpose of this rule?

The "alumni exception" applies to records that are "created or received by an educational agency or institution after an individual is no longer a student in attendance and that are not directly related to the individual's attendance as a student."[62] The purpose of this rule is to "allow educational agencies and institutions and their alumni organizations to perform their traditional functions of fund-raising and publishing information concerning the accomplishments of alumni."[63]

Does the "alumni records exception" apply to all records created after a student is no longer enrolled?

Not necessarily. The exception is defined not only by the point in time at which they are created but also by the nature of the records themselves. For example, the alumni records provision does not include records created after an individual is no longer a student, but which are concerned primarily with the activities of that individual as a student.[64]

An example—Sally Student graduated from City College on July 27th, where as a student she had been involved in a controversy with the College over a student group. Several months later, Sally makes a request to inspect her educational records, and a dispute arises over whether she is entitled to inspect a draft and final version of a letter from the attorney for the college to an individual (not a client) and dated August 28th. The College contends that since the final draft of the letter was created after Sally graduated, the alumni records exception provides. However, FPCO rejected this position finding that since the letter appeared to be directly related to Sally's activities while she was a student, the alumni records exception was inapplicable.[65]

What if the student did not graduate from the institution, but simply left and is no longer enrolled—may the "alumni" exception be used to publicize their accomplishments after leaving the institution?

Through almost universal common application, the term "alumni" applies exclusively to graduates of institutions; however, the accepted definition of "alumni" includes "former students."[66] Moreover, while this exception is commonly denominated the alumni exception, the actual regulatory text refers to "an individual after he or she is no longer a student at that agency or institution."

May an institution disclose information falling within the alumni provision, or refuse an eligible student's request to inspect these same records, without regard to either FERPA's access or confidentiality rules?

In terms of the Department's specific position on this issue, the Department does acknowledge that records contained within the alumni records exception are not subject to the right of parents or eligible students to challenge the accuracy of educational records under FERPA.[67] Theoretically, this is consistent with the view that neither the access rights nor confidentiality duties of FERPA apply. However, in the absence of direct authority on this point, we do advise caution in the disclosure of information about a former student which may be a basis for complaints under state law (such as libel or slander).

Does the "alumni exception" permit disclosure of directory information by the Institution to an alumni association which is not a part of the institution?

This depends upon the whether the institution has published a directory information notice, and the response of individual students to this notice. In a 1999 letter, the Department treated a former student's election not to participate in the university's directory information policy as also barring the release of this directory information to a non-institutional, alumni association.[68] On the other hand, disclosure of this information to an office within the institution (for example, the office of alumni affairs) may well be permissible under the exception for disclosing information to school officials with a legitimate educational interest. (See Chapter IV for a further discussion of this provision).

Practice Pointer. Once the outside, alumni association has properly obtained the directory information of former students, FERPA itself does not impose any express prohibitions on the sale or distribution of this information. Certainly, a common practice has been the sale of these lists of former students to various vendors and as part of the fundraising activities of the alumni association, in addition to the direct solicitation of alumni for fundraising purposes.

Has the list of records excluded from FERPA's definition of an educational record been amended or changed over time?

Yes. Most recently in 2008, the Department added a sixth category of records excluded from the concept of educational records under FERPA in an effort to respond to address confusion after the Supreme Court's decision in Owasso. The most recent category of records excluded from the FERPA definition of an education record is that of "grades on peer-graded papers before they are collected and recorded by a teacher."[69]

What about group or team projects—does FERPA prohibit a teacher from discussing the grades of an individual student or the group of students?

As long as the grades have not yet been recorded by the teacher, the Department has said, FERPA does not prohibit the teacher from discussing either the grade of the group or team, or individual students grades on the group activities. For purposes of the FERPA, the Department takes the position that the grades do not become educational records "maintained" by the institution "at least until the teacher has recorded the grades."[70]

MAINTAINING EDUCATIONAL RECORDS—THE GROUND RULES

Does FERPA itself require an institution or school district to actually maintain ANY records in particular?

Generally, no. FERPA applies to records the district does maintain, but it does not independently create any duty on the part of the district to maintain any particular records.[71] However, once the district makes the determination to maintain some educational records about students, FERPA then requires some records be maintained regarding these educational records (such as records of who accesses student records). FERPA itself does not initially require institutions to maintain transcripts, disciplinary histories, or other information traditionally falling within educational records. Of course, State law and/or local policy may and often does require that the district maintain certain educational records, and further prescribes the minimum period of time such records must be maintained.

Does FERPA set forth any rules as to what information the district may or should collect in a student's educational records?

Generally, no. FERPA is concerned with access, confidentiality, and amendment rights of parents and student as the personally identifiable information contained within an educational records, but "FERPA does not prohibit a school or District from gathering information and records from any source and including such information in a student's education records."[72]

Under FERPA, can the nature and amount of information collected, protected, and accessible to parents and students be different from one state to another state, and even from one school district to another?

Absolutely, since State or local laws, policies, practices, and customs may require or encourage the collection of information about students that is unique, the information which will fall under the umbrella of "educational records" can certainly be different in other schools or states.

What does it mean to "maintain" a record for purposes of FERPA?

While FERPA itself does not define the term "maintain," the Supreme Court in *Owasso* noted that "the ordinary meaning of the word 'maintain' is 'to keep in existence or continuance; preserve, retain . . . the word 'maintain' suggests FERPA records will be kept in a filing cabinet in a records room at the school or on a permanent secure database, perhaps even after the student is no longer enrolled."[73]

Who is considered to be "a person acting for" the district or school under FERPA?

In *Owasso*, the Court said, "The phrase 'acting for' connotes agents of the school, such as teachers, administrators, and other school employees," and rejected the argument that students who graded each other's work were acting for the district in doing so.[74]

Did the Supreme Court in Owasso add anything else to the definition of an "educational record"?

Yes, the Court also examined FERPA's requirement that the district maintain a record of access for each student's records, and said, "this suggests Congress contemplated that education records would be kept in one place with a single record of access . . . FERPA implies that education records are institutional records kept by a single central custodian, such as a registrar, not individual assignments handled by many student graders in their separate classrooms."[75]

Did any of the Supreme Court justices disagree with this decision?

While Justice Scalia did agree that peer-grading does not violate FERPA, he also wrote a separate concurrence in which he rejected the "central custodian" theory of educational records apparently adopted by the majority of the Court. Justice Scalia's main complaint with the "central custodian" theory appears to be that it does not explain why Congress included an exception to the definition of educational records for "sole possession" records, since by almost any definition "sole possession" records are never maintained by the central custodian of records.[76]

What types of security does FERPA require districts to utilize when maintaining educational records?

The Department's current position is that "an educational agency or institution must use physical, technological, administrative, and other methods, including training, to protect education records against unauthorized disclosure in ways that are reasonable and appropriate to the circumstances in which the records are maintained."[77] In 2008, the Department further stated (or clarified) that FERPA requires use of "reasonable methods" and this requirement is intended to be "sufficiently flexible to permit each educational agency or institution to select the proper balance of physical, technological, and administrative controls to effectively prevent unauthorized access to education records, based on their resources and needs."[78] In one instance where a small district proposed to share a computer network with other county agencies, thus allowing access to student educational records by personnel outside the district, the Department "would consider a record management system that allows unauthorized individuals to have access to education records to constitute a policy or practice of violating FERPA."[79]

An Example—In one case several years ago, a female student (also the daughter of the school secretary) was in the office waiting on her mother after the rest of the student body had been dismissed for early release. Without the knowledge of her mother (or any other school personnel), the student went through the apparently open, swinging doors into the school record room. In the record room, the student looked up the file of a male classmate (apparently open and easily accessible) and discovered documentation that he had been adopted. After telling the student that she knew his "secret," the female student told at least one of her friends as well as the male student that he was adopted—information of which he was previously unaware. In this case, however, the court dismissed a lawsuit filed by the male (adopted) student and his parents, paying scant attention to whether or not the district had provide a security system for student records.[80] In light of the Department's language in 2008, we are not entirely comfortable that FERPA today would excuse the apparent absence of any security system at all in connection with student records.

Do FERPA's record management requirements prohibit the district from allowing students and parents to sort through, for example, student report cards in order to find their report card?

Absolutely, this would be inadequate in terms of the security provided to paper records.[81] By extrapolation, we believe maintaining student folders with open access in the classroom, when such folders include student's standardized test scores and other education records, would also be inadequate.

What about postcards mailed to parents notifying them of their child's lack of progress in one or more academic subjects?

FPCO has taken the position that such a postcard "results in an unauthorized disclosure under FERPA because anyone who reads the card would know that the student is not successfully completing her . . . classes . . . [since] such information would generally come from a student's education records, so the disclosure of the information without the parent's prior written consent would not be permitted under FERPA."[82]

Does FERPA have any specific rules governing the destruction of educational records?

FERPA does prohibit the district from destroying educational records "whenever there is an outstanding request to inspect or review the records,"[83] and IDEA imposes some added duties in connection with the retention and destruction of the educational records of disabled students. (See Chapter VIII for a further discussion of these rules). Furthermore, many states laws require districts to maintain certain records about students, and in addition, many states have record retention requirements which require districts to adopt policies specifying which records will be maintained and the period of time the records will be maintained.

Does FERPA require the district to notify parents prior to the destruction of educational records generally?

No. In fact, the Department specifically rejected this requirement in 1988, saying that "such a requirement would impose an unnecessary burden on educational agencies and institutions."[84] Note, however, that IDEA has imposed some duties in this regard in the case of special education records, and certainly nothing in FERPA would prohibit a District from applying those procedures to all students.

DISCLOSING EDUCATION RECORDS—THE BASICS

What does it mean to "disclose" personally identifiable information?

Disclosure is defined as "to permit access to or the release, transfer, or other communication of personally identifiable information contained in education records to any party, by any means, including oral, written, or electronic means, to any party except the party identified as the party that provided or created the record."[85]

Has the definition of "disclosure" under FERPA been changed recently?

Yes. In 2008, the Department added an exception for parties which provided or created the record in the first instance (discussed above), and which permits the district to discuss or share records with the initial provider or creator of the record in the first instance without obtaining consent of the parent or eligible student. The purpose of this amendment was to facilitate the verification and authentication of educational records, and improve the ability of schools to successfully investigate suspected fraud in connection with the creation of records.[86]

Does FERPA require that the district keep a record of any return or release of records to an original source?

No, there is no record-keeping requirement in connection with this provision, though the party to whom the record is returned is subject to the redisclosure provisions and limitations of FERPA.[87]

Does FERPA protect sensitive information about a student which does not come from a student's educational records?

Several courts have considered this question and said clearly no, "FERPA does not protect information which might appear in school records but would also be 'known by members of the school community through conversation and personal contact.' Congress could not have constitutionally prohibited comment on, or discussion of, facts about a student which were learned independently of his school records."[88] However, educators are again cautioned that state certification and ethics rules often do include a broader duty of confidentiality than FERPA, and that they should consult counsel familiar with these rules in the state prior to disclosure.

When the district obtains consent to disclose personally identifiable information, what information should be included in this consent?

The consent to disclose personally identifiable information must be in writing, and should include the following information: (1) the specific records which may be disclosed, (2) the purpose for the records disclosure, and (3) the identity of the party or class of parties to whom the records may be disclosed.[89]

Must the district provide a parent or eligible student copies of the records which may be disclosed pursuant to their written consent?

Yes, FERPA requires that a copy of these records be provided to the parent or eligible student if they "so request." In the case of student who is not an eligible student, the district is required to provide a copy of the records to the student if the parent "so requests."[90]

When is the prior, written consent of a parent or eligible student not required before the disclosure of educational records?

FERPA recognizes a number of instances (17) in which personally identifiable information may be disclosed without the consent of parents or eligible students.[91] For a complete discussion of each these exceptions, please see Chapters IV and VI.

Does FERPA prohibit the posting of student grades?

As long as the student's names are deleted and the student's identities are not otherwise disclosed or easily traceable (for example, the use of social security or partial social security numbers is prohibited), this practice does not violate FERPA.[92]

What about posting samples of student work—is this prohibited by FERPA?

After the lower court decision in *Owasso* (which found that peer grading was a violation of FERPA), there was much public discussion and concern as to whether posting a student work sample would also be a FERPA violation. However, when the Supreme Court overturned the lower court's decision in *Owasso*, the Court spoke very critically of, and appears to reject the view that, "If a teacher in any of the thousands of covered classrooms in the nation puts a happy face, a gold star, or a disapproving remark on a classroom assignment, federal law does not allow other students to see it."[93] Consequently, we do not believe posting samples of students work is a FERPA violation.

Is the teacher's grade book considered an educational record?

As a result of the 2008 revised regulations, we believe the answer to this issue is clearly yes. Notably, the Court in *Owasso* considered the teacher's grade book as an educational record, though they went out of their way to note specifically that they were not deciding this question. However, the 2008 regulatory exclusion of "grades on peer-graded papers *before* they are collected and recorded by a teacher" creates the obvious inference that *after* the teacher records these grades (presumably in the grade book); the grades in the grade book are now educational records under FERPA.[94]

May a school hold a celebration or party only for students who achieve certain academic benchmarks, for example, to provide a reward to students who perform at or above grade level on standardized tests under NLCB?

Given FPCO's position on the question of postcards discussed above, it is our interpretation that any reward publicly made available only to students who demonstrate a given level of academic achievement also has the consequence of communicating to all the other students the identity of those who failed to meet the academic expectations of the school.[95] However, one method of addressing this issue is to specifically designate this information as directory information (analogous to an honor or award) at the beginning of the school year, thereby permitting the publication and recognition of students who have achieved this honorary status.

Do FERPA disclosure limitations apply to parties or entities other than educational agencies?

In a case brought by parents who sought to pursue their IDEA and FERPA claims anonymously, a federal court pointed out that while FERPA restricts educational agencies from releasing personally identifiable information to anyone other than the parents of a child, FERPA does not limit disclosure by other parties (including the parents).[96]

What about attorney-client communications contained in a student's file—are parents or eligible students entitled to inspect these communications?

The Department has recognized that while neither the FERPA statute nor the regulations provide for a denial of access to records maintained in a student's educational file on the basis of attorney client privilege or the work product doctrine, "nonetheless, an educational institution may deny a request to inspect and review on these grounds in certain instances."[97]

When may the district deny a student access to information contained in their educational records on the basis of attorney-client privilege or work product?

The Department has established five conditions, all of which must be met in order for the district to assert that particular documents are protected. These conditions are: (1) the asserted holder of the privilege is or sought to become a client; (2) the communication is between a client and a member of the Bar (or subordinate) who is acting as a lawyer in connection with the communication; (3) the communication relates to facts disclosed by the client to the attorney for the purpose of securing a legal opinion or advice (and not to commit any illegal act or tort); (4) the communication is in fact confidential and not made in the presence of anyone outside the specific attorney-client relationship; and (5) the privilege has been claimed and has not been waived.[98]

ENDNOTES

1. 34 C.F.R. § 99.3.
2. 34 C.F.R. § 99.3.

3. Letter to Lee Tyner, Jr. (February 12, 2002). The Department extended this position in its own amicus brief before the Supreme Court in the *Owasso* case discussed further below.

4. 34 C.F.R. § 99.3.

5. *Tarka v. Franklin,* 891 F.2d 102 (5th Cir. 1989). The 5th Circuit does note, however, that "auditing students are entitled to some protection under FERPA…the specific rights afforded to auditing students under FERPA are not expressly enumerated." Id. at 107. The court in Tarka mentions, but does not endorse, the view of the prevailing defendants in the case that auditing students are entitled to information regarding the audited class only.

6. *Kirwan v. The Diamondback,* 352 Md. 74, 721 A.2d 196 (Court of Appeals of Maryland, 1998).

7. For example, in *Rome City School District Disciplinary Hearing v. Grifasi,* 10 Misc.3d 1034, 806 N.Y.S.2d 381(N.Y.Sup., 2005) the court found that a school district security tape was not an educational record under FERPA, reasoning that FERPA was primarily concerned with records relating to the educational performance of students (and which was distinct from the security tape). And in *State of Louisiana v. Donald Mart,* (La.App. 1 Cir. 6/20/97), (697 So.2d 1055), the court held that school bus video tape of a student being attacked on a school bus was not an education record under FERPA, and that a request for access to the tape under State Sunshine laws. In 2006, a Texas Attorney General Opinion of July 18, 2006 to William Bednar also concluded that a school cafeteria video of students involved in an altercation in the cafeteria was an education record for each of the students so involved, but not to other students who may have been incidentally captured in the video. See also the *Medley v. Shelby County* case discussed below.

8. Email from Thomas Hutton of the National School Boards Association on December 26, 2006. In the Rome City case, there is also reference to an unpublished FPCO letter from 2004 opining that a video tape of one student fighting was an education record which the parents of that student would be entitled to inspect.

9. Of course, this technology driven approach to defining the lifespan of an educational record may be a double-edge sword. As it becomes more and more possible to store an entire school year's worth of video footage in smaller and smaller computer files, the district may inadvertently find that the period of time during which parents or eligible students may seek access to existing files has been greatly (if unintentionally) expanded. In these cases, the issue may again become whether these files or tapes are education records in the first place.

10. *Medley v. Board of Educ.,* Shelby County 168 S.W.3d 398 (Ky.App., 2004).

11. 34 C.F.R. § 99.3.

12. Id.

13. Federal Register Vol 65 No. 130, 41855 (July 6, 2000). In 1999 and 2000, the Department proposed some changes to the definition of "sole possession records," specifically adding a requirement that the records be "typically maintained by the school official unbeknownst to other individuals." In addition, the Department proposed to exclude from the definition of sole possession records "records that contain

information taken directly from a student or that are used to make decisions about the student." See Federal Register Vo. 64 No. 104, 29534 (June 1, 1999). The purpose of these proposed changes, according to the Department, was to clarify that the sole possession records "do not include evaluations of student conduct or performance." Id. 41856. However, these proposed changes were <u>not</u> adopted in the July 2000 final version of the rule.

14. *See K.C. & A.C. v. Fulton County School District,* Civil Action File No. 1:03-CV-3501-TWT (N.D. Ga. 2006).

15. 34 C.F.R. § 99.8(a)(1).

16. 34 C.F.R. § 99.8(b)(1)(i–iii).

17. Federal Register Vol. 60, No. 10 3466 (January 17, 1995).

18. Federal Register Vol. 60, No. 10 3467 (January 17, 1995).

19. Id.

20. Id.

21. 34 C.F.R. § 99.8(b)(2).

22. Federal Register Vol. 60, No. 10 3466 (January 17, 1995).

23. Letter to Judith S. Bresler (February 15, 2006).

24. Id.

25. Id.

26. Letter to Attorney for School District, 40 IDELR 99 (October 31, 2003). In this letter, FPCO the student-defendant sought the production of these statements in connection with his IDEA due process hearing, and in consideration of both his rights under IDEA as well as his due process rights generally, FPCO rather forcefully concluded that FPCO's confidentiality provisions trumped both such interests.

27. Federal Register Vol. 73, No. 237 74832-3 (December 8, 2008).

28. 34 C.F.R. § 99.8(c)(2).

29. *U.S. v. Miami University,* 294 F.3d 797 (6th Cir. 2002); *DeFeo v. McAboy,* 260 F.Supp.2d 790, 794 (E.D. Missouri 2003).

30. Federal Register Vol. 60, No. 10 3465 & 68 (January 17, 1995). It also notable that the Department seemingly rejected a request that victims of criminal offenses be updated as to the progress of an investigation (as opposed to a closed investigation), though presumably such "updates" would be permissible if the College's own policy so provided. See Federal Register Vol. 60, No. 10 3468 (January 17, 1995).

31. *Jensen v. Reeves,* 3 Fed. Appx. 905, 910 (10th Cir. 2001). In an interesting opinion, a federal compliance officer appears to have accepted this rationale as consistent with the health and safety exception under FERPA. See Douglas County School District RE-1; Complaint 2004:502, 41 IDELR 258, Colorado State Educational Agency (June 2, 2004).

32. Letter to S. Daniel Carter (March 10, 2003); 34 C.F.R. § 99.31(a)(13) & (a)(14).

33. *DeFeo* (supra) at 795. *Board of Education of Colonial School District v. Colonial Education Association,* 1996 WL 104231 (Del.Ch. 1996) (referring to type of records contemplated by FERPA as "records relating to individual student academic performance, financial aid or scholastic probation); *Bauer v. Kincaid,* 759

F.Supp. 575 (W.D. Missouri 1991). See again also the distinction drawn by some courts between security video and educational records, above.

34. *Risica v. Dumas,* 466 F.Supp.2d 434, 441 (D. Conn. 2006).

35. Federal Register Vol. 60, No. 10 3468 (January 17, 1995); 34 C.F.R.§ 99.31(a)(9).

36. 34 C.F.R. § 99.3

37. Id.

38. Letter to Joseph Ambash, undated but responding to inquiry dated February 12, 2002.

39. Federal Register Vol. 53, No. 69 11950 (April 11, 1988).

40. Letter to David Strom (August 21, 2000). In this letter, the example provided by the Department is that of a secretary to the president of the university and who takes a course from the university. In this instance, her employment is not the result of her status as a student. Id. Indeed, the converse is more likely to be the case—her presence as a student may be derivative from her employment status.

41. Letter to Joseph Ambash, undated but responding to inquiry dated February 12, 2002.

42. Letter to Ms. Marya Ryan (November 26, 2004).

43. 34 C.F.R. § 99.3.

44. Of course, Camille's lawyer may subpoena the records after a lawsuit has been filed and pursue access by way of the subpoena exception discussed in Chapter VI.

45. Federal Register Vol. 73, No. 237 74840 (December 9, 2008). While the Department's concern over the confidentiality of treatment records is laudable, the particular legal interpretation on this point is questionable. Under the statute, treatment records are excluded from the FERPA records entirely, and we have some question as to the Department's position that neither parents nor eligible students enjoy FERPA access rights to these records, though the Institution is still governed by FERPA's confidentiality provisions. For instance, does the Department's reliance upon the non-disclosure exceptions mean that a postsecondary institution may disclose any treatment records to parents of a tax dependent, eligible student without regard to any health or safety emergency?

46. But note that HIPPA does not apply to such medical treatment records, as these are excluded from the definition of "protected health information" Federal Register Vol. 69, No. 77 21672 (April 21, 2004).

47. Letter to Melanie Blaise (November 29, 2004).

48. Note that the third condition of the professional treatment exception must also apply—that is, the records may not have disclosed to anyone else not involved in the delivery of the treatment of the student.

49. In the absence of further or subsequent guidance from the Department, one approach to defining the list of individuals engaged in a covered or related "profession" is to consult state licensing rules and regulations. Physicians, psychiatrists, and psychologists are typically licensed and regulated by the state, and to the extent the state also recognizes and regulates "related professions," the state may be argued to have defined this list of individuals.

50. Letter to Ms. Marya Ryan (November 26, 2004).

51. 34 C.F.R. § 99.3(b)(4)(iii).

52. Letter to David Cope (November 2, 2004).

53. Id; Joint Guidance on the Application of the Family Educational Rights and Privacy Act and the Health Insurance Portability and Accountability Act of 1996 to Student Health Records, p.3. (November 2008). Apparently, the most common situation where a district might be subject to HIPAA is when a school employs a health care provider which bills Medicaid electronically for services rendered to a student. If the provider maintains health information outside of education records under FERPA, then the HIPAA privacy rule would apply; however, if the provider only maintains this information in education records, then the FERPA privacy rule applies and the school would be expected to "obtain parental consent in order to disclose to Medicaid billing information about a service provided to a student." Joint Guidance, p. 4.

54. Letter to Ms. Martha Holloway (February 25, 2004); see also Joint Guidance, p. 4.

55. Id. Of course, FERPA would not prohibit the release of information that is not personally identifying to public health officials. In this letter, FPCO also opined that "certainly an outbreak of diseases such as measles, rubella, mumps, and polio not only pose a threat of permanent disability or death for the individual, but have historically presented themselves as epidemic in nature.'" Thus, disclosure of personally identifiable information from students' education records to state health officials for such reasons would generally be permitted under FERPA's health or safety emergency provision." See Chapter VI for further discussion of the health or safety exception.

56. Letter to Ms. Melanie Baise (November 29, 2004).

57. Id.

58. Id. See also Federal Register Vol. 73, No. 237 74837 (December 9, 2008).

59. Letter to Ms. Melanie Baise, *supra*. Of course, reporting of anonymous or de-identified data about, for instance, a student with cancer, may well fall outside this rule. The problem, however, is that many public health reporting requirements to include patient name, date of birth, sex, race, and contact information among the pieces of data required.

60. Please see "Balancing Student Privacy and School Safety: A Guide to the Family Educational Rights and Privacy Act for Colleges and Universities," published by the Department in October 2007, as well as Federal Register Vol. 73, No. 237 74840 (December 9, 2008).

61. 34 C.F.R. § 99.10(f). However, the permissive regulatory language on this point certainly would not prevent the agency or institution from allowing the eligible student to inspect treatment records—we do not believe that any confidentiality interest on the part of the physician or other professional is recognized as against the student.

62. This long-standing view of the Department was incorporated into the regulations in 2008 at 34 C.F.R. § 99.3(b)(5). See Federal Register Vol. 73, No. 237 74811 (December 9, 2008). One particular type of record (settlement agreements) appears to have been the subject of considerable concern, and within the Comments it is clear that the Department views a settlement agreement entered into after a student is no longer in attendance, but relating to directly that individual's attendance as a student, most certainly does not fall within the alumni records exception.

63. Federal Register Vol. 53, No. 69 11950 (April 11, 1988). In carving out this exception, the Department specifically noted that since it was unusual for an alumni organization to publish or use negative information about alumni, any expected abuse was "minimal and insufficient to justify imposing an additional regulatory burden." Id. It is interesting that in contemplating this exception, the Department appears to have given extensive consideration to the "harmful" prong of the personally identifiable information analysis, but not much thought to the "invasion of privacy" aspect of this analysis.

64. Letter to Dr. Tana Hasart (June 1, 1999).

65. Id. It is also worth noting that the Department apparently took the position that the alumni provision would only apply if the records concerned "were solely about the [Complainant] after she ceased to be a student."

66. The American Heritage Dictionary of the English Language (4th Ed.) (2006). In disputed cases, it may also be important if the institution has previously adopted any given definition of the term "alumni" which it may be argued the student has accepted by their enrollment in accordance with the rules and policies of the institution.

67. Federal Register Vol. 73 No. 237 74811 (December 9, 2008).

68. Letter to Dr. Peter Likens (March 11, 1999). This letter is interesting in that it is at least arguable that since alumni records are recognized as an exception to the very definition of education records, one might argue that the university's directory information policy and any individual student's response thereto is irrelevant to the creation and use of these records. In this case, the issue may best be understood as a narrow reading of the university's authority to disclose information about the student to the association which did not, in fact, relate to the individuals activities after he left the university, but rather, consisted essentially of the transfer of his directory information to the association.

69. 34 C.F.R. § 99.3(b)(6).

70. Federal Register Vol. 73, No. 237 74812 (December 9, 2008).

71. As an historical note, we find it interesting that at one time FERPA did require that institutions to adopt a policy regarding the retention of educational records. However, this provision of FERPA has since been repealed. In many cases, however, State records laws or regulations now impose a similar requirement that districts adopt some manner of policy in this regard.

72. FPCO Letter (July 16, 2002).

73. 534 U.S. 426, 433 (2002).

74. 534 U.S. 426, 433 (2002).

75. 534 U.S. 426, 434–35 (2002). However, it should be noted that the Department takes a narrower reading of the Supreme Court's opinion in *Owasso* than some of the federal courts which have interpreted this decision. For example, in one post-*Owasso* opinion letter the Department found that "student term papers that have been collected and maintained by a teacher or other school official acting on behalf of the College" are educational records. See Letter to Michael Riley (October 11, 2005). See also the Letter to Lee Tyner referenced above.

76. 534 U.S. 426, 436–7 (2002).

77. Letter to Dr. Brad Bartel, (October 11, 2005).
78. Federal Register Vol. 73 No. 237 74817 (December 9, 2008).
79. Letter to Alan McGraw (October 7, 2005).
80. *Appleberg v. DeVilbiss,* Civil Action No. A.00-0202 BH-C (S.D. Ala. 2001).
81. Letter to McGraw, supra.
82. Letter to Don Bell (June 28, 2004). Quite frankly, we have reservations regarding the breadth of FPCO's interpretation that information such as the student's lack of success (but not the student's actual grade) is impermissible in the absence of prior written consent.
83. 34 C.F.R. § 99.10(e).
84. Federal Register Vol. 53, No. 69 11953 (April 11, 1988).
85. 34 C.F.R. § 99.3
86. Federal Register Vo. 73 No. 237 74810 (December 9, 2008).
87. Id.
88. *Frasca v. Andrews* F.Supp. 1043, 1050 (E.D. N.Y. 1979); *Daniel S. v. Board of Education of York Community High School,* 152 F.Supp.2d 949 (N.D. Ill. 2001).
89. 34 C.F.R. § 99.30(b).
90. 34 C.F.R. § 99.30(c).
91. 34 C.F.R. § 99.31
92. Letter to Dr. Evangelos J. Gizis, undated but responsive to allegation received from student dated August 21, 2000. Importantly, the Department has long construed a violation to include the use and disclosure of even a student's partial social security number in connection with the practice of posting grades. Id.
93. 534 U.S. 426, 435 (2002). The Court goes on to say that "we doubt Congress meant to intervene in this drastic fashion with traditional state functions." Id.
94. 34 C.F.R. § 99.3(b)(6).
95. In addition, the discussion by the Department in the comments to the 2008 regulations concerning a disclosure within the school or institution, and disclosures to the general public, provides an additional basis on which to distinguish the postcard case from the celebration, within the school setting, of students who have achieved a level of academic excellence.
96. *S.R. & M.C. v. Board of Education of the City School District of New York,* 08: CIV 1035 (LAK); 49 IDELR 255 (February 25, 2008). Consequently, the court found, FERPA did not provide the parents with any right to pursue their suit anonymously, since FERPA simply didn't address disclosures made by the parent in the prosecution of their own suit.
97. Letter to Dr. Hoke Smith (June 22, 1998) & Letter to Dr. Hasart (June 1, 1999).
98. Letter to Dr. Hoke Smith (June 22, 1998).

Chapter 3

Educational Records: Parent and Student Rights

Contemporary education policy and law have contained a distinctive element and emphasis upon the concept of an enhanced parental role, involvement, and choice in their child's education. In the area of choice, the Supreme Court has upheld the fundamental constitutionality of voucher's in the seminal case of Zelman v. Harris.[1] Throughout the No Child Left Behind Act, we see numerous indicia of a federal inclusion of parental choice as a major component of educational policy.[2] In the area of educational records, we also see key aspects of parental choice (directory information, disclosure of personally identifiable information) accompanied by detailed rules governing the furnishing of notice to parents as to their statutory rights in this regard. Indeed, and perhaps because the majority of parents do not exercise their right to choose something different for their child's education, the origin of many disputes in this area focus upon the issue of whether or not the District understood the rights afforded to parents, and/or whether the District properly notified parents of these rights.

OVERVIEW, BASIC CONCEPTS, AND DEFINITIONS

What are the rights of parents and eligible students under FERPA?

FERPA provides basically four separate rights to the parents of student (or eligible students), which include the right to inspect and review educational records, the right to consent (or not) to disclosures of the student's educational records which require consent, the right to seek an amendment to educational records which are "inaccurate, misleading, or otherwise in violation of the student's privacy rights," and the right to file a complaint with the Department of Education over any alleged violation of FERPA by the District.[3]

How must the District notify parents and eligible student about these rights?

FERPA requires that the District notify parents and eligible students of each of these four basic rights, including the procedure for inspecting and requesting an amendment of records, as well as the District's criteria for identifying school officials with a "legitimate educational interest" to whom records may be disclosed without consent. [4] However, the method for providing this notice is not specified, as FERPA simply requires the District to "provide notice by any means that are reasonably likely to inform parents of their rights . . . these means could include publication in the school activities calendar, newsletter, or student handbook."[5]

Is there any difference between the notice of FERPA rights and the Directory Information policy and notice requirements discussed in Chapter V?

Yes, as the District is required in all instances to provide the general notice of FERPA rights to all parents and eligible students discussed above. However, the District's decision to adopt a Directory Information policy is discretionary, and therefore the notice associated with a Directory Information policy is only required if the District has made a conscious decision to adopt such a policy.

Is the District required to translate the notice of FERPA rights into languages other than English, and if so, when does this responsibility arise?

FEPRA requires the District to "effectively notify parents who have a primary or home language other than English," but does not provide any further detail as to what exactly this means.[6] However, under Title VI as interpreted by the Office of Civil Rights in the Department of Education, the District is required to provide parents of students with school notices and other information in a language they can understand. On May 25, 1970 the Department of Health, Education and Welfare issued the "May 25th memorandum" to school Districts with more than 5 percent of national origin minority students, and which included the provision that "national origin-minority group parents [be notified] of school activities which are called to the attention of other parents. Such notice in order to be adequate may have to be provided in a language other than English."[7]

Practice Pointer—Perhaps the most specific guidance in terms of the particular documents the District may be required to translate into a language other than English comes from a settlement the Office of Civil Rights reached with the Tucson Unified School District in 2002. In that agreement, the Tucson

Schools agreed to translate the following list of documents for prominent language groups:

1. Registration form
2. Emergency notification card
3. Home language inventory
4. Field trip permission form
5. **Privacy policy**
6. Letter from the Director of Health Services
7. Health services registration form
8. Report cards
9. Guidelines of Student Rights and Responsibilities
10. Notice of discipline to parents
11. Class schedule
12. Progress notes (glossary)
13. Specified Special Education forms
14. Specified Section 504 forms[8]

The inclusion of the privacy policy in this settlement agreement is the best authority, we believe, for the conclusion that Title VI requires the translation of the District's general notice of FERPA rights into a language other than English for prominent language groups.

INSPECTION AND DISCLOSURE ISSUES

Who is considered a "parent" under FERPA?

Under FERPA, a parent "means a parent of a student and includes a natural parent, a guardian, or an individual acting as a parent in the absence of a parent or a guardian?

Is a step-parent considered a parent under FERPA?

Generally yes, as long as the step-parent is present in the day-to-day life of the student, they will be considered a parent under the Act. The Department has said "a step-parent has rights under FERPA where the step-parent is present on a day-to-day basis with the natural parent and the child and the other parent is absent from that home."[9] In the case of the non-custodial parent, however, it is important to note that since the spouse of this natural parent is not typically present on a day-to-day basis in the home of the child, that step-parent is not a FERPA "parent" to the child. Additionally, while the non-custodial natural parent may consent to the release of educational records to his or her spouse, FERPA does not (in the case of regular education students) require the District to provide access to this non-custodial step-parent.[10]

In the case of someone other than the natural parent of a student, does FERPA require this other person to obtain a guardianship over the student in order to qualify as a parent?

No, FERPA specifically recognizes that "an individual acting as a parent in the absence of a parent or guardian" can qualify as a "parent" for purposes of FERPA. While in some states the District may require other individuals to obtain guardianship in order to enroll a child in the District, FERPA provides parental access rights to individuals who may not be legal guardians of a student, but who are "acting as a parent in the absence of a parent or guardian." This would also apply, for instance, in the case of foster parents who are acting as a child's parent and who would therefore have the rights afforded to a parent under FERPA.[11]

An Example—Kindergarten Kate is the daughter of single mom Mary. Mary is in the Army National Guard, and when Mary is called up to active duty and deployed to Iraq for 12 months, Kate's grandmother Ginny moves into their home and becomes primarily responsible for the care and supervision of Kate. Under FERPA, Ginny may access Kate's educational records since she is 'acting as a parent in the absence of a parent." However, the process (if any) that the District may require in order to secure parental consent for school activities (such as a field trip) is distinct from determining who may qualify as a parent for FERPA purposes.

What does it mean to say that the parent or guardian is "absent" for purposes of determining a parent under FERPA?

A parent is considered absent "if he or she is not present in the day-to-day home environment of the child."[12] However, please note that in the case of a natural parent, being "absent" does not remove that parent's FERPA rights—only a court order specifically removing the rights of a natural parent has this effect. The absence of the parent/guardian permits an individual to qualify as a FERPA parent.

When natural parents disagree, separate, or divorce, does FERPA give either parent the right to restrict access to the educational records of their child or children?

No, FERPA provides that "an educational agency or institution shall give full rights under the Act to either parent, unless the agency or institution has been provided with evidence that there is a court order, State statute, or legally binding document relating to such matters a divorce, separation, or custody that specifically revokes those rights."[13]

How does a school know when a court order or other legal document revokes one parent's rights to access their child's educational records?

The District (or the District's attorney) must examine the document to determine whether one parent's rights have been so limited or revoked. In one case, the court examined language in a divorce decree which awarded "the right to make all decisions regarding the child's health and safety while in his care during the school year." In this case, the court held that this language meant the mother did not have the right to initiate a hearing to challenge the content of their child's educational records.[14] It is also important to determine whether the document or order being examined represents the current and controlling language of the court in the parties' domestic litigation.

Practice Pointer—In any instance in which the examination and interpretation of court documents is instrumental in deciding a question under FERPA, it is very important that the District be certain that the most recent, authentic court document is being presented. In most instances, this will require at a minimum that the District's counsel contact the clerk of the court where the document was filed. In some cases, it may also be necessary or prudent to communicate with the attorney(s) for one or both parties to confirm the accuracy of the document at issue.

Does FERPA give natural, divorced, or separated parents any rights to access their children (not the child's records) at school—for example, to join their children for lunch?

No, FERPA simply does not address a natural parent's (whether married, divorced or separated) physical ability to access or visit with their child during the school day. In general, school District policies applicable to parents visiting students during the day may continue be applied and extend to both natural parents even after their separation or divorce. However, sometimes the separation or divorce agreement will curtail one parent's rights or abilities in this respect and in certain situations concerns for the security or safety of the child may dictate a case-by-case approach.

Is there any information in a student's education records which a parent does not have a right to access under FERPA?

Generally no, so long as the information does in fact constitute an educational record of the student and does not fall within one of the exceptions to the definition of educational records discussed in Chapter II, the parents of a student have a FERPA right of access to this information.[15] For example, counselor's notes may well fall under the sole possession exception previously discussed, and so not qualify as education records at all, in which case there is no FERPA right of access to these records.

What if the purported restriction on parental access is not another provision of FERPA, but a State law, will this prevent a parent from exercising their FERPA right of access?

Generally no, since FERPA as a federal statute conveying rights upon parents will be interpreted to prevail over conflicting State law. For example, in one case involving a State law which purported to give students a right to seek confidential medical services and to have this information withheld from their parents, FPCO specifically held the District must permit parental access to such records.[16]

What is the District's obligation to verify or authenticate the identity of someone who claims to be the parent of a student?

The FERPA regulations now require the District to use "reasonable methods to identify and authenticate the identity of parents, students, school officials, and any other parties to whom the agency or institution discloses personally identifiable information from education records." [17] However, the Department has also stated that "educational agencies and institutions should have the flexibility to decide the methods for identification and authentication of identity best suited to their own circumstances."[18] It also notable that the Department specifically rejected in 2008 the suggestion that some school staff themselves might be exempted from this requirement.

An Example—Is it reasonable to use a sliding scale of security, depending upon the nature of the personally identifiable information? Though perhaps obvious, the Department's position is a definitive "maybe" when discussing the difference between methods used to verify the identity of an individual before disclosing a social security number or credit card information, as compared with, disclosing a student's name or directory information.[19]

What are some examples of the steps a District might take to verify and authenticate the identity of individuals requesting access to records?

The Department has discussed a variety of techniques a District might use in this regard. Among these are personal recognition by the individual school official, photo identification, PIN, password, answer to a personal question, smart card or token, or biometric factor (finger, iris, or voice print).[20] However, there is also a fundamental recognition that the technology available for these purposes as well as the generally accepted standards for protecting certain information (such as financial or health information) are constantly evolving.

Are there any limitations upon the educational records that may be disclosed to the parents of a student under 18 years old or to an eligible student themselves?

Unlike most of the other non-consensual disclosure provisions which include some substantive limitations upon how much and the nature of the information which may be disclosed (see the discussion of the health or safety exception below), as long as the records involved are *bona fide* educational records under FERPA, the parent of a student or an eligible student would be entitled to inspect any or all of those educational records. However, remember that FERPA *does not* extend a universal right of access and inspection to *all* records of a student. Recall that counselor's notes and treatment records of students may often fall within the "sole use" exception, be outside the definition of educational records, and typically would not be subject to any FERPA right of access.

May the District disclose educational records to the attorney for parents of a student, or the attorney of an eligible student?

Yes. In many cases, attorneys will obtain and forward to the District a release for educational records, though the Department in the past has only recommended that a written designation of the attorney by the parent or eligible student is necessary.[21] As discussed below, however, it is important to remember that FERPA inspect rights are generally satisfied by providing access to records—copies of actual records are not generally required under FERPA. While the District may choose to provide copies of educational records requested by the attorney for a parent or eligible student, the mere fact that the request is generated by an attorney (as opposed to the parent or eligible student) does not change the District's duty under FERPA. Remember, a request by the student's attorney is not the same as a subpoena or court order directing that the records be produced.

Is the District liable if it intentionally, though inadvertently, discloses information to someone believed to be a parent of a student, but who is later discovered was not a parent?

Yes, if the District fails to employ "reasonable methods" to verify and authenticate the identity of an individual who claims to be a parent, then this is a FERPA violation.

If the District accidentally discloses information from a student's educational records to someone who is not the parent, is this a FERPA violation?

Yes, according to the Department—when 'agencies and institutions disclose education records to the wrong party because someone misaddresses an envelope, or puts the wrong material in a properly addressed envelope . . . this is a failure to properly identify the authorized recipient."[22]

An Example—On the last day before Thanksgiving, Tammy Teacher is writing an email to Teresa, the mother of one of her second grade students, Terrible Timmy. After spending almost 45 minutes going back forth between drafting the email and checking the internet for last minute flight schedules and prices to Ski Central, Tammy spell checks her message, pulls up the email address for Theresa, who is actually the parent of Terrific Teri, and clicks send on the email message detailing Timmy's declining and disruptive behavior throughout the Fall semester. Tammy shuts down her computer and heads off to Wal-Mart in search of discount winter wear. The following Monday, Principal Paula asks Tammy to come to her office for a meeting.

How long does the District have to comply with a request for access to educational records by a parent or eligible student?

The District is obliged to respond to such a request "within a reasonable period of time, but not more than 45 days after it has received the request."[23] However, as discussed in Chapter VIII, there are additional (and shorter) timelines which may apply when parents of students with disabilities have requested access to special education records. And of course, FERPA does not prevent a District from responding to parental requests for access much sooner than 45 days.

Practice Pointer—In some Districts or schools, there has developed a culture or expectation that parental requests to inspect records will be responded to within a day of receiving the request, and personnel will place aside other duties until this request has been satisfied. While certainly permissible, this is more than FERPA requires of the District in the vast majority of cases. In addition, an overly hurried approach to responding to parental request does include certain risks—either the response may be incomplete because one individual who happens to be involved in creating or maintain records is not available that day, or the response may include information that technically is not a part of the student's educational records. In the worst case, a quickly compiled response to a parental request for access (and copies) of educational records may accidentally include confidential information about other students which was not identified and removed or redacted.

Is the District required to provide parents a copy of a student's educational record?

Generally no, the District is only required to provide parents with access to records for purposes of inspection, rather than copies of records themselves. In three specific instances, FERPA does require a copy of the educational records be provided the parent or eligible student. One instance is when records are transferred from the District to another agency or institution—the District must provide a copy of the records upon request. Another instance is whenever the parent or eligible student gives written consent to a disclosure of the records and requests a copy of the records. Finally, FERPA provides that the District should provide copies of records when the failure to do so would "effectively result in a denial of access."[24] Outside of these specific cases, however, FERPA itself does not require that the District provide copies of a student's educational records to a parent or eligible student. (For additional instances when IDEA may require the parents of students with disabilities be provided with copies of education records, please see Chapter VIII).

So when parents seek to exercise their FERPA access rights, is the District required to make a copy of educational records whenever requested?

Not at all. FERPA initially requires only that the District provide "access" to the records. If, however, "circumstances effectively prevent the parent or eligible student from exercising their right to inspect and review" the educational records, the District is then required to either (1) provide a copy of the records to the parent or eligible student or (2) provide some "other arrangements" to facilitate the inspection and review of these records.[25]

When do circumstances effectively prevent a parent from exercising their FERPA inspection and access rights such that copies may be required?

In most cases, this appears to have been defined in reference to the geographical proximity (or not) of the parent to the school.

An Example—Doug the dad lives in New York City, though his ex-wife and their ten year old son Dudley live in Florida. Doug requests a copy of Dudley's standardized test scores from the Fall. The District's normal practice is not to provide parents with copies of these particular records, but rather to allow parents to make an appointment with the counselor to come to school and visually review the test results. In this instance, however, Doug has a very reasonable claim that this practice will effectively prevent him from exercising his rights as a parent to inspect his child's education record, and the District would be well advised to make a copy of this record available to Doug.

If a parent lives beyond commuting distance of the school, does the District have any alternative to providing copies of the records?

Yes, the District may forward the records to another school proximate to the parent, and the parent may inspect the records at that location before the records are returned to the District. In the example discussed above, the School may send a copy of Dudley's standardized test scores to the New York City elementary school closest to Doug the Dad, and Doug may make an appointment to come to that school to inspect the records before they are returned to Florida.

May the District charge a fee to parents or eligible students for copying educational records?

Yes, FERPA generally allows the District to charge a copying fee, "unless the imposition of the fee effectively prevents a parent or eligible student from exercising the right to inspect and review the student's education records."[26] In discussing this fee, the Department has explained that Districts "are entitled to charge reasonable fees for the actual cost of reproduction, secretarial time, and postage."[27]

May the District charge for the costs involved in searching for and retrieving educational records?

No, FERPA specifically prohibits charging parents or eligible students a search or retrieval fee, as this is considered "part of the accepted and normal business of educational agencies and institutions."[28]

What is meant by the reference to charging for secretarial time, and how does the District establish the amount of costs that may be charged under this provision?

Under FERPA, the District may charge for the secretarial time of the individual who will put down their regular duties and make copies of the educational records requested by the parent. In most cases, this effectively means the hourly rate multiplied by the actual time required to physically make the copies of the records requested. If the school secretary spends 30 minutes making copies of a fairly involved student file, and his hourly rate of pay is $15/hour, then the school may charge $7.50 plus the cost of the copies themselves to the parent who has requested these copies. However, in many instances it has been our experience that the District does not actually pursue the charge for secretarial time (perhaps unaware FERPA allows for this), but rather, simply imposes a reasonable charge for the copies themselves.

If education records cannot be located, have been lost or destroyed, does FERPA require the District to recreate these records?

No, FERPA does not require the re-creation of education records which have been lost or destroyed.[29]

Are parents or eligible students entitled to an explanation or interpretation of the educational records produced?

Importantly, yes, though sometimes school personnel are unaware or resistant to doing so, especially when dealing with challenging parents. However, FERPA does specifically require the District to "respond to reasonable requests for explanations and interpretations of the records."[30] Notably, the regulations do not require that any such explanation or interpretation be produced in writing. Of course, when dealing with a contentious school-parent relationship, it is sometimes prudent for the District to respond in writing (or at least, document the meeting or conversation when the explanation was offered) so that a record of the response has specifically been created.

Does FERPA require the District to honor standing requests from parents to receive certain information?

No, the District is not required to honor such standing requests under FERPA, such as parent's request that they be provided with copies of disciplinary reports or records of disciplinary referrals involving their child. Instead, the burden is on the parent to initiate each individual, specific request for records.[31]

What are the responsibilities of parents and the District whenever a parent believes that some educational records of their student have not been made available?

The parent bears primary responsibility for clearly specifying the records they are seeking. Though the District is required to undertake a "reasonable" search of the records, if a parent believes some records were not made available, it is the parent's duty to "submit a follow-up request clarifying the additional records he or she believes exist."[32]

What if the records requested contain personally identifiable information about other students?

The District must always remove any personally identifiable information about other students from records made available to parents of a particular student. If for some reason this is not possible, FERPA also permits the Districts to summarily advise the parents of the nature and content of the records at issue rather than providing physical access or a copy of the records themselves.[33]

Who is a student for purposes of FERPA?

A student is defined as "any individual who is or has been in attendance at an educational agency or institution and regarding whom the educational agency maintains education records."

Practice Pointer—In 2008, the definition of "attendance" under FERPA was amended so as to "include(s), but is not limited to (a) Attendance in person or by paper correspondence, videoconference, satellite, Internet, or other electronic information and telecommunications technologies for students who are not physically present in the classroom; and (b) The period during which a person is working under a work-study program."[34]

Does this mean that an individual who applies for discretionary admission to the District, for instance, an out of District student who applies for admission pursuant to the District's non-resident student policy, and then who for whatever reason does not actually attend school in the District, is not considered a "student" for purposes of FERPA?

Yes, this is literally correct. However, we caution that at the application or pre-admission stage it is (frequently) unknown as to which prospective students will actually enroll and attend the school or institution, so that an agreement to maintain the confidentiality of information received in connection with application of the prospective student is often extended as a matter of District or institutional policy. In other cases, the District or institution may have agreed with another FERPA covered entity to maintain the confidentiality of the subject information (i.e. a student's high school transcript) as condition of a copy of the record being forward to the District or institution. Consequently, it is frequently the case that either by policy or agreement the District or institution may have voluntarily accepted a duty to maintain the confidentiality of documents received by individuals who do not actually enroll and attend so as to be become "students" within FERPA's strict terms.

What about individuals (18 years old or older) who apply but are not granted admission to a college or University—are they entitled to inspect the records of the institution related to their application?

No, since the individual in this instance did not actually attend the institution, they are not a student with standing under FERPA to access any educational records which may be maintained by the institution.[35]

Are the records of student teachers maintained by the District considered educational records under FERPA?

Generally no, since student-teachers are not "students" of the District for purposes of FERPA. However, if the District maintains records on student-teachers "on behalf of" the college or University where the student-teacher is enrolled, then the individual student does have FERPA rights (including rights of access) which may be asserted as to the college or University.[36]

Does FERPA apply to and govern the handling of educational records submitted by individuals to the District during the course seeking or obtaining employment?

No, FERPA does not apply to personnel records in this respect, and when an individual voluntarily disclosures (or causes to be disclosed) their educational records to an agency or institution where they are not a student, but an employee, those educational records are considered personnel records and not educational records, and are not governed by FERPA even when the employing agency itself is a covered institution. [37]

An Example—Mark the Math Teacher is the newest member of the Math Department at City High, and in accordance with the Principal's long-standing practice, is assigned to teach both the regular and support sections of 9th grade math. Perhaps not surprisingly, a number of students in Mark's classes do not do well during the fall semester. Despite the fact that many of these same students also struggled mightily with math in middle school, a number of parents are convinced that the problem must be that Mark is not a very good teacher. One of the parents even asks to review a copy of Mark's college transcript—especially his math classes. While State law may provide some basis on which to withhold part or all of Mark's college transcripts, FERPA itself generally would not prevent the release of this information as these records were not created during and concerning Mark's tenure as a student at City High School.[38]

Practice Pointer—While FERPA does not prohibit the release of employee personnel records, including academic transcripts from the employee's graduate or undergraduate program, State privacy or open records laws may not necessarily entitle media, private persons or others access this information. For example, in Texas the legislature amended the State Open Records Act to except from the disclosure "transcripts from institutions of higher education maintained in the personnel files of professional public school employees."[39] This represents a state-level protection from disclosure for employee transcripts, rather than an objection to disclosure based upon FERPA per se.

What about the statements of student witnesses or victims relating to the alleged misconduct of District personnel—are these statements considered part of the personnel file, or are they educational records of the students?

This is a difficult question to which different courts may and have reached different results. In some cases, both parties agree that the actual names and other personally identifying information about individual students will be redacted from statements, in other cases, the court may order that such protections be taken to protect the privacy interests of students. However, in one case where the issue was whether FERPA prohibited the District from releasing unredacted copies of student witness statements about an incident where the teacher was alleged to have slammed a door into the arm of a student, a court held that the student's statements were not education records under FERPA at all.[40]

Do "former students" have the same FERPA rights as current students?

No. Perhaps most significantly, the regulations specifically provide that an institution may disclose directory information about former students without going through the notice and opt-out provisions otherwise applicable to directory information.[41] However, in the event that a former student did opt out of the directory information policy while a student, the 2008 regulations now clearly provide that "the agency or institution must continue to honor any valid request to opt out of the disclosure of directory information made while a student was in attendance unless the student rescinds the opt out request."[42] Furthermore, it is important to note that there is nothing in FERPA which minimizes or removes the FERPA rights of former students in terms of their access to educational records, their right to seek amendments or file a complaint as to those records, and to consent (or not) to the disclosure of personally identifiable information contained within their educational records.

Who is an eligible student under FERPA?

An eligible student is a student who has turned 18 years of age, or who is attending any postsecondary institution.

If a student under the age of 18 is declared emancipated under State law, are they now considered an eligible student for FERPA purposes?

No, FERPA recognizes only two ways in which a student becomes an "eligible student," and emancipation under State law is not one of these.[43]

Does FERPA prohibit the release of information or educational records to the parents of college students?

No, FERPA specifically allows a postsecondary institution to disclose education records to a parent who claims a student as a dependent for tax purposes and who meets the definition of a "parent" under FERPA. [44] Importantly, however, this disclosure is permissive on behalf of the postsecondary institution, and is no longer the FERPA right of access enjoyed by the parents of students under the age of 18 or who are still enrolled in the K–12 setting.

Practice Pointer—In response to the tragic shootings at Virginia Tech, and in the 2008 regulations, the Department has also specifically identified parents of postsecondary students as individuals to whom personally identifiable information may be disclosed in a health or safety emergency.[45] For a further discussion of the contemporary interpretation of the health & safety provision in the wake of the Virginia Tech tragedy, please see Chapter VI.

What about a student who is under the age of 18, but who is enrolled in a post-secondary institution?

If the student is a dependent for tax purposes, as is frequently the case with younger students, the permissive disclosure provisions discussed above would apply. In the event the student was not a dependent for federal tax purposes, and did not consent to the disclosure of information contained within their educational records to their parent(s), the student is an eligible student and now controls the exercise of their FERPA rights. To the extent that a non-consensual disclosure provision may apply, the most likely FERPA provisions are the health and safety emergency or when the institution determines that the student has violated the rules of the institution relating to the use of alcohol or controlled substances. As discussed further in Chapter VI, the post-secondary institution may disclose information from the student's educational records to their parents in both of these instances.[46] In any particular case, of course, other nonconsensual disclosure provisions of FERPA (such as the subpoena exception, or directory information) may apply, and so each situation must be examined individually.[47]

Is a student with a disability over the age of 18 considered an eligible student, or do their parents continue to enjoy FERPA rights?

On this issue, the Department has stated that in the absence of a guardianship, "it would be reasonable to presume that the parents of such a student are the persons who are in the best position to act on behalf of the student."[48] Of course, this "presumption" is inherently subject to rebuttal, and in closer cases the best course may well be document the consent of both the parents and the possibly eligible student.

When is the District required to obtain the consent of a parent or eligible student?

The District should obtain consent prior to any disclosure of personally identifiable information from a student's educational record, unless the disclosure falls within one of the exceptions discussed in Chapters IV or VI.

How should the District document the consent received from a parent or eligible student?

Whenever consent is required, the District must obtain this consent in writing, and this written consent must (1) identify the specific records to be disclosed, (2) the purpose of permitting the disclosure, and (3) specify the party or parties to whom disclosure is permitted.[49] In addition, we recommend that the District make certain the consent is properly dated.

Does FERPA require that a request to disclose educational records pursuant to any of the non-consensual disclosure provisions be made in writing?

No, FERPA itself does not require that such a request be in writing.[50] For instance, in the case of a health or safety emergency it is often impracticable to reduce a request to writing. Of course, this is a different and separate issue from the District's obligation to keep a record of certain non-consensual disclosures. And in the case of any non-consensual disclosures, FERPA does not prevent the District from requiring that any permissive, nonconsensual disclosures be submitted in writing and even on a particular form.

An Example—Roger the Registrar at City College receives a request to inspect the academic transcript of Stephen Sophomore by Stephen's father. In addition to validating the identity of the individual claiming to be Stephen's father, as well as Stephen's status as a dependent for income tax purposes, Roger has also developed form which qualifying parents must complete and submit in order to inspect their children's education records. Since the disclosure by postsecondary institutions to parents of tax dependent students is permissive on the part of the institution (and not a right of access, as in the K–12 setting), FERPA does not prevent Roger from developing and requiring the use of this form.

Is parental consent required before school officials may disclose and discuss with one another information contained within a student's educational records?

One of the nonconsensual disclosure provisions of the Act allows the District to designate school officials with a legitimate educational interest, and having done so, individuals covered by this definition may share information from student educational records without obtaining parental consent. Generally speaking, the school official with a legitimate educational interest will be one who requires access to the educational records of a student in order to perform his or her professional duties. For a further discussion of school officials and the legitimate educational interest provision, please see Chapter IV.

Is this another area where the application of FERPA may be different from one LEA to another when, for instance, one LEA defines the lead teacher of academic department as an individual with a legitimate, educational interest in reviewing the educational records of students enrolled in classes within the department, while another LEA either intentionally or unknowingly fails to do so?

Yes. In the first LEA mentioned above, the school may charge the lead teacher with overseeing the monitoring of all student progress in all departmental classes, as well as the identification, coordination and/or implementation of early intervening services for students who are struggling. As a result of establishing this arrangement and properly notifying parents of the lead teacher's status as an individual with LEI to access their child's educational records, the District has complied with FERPA in this instance. In the second scenario (no such designation or notification), the District would face at least a technical breach of FERPA's confidentiality requirements if the educational records of individual students were nonetheless shared with the lead teacher.[51]

May the District require that parents or eligible students provide consent as a condition of participation in a particular program?

The Department's position as to this point generally appears to be no, such consent may not be required as a condition of program participation. [52]

FERPA HEARINGS, REQUEST TO AMEND RECORDS, AND COMPLAINTS

What are the rights of parents or eligible students to seek an amendment to the educational records of a student?

A parent or eligible student has the right to request that educational records be amended if they believe the records are "inaccurate, misleading, or in violation of the student's rights of privacy." The District must make a determination as to whether or not to amend the record, and if the District determines not to amend the record, the District must notify the parent or eligible student of their right to a hearing.[53]

Does this mean a parent or eligible student can request a hearing to challenge a teacher's decision about a student's grade?

No, FERPA does not create any right on the part of students or parents to challenge a teacher or professor's "grading process," and was not intended "to overturn established standards and procedures for the challenge of substantive decisions made by an educational institution," but rather, "to require only that educational agencies and institutions conform to fair recordkeeping practices." [54] Some courts have described this as no more or less than the correction of a "ministerial error" in a student's record.[55]

An Example—Ned Neverwrong applies and is accepted for admission to Elite University. At Elite, freshman students are allowed to exempt certain first year classes (and received credit for the class) if they perform exceptionally well on Elite Challenge Exams. Ned takes the Challenge Exam Physics, and both Ned and his parents, Nancy and Nat, are stunned to learn that the professor who graded his exam considered his results "good," but not "exceptional." The Neverwrongs ask for a hearing to challenge the professor's grading of Ned's exam. Unfortunately, the Neverwrongs have no chance.[56]

How long does the District have to make the decision as to whether or not to amend the student's educational records?

The regulations only specify that this decision must be made "within a reasonable time after the agency or institution receives the request."[57]

When does a parent or eligible student have the right to request this hearing?

The regulations provide that "on request," the District shall give the parent or eligible student the opportunity for a hearing to determine whether the educational records are "inaccurate, misleading, or in violation of the privacy rights of the student."[58]

Does FERPA set forth any rules for the conduct of this hearing?

Yes, FERPA requires the District give reasonable advance notice to the parent or eligible student of the place, date and time of the hearing. The District is responsible for holding this hearing, which may be conducted by "any individual, including an official of the educational agency or institution who does not have a direct interest in the outcome of the hearing."[59] The directive that the hearing officer not have a direct interest in the outcome of the hearing is mandatory.[60] In discussing this point, FPCO has emphasized the Congressional intent that District "have some flexibility in conducing these hearings," and that a "rule of reason would be followed by the participants involved."[61]

Is the school official who makes an initial decision against amending an educational record automatically disqualified from conducing this hearing?

No, this individual is not automatically disqualified. However, FPCO has also stated that "ordinarily a school or agency would not assign as hearing officer either the individual who determined not to amend education records or someone who is in a direct reporting or close collegial relationship with that individual."[62]

What rights do parents or eligible students have at this hearing?

In addition to notice of the date, time, and place of the hearing, FERPA provides that parents or eligible students shall have the right to a "full and fair opportunity to present evidence relevant to the issues raised" and that they may at their own expense be "assisted or represented by one or more individuals . . . including an attorney."[63]

What about the District's decision—are there any specific requirements relating to either the format or content of this decision?

Yes, the District's decision must be writing, must be reached "within a reasonable period of time after the hearing," and shall be "based solely on the evidence presented at the hearing" and include both "summary of the evidence and the reasons for the decision."[64]

What may happen as a result of this hearing under FERPA to contest the accuracy of an educational record?

The District may determine that the record is, in fact, inaccurate, misleading or violates the privacy rights of the student, in which case the District shall "amend the record accordingly" and notify the parent or eligible student of the amendment in writing. In the alternative, the District may decide that the complaint is not correct, in which case the District shall "inform the parent or eligible student of the right to place a statement in the record commenting on the contested information or State why he or she disagrees with the decision of the" District.[65]

What obligation does the District have regarding the statement submitted by the parent or eligible student?

The District must keep the statement with the contest part of the record as long as the record itself is maintained, and must also disclose the statement whenever that portion of the student's education record is disclosed.[66] The purpose of the rule on this point is to guarantee that the parent's statement is also disclosed whenever the contested educational record is disclosed. Along these same lines, FPCO has specifically rejected the idea that multiple parental statements might be kept together in a separate location within the file.[67]

Does this obligation apply to disclosures to other school personnel, even those with legitimate educational reasons to access a student's file?

Yes, disclosures to school officials with legitimate educational interests in accessing a student's file are still "disclosures" under FERPA, even though they are a recognized instance when consent of the parent or eligible student is not required. Consequently, a statement by a parent submitted in accordance with the process described above must also be disclosed to other school officials who properly access this educational record of the student.

What if the District determines that the parent or eligible student's complaint does not identify one of the permissible basis upon which to seek the amendment of an educational record—does the District have to notify the parent's in writing of this decision, and do the parent's still have a right to place a statement in the file?

Though the regulations are silent as to this situation, the authors believe the better practice would be for the District's decision to State and explain this decision in writing in the same manner in which the District would otherwise reach a decision under this process. At this point, a parent would have the right to attach a statement of their own and expressing their disagreement with the decision. In the alternative, the District may also issue a decision which essentially and simply "dismisses" the parent's complaint and take the position that since no substantive ruling was made as to the accuracy of the underlying record, the parent's right to attach a statement or explanation does not attach.

Does a parent or eligible student have to ask for a hearing before they have the right to place a statement of explanation in the student's file?

Unless the District agrees to waive the hearing requirement, then a parent or eligible student must first go through the hearing process, as the Department has stated that "Congressional intent was that a parent or student should exhaust the administrative remedy afforded by the hearing process before exercising the right to place an explanatory statement in the record."[68] In some cases, however, we suspect that the District may decide that simply permitting the inclusion of the parent or eligible student's statement is less burdensome (and less costly) than going through the hearing process.

How does a parent or eligible student go about filing a complaint with the Department?

A complaint must be in writing and filed with the Family Policy Compliance Office of the Department, in Washington D.C., and should contain enough factually specific information that the Office can identify and investigate the alleged violation.[69] In 2008, the Department made clear that this initial complaint is not required to allege a "policy or practice" of violating FERPA, though of course FPCO "may elect to investigate and determine whether conduct that violates a specific FERPA requirement also constitutes a policy or practice of the agency or institution."[70]

Practice Pointer—The Complaint process is actually much more encompassing than the amendment and hearing rights discussed above. Under the hearing process the parent or eligible student may only seek an amendment of records which already exist in reference to information which is allegedly inaccurate, misleading, or invasive of the student's privacy rights. However, a complaint may be filed over any alleged violation of FERPA, including for example, the denial of access to a parent or eligible student, the improper release of information to third parties, or the failure to provide notice of a District's directory information policy.

Is there a requirement that a FERPA complaint be filed in a particular time frame?

Yes. Under the regulatory language, a timely complaint is considered to be a complaint filed within 180 days "of the alleged violation or that the complainant knew or reasonably should have know of the alleged violation."[71] However, the Department reserves the right to extend this time limit for "good cause," as may be determined by the Department.[72]

Are the FERPA complaint procedures only available to parents or eligible students?

No, the language of the regulations specifically State that "a person may file a complaint," so that, for example, a teacher could file a complaint if they believe the District had a violated FERPA in some regard.[73] Furthermore, the 2008 regulations make clear that the Department itself may initiate its own investigation of the District, even in the absence of a complaint filed by a parent, eligible student or other person.[74] The reason for this change, according to the Department, was that "sometimes FERPA violations are brought to the attention of the Office by school officials, officials in other schools, or by the media [and] [i]t is important that the Office have the authority to investigate allegations of noncompliance in these situation."[75]

An Example—Disgruntled Doug is notified that he will not be renewed by City School District. Doug is told that his non-renewal is for "budgetary reasons" due to a slowdown in the economy and State-wide funding cuts. However, Doug suspects that the true reason for his non-renewal is his difficult working relationship with the Director of Special Education, especially after he pointed out her "misstatements of fact" during a recent I.E.P. meeting. After filing for and being awarded his unemployment compensation, Doug begins to think long-term about his financial prospects. While thinking about his prospects, Doug recalls the Special Education Director frequently spoke about named, individual students with any school personnel who happened to be in her office, as well as on the phone with her friends and "colleagues" around the State. Doug (almost) breaks into a sweat in the hurry back to his lawyer's office.

If a complaint is filed against the District, what may the Department require the District to submit in response?

The 2008 regulations have clarified that the Department may require the District to submit "reports, information on policies and procedures, annual notifications, training materials, and other information necessary to carry out its enforcement responsibilities."[76] Perhaps by implication only, this more fully articulated list of materials that may routinely be required when responding to alleged FERPA violations does provide some suggestion that certain materials (for example, policies and training materials) should actually exist.

What is the standard used by the Department in determining whether the District has violated FERPA?

In order to seek to withhold, terminate or recover federal funds, the standard for identifying a FERPA violation is a "pattern or practice" of violating the law. This means that a single, inadvertent, or mistaken FERPA violation will almost always be insufficient to sustain a complaint under the Act. However, the 2008 regulations were amended to clarify that FPCO may still investigate an alleged, singular violation of FERPA and potentially issue a letter of finding as to a singular violation. However, FPCO may not pursue any of the funding remedies for a FERPA violation unless it is also determined that the violation also constitutes or was caused by a "policy or practice" of the institution.[77]

How may the Department go about enforcing a determination that a District actually has a "policy or practice" of violating FERPA?

Initially, the Department generally seeks to obtain the voluntary agreement of the District to remedy the violation—usually within the context of a compliance agreement. In the event this is unsuccessful, the Department has the authority to seek termination federal funding administered by the Department of Education, withholding of such funding or issuance of a "cease and desist" order. [78] Finally, the Department may also seek injunctive relief[79]—essentially a court order directing the District to comply with FERPA in some particular manner.

SO SUE ME—PURSUING FERPA CLAIMS IN COURT

May parents or eligible students file a federal lawsuit against either the District or school officials for a violation of FERPA?

On the same day the Supreme Court decided *Owasso v. Falvo*, the Court also decided the case of *Gonzaga University v. Doe*.[80] In *Gonzaga*, the Court held that FERPA is a funding statute that did not confer upon individuals a right to sue a covered entity (District or university) for a violation of the confidentiality provisions of FERPA under Section 1983. For the most part, this case has barred subsequent federal litigation against the District based solely on an alleged FERPA violation. However, in Chapter VIII we discuss the additional, confidentiality provisions of IDEA and Section 504 which continue to serve as a basis for the pursuit of federal litigation.

Sidebar. In *Gonzaga University*, a student "John Doe" sued the university after he learned that he was denied a teaching certificate, apparently based upon the disclosure of allegations of sexual misconduct by him against a female, undergraduate student by a "teacher certification specialist" who worked for the University. In rejecting Doe's suit, the Court noted that the Department has established an office to investigate and enforce FERPA's statutory and regulatory standards—the Family Policy Compliance Office (FPCO).[81]

Can a District or school official be sued under State law for conduct that allegedly violates FERPA?

Yes. There are some cases in which lawsuits alleging of FERPA violations have been filed on the basis of FERPA and which have included allegations of related State law violations. For instance, some states have a statutory similar provision to FERPA relating to the parental rights of access to their children's educational records. Whether this State law provision allows for a lawsuit to be filed (as opposed to some administrative remedy such as filing a complaint with the State Department of Education) is a State law question which must be addressed on a case-by-case basis.[82]

Are there other State laws which may be used as the basis upon which to sue a District or school official for alleged breaches of FERPA's confidentiality provisions?

Yes. In some states, it may also be possible to sue the District or an individual for invasion of privacy, and the inappropriate disclosure of information required to be confidential under FERPA could give rise to a lawsuit on this basis. In addition, the disclosure of information about a student which is false and damaging to the student may give rise to claims for defamation (including libel or slander).

Practice Pointer—Although it is a question of State law, the type of lawsuit discussed above is considered a "tort" which must be predicated on some duty on the part of the District or school officials. In this particular scenario, the argument would be that the parent or eligible students had a reasonable expectation of privacy since the District or school officials had a duty under federal law (FERPA) to maintain the confidentiality of personal information about the student. In addition to State law variations as to whether such a claim is viable, of course, the nature of the confidential information disclosed and other particular facts and circumstances surrounding the case in question will heavily influence the possibility of litigation in this area.

Are there legal protections for districts and school officials who are sued under any of these State law claims?

In many states, there are varying degrees and forms of immunity which extend some protections of Districts and school officials in these cases. In some states, this protection may be so complete and absolute as to render the concern over such claims fairly minor. In other states, claims may be permitted only when the parent or student alleges intentional conduct on the part of school officials, while in some states the simple negligent failure to maintain confidential certain information may be a realistically available basis on which to file suit. In all of these situations, the breadth and depth of immunity as a defense to suits of this kind must be examined on a case-by-case basis.

ENDNOTES

1. *Zelman v. Simmons-Harris*, 536 U.S. 639 (2002).

2. These include the opportunity of students to transfer to better performing schools if their own school does not meet State standards for two consecutive years, the opportunity to receive supplement instruction for some students when their school does not meet standards for three years, and the option of transferring out of a school found to be persistently dangerous, as defined by the state. See generally "Four Pillars of NCLB" accessed from the U.S. Department of Education website www.ed.gov/nclb/overview/intro/4pillars.html on January 1, 2009.

3. 34 C.F.R. § 99.7.

4. 34 C.F.R. § 99.7(a)(3); 34 C.F.R. § 99.31(a)(1).

5. Letter to Anonymous (March 10, 1999).

6. 34 C.F.R. § 99.7(b)(2).

7. May 25, 1970 Memorandum, accessed on January 5, 2009 from http://www.ed.gov/about/offices/list/ocr/docs/lau1970.html.

8. Letter to Dr. Estanislado Y. Paz, Superintendent of the Tucson Unified School District on June 18, 2002, memorializing settlement agreement in OCR Complaint Case Number 08011157-D, accessed on January 5, 2009 from http://www.ed.gov/

about/offices/list/ocr/letters/tucsonusd08011157.html. The Tucson letter does include some 'qualifying' language to the effect that the district's obligation to translate these documents is "to the extent feasible," but would also include any other documents routinely provided to parents.

9. Letter to Parent (August 20, 2004).

10. Id. This is consistent with the general rule under FERPA that a "school is not required by FERPA to disclose information from a student's education records to a third party, even if the parent has provided consent." Id. Of course, this does not prohibit the school from making such a disclosure, though we strongly recommend that the consent upon which this disclosure is based be documented. The major exception to this provision is discussed in Chapter VIII below, where IDEA does specifically provide the parents of disabled student with the right to have their child's educational records inspected by a third party.

11. Federal Register Vo. 61, No. 226 59294 (November 21, 1996).

12. Id.

13. 34 C.F.R. § 99.4.

14. *Taylor v. Vermont Department of Education,* 313 F.3d 768 (2d. Cir 2002). However, it should be noted that there is a possible distinction between the language in a domestic relations order which limits a parent's right to make decisions about a child's education, as compared to that parent's right to access educational records in the first instance. In fact, in some cases the court will specifically require the parents to confer and consult, while vesting final decision-making authority in one parent. In these instances, the district should be careful not to read the court's language too broadly, since it is arguable that a parent without ultimate decision-making authority cannot meaningfully confer with the other parent without first having access to their child's educational records. It is also worth noting that, at least in some jurisdictions, the language found in domestic relations agreements and orders is fairly standardized, and it can be important for the district to become familiar with how local judges interpret the language in their own orders or court-approved agreements.

15. Letter to Robert H. Henry (March 14, 2005).

16. Id.

17. 34 C.F.R. § 99.31(c).

18. Federal Register Vol. 73, No. 237 74840 (December 9, 2008).

19. Id.

20. Federal Register Vol. 73, No. 57 15585 (March 24, 2008). In the NPRM, the Department more forcefully appears to State that the greater the harm that might result from disclosure, "the more protections the agency must use to ensure that its methods are reasonable." Id.

21. Letter to Ms. Doris Dixon (October 22, 1998). This letter actually discusses release of educational records by the NCAA to attorneys for parents or eligible students, but the Department's interpretation as it concerns the necessity of an actual release, as opposed to a written designation by the party holding FERPA access rights, should be the same in both instances.

22. Federal Register Vol. 73, No. 57 15585 (March 24, 2008).

23. 34 C.F.R. § 99.10(b).
24. Federal Register Vol. 53, No. 69 11953 (April 11, 1988). See 34 C.F.R. § 99.10 and when the parent lives outside commuting distance of the school.
25. 34 C.F.R. § 99.10(d).
26. 34 C.F.R. § 99.11(a).
27. Federal Register Vol. 53, No. 69 11953 (April 11, 1988).
28. 34 C.F.R. § 99.11(a); Federal Register Vol. 53, No. 69 11953 (April 11, 1988).
29. FPCO Letter of July 16, 2002.
30. 34 C.F.R. § 99.10(c).
31. Letter to Parent (August 20, 2004).
32. Id.
33. 34 C.F.R. § 99.12(a).
34. 34 C.F.R. § 99.3. This purpose for this change was to "prevent the regulations from becoming out of date as new formats and methods are developed" for the delivery of instruction. Federal Register Vol. 73, No. 237 74807 (December 9, 2008).
35. Letter to Anonymous (March 10, 1999).
36. Letter to University Student (November 1, 2005).
37. *Klein v. Mattox* 830 F.3d 576 (1987); *Hovet v. Hebron Public School District,* 419 N.W.2d 189 (Supreme Court of North Dakota, 1988).
38. On a related note, the No Child Left Behind Act provides parents with a right to know certain information about their child's teacher, including the certification status and degree major of the teacher. However, this is not typically the type of information which is of greatest concern to individual educators, who may not unreasonably feel that it is one thing to reveal that they majored in political science as opposed to history, quite another to disclose the C- they received in the Spring Semester of their senior year.
39. *Houston Independent School District v. Houston Chronicle Publishing Company,* 798 S.W.2d 580 (Court of Appeals of Texas, 1990). In addition to limitations or exclusion under State Open Records or Sunshine Acts, the reader is also recommended to consider the different weight the state(s) may apply to an individual privacy interest in this information.
40. *City of Boston School Committee v. Boston Teacher's Union,* 2006 WL 4125023 (Mass. Super. 2006) (note again that this case dealt with the unredacted student statements). See also *Wallace v. Cranbrook Educational Community* 2006 WL 2796135 (E.D. Mich. 2006) and *Ellis v. Cleveland Municipal School Dist,* 309 F.2d 1019 (N.D. Ohio 2004), cited in *Boston* and standing for the similar proposition.
41. 34 C.F.R. § 99.37(a).
42. Id. In several additional places, FERPA arguably limits the notice to which former students are entitled. See Federal Register Vol. 53, No. 69 11951–2 (April 11, 1988).
43. See also the Analysis of Comments and Changes, Federal Register Vol. 69, No. 77 21671 (April 21, 2004), where the Department again listed only these two conditions—a student who turns 18 years of age or attends a postsecondary institution—as the manner in which a student becomes an eligible student.

44. 34 C.F.R. § 99.31(a)(8); In determining whether a student is a dependent for tax purposes, the institution should refer to the most recently filed tax return. It is also worth noting that in this situation, the disclosure to the parent is permissive, not mandatory. See Federal Register Vol. 65, No. 130 (July 6, 2000).

45. 34 C.F.R. § 99.36(a); Federal Register Vol. 73, No. 237 74838–9 (December 9, 2008).

46. 34 C.F.R. § 99.31(a)(14). Letter to Dr. Omero Suarez (January 16, 2004). Note also that in the wake of the tragic shootings at Virginia Tech University, FERPA has issued guidance substantially liberalizing the disclosure of information to parents of college students. See Chapter VI for further discussion of these developments.

47. Federal Register Vol. 73, No. 237 74813 (December 9, 2008).

48. Federal Register Vol. 53, No. 69 11951 (April 11, 1988).

49. 34 C.F.R. § 99.30(b).

50. Federal Register Vol. 53 No. 69 11954 (April 11, 1988).

51. Of course, given the instructionally focused nature of this hypothetical situation and the likely absence of any harm to the student associated with this particular practice, we believe that the district may still prevail against a charged violation before many judges. The Department, we suspect, is more likely to aggressively pursue the technical violation.

52. Letter to Julie Ann Evans (August 15, 2005).

53. 34 C.F.R. § 99.20.

54. *Tarka v. Cunningham,* 917 F.2d 890 (2nd Cir. 1990); *Adatsi v. Mathur,* 935 F.2d 272 (7th Cir. 1991); Letter to Parent (August 13, 2004). See also Federal Register Vol. 53, No. 69 11952 (April 11, 1988), where the Department stated that "the Act was not intended to be used to replace previously established procedures to appeal the grade." Of course, the Department went on to note, the district could permit a parent or eligible student to use this FERPA hearing to challenge or appeal a grade if they so elected. In the absence of a local decision to expand the scope of FERPA hearings generally, courts are reluctant to intervene in grading disputes between schools and parents. In some instances, controlling authority may be found in school or district grading policies or practices, when they exist, as well as Code of Ethics for educators, which typically include prohibitions on the misrepresentation or falsification of information submitted to the school. Evidence of a teacher's repeated failures in this regard may also be grounds for teacher discipline on the grounds of incompetency under state tenure statutes.

55. *Guillaume v. Rector and Visitors of the University of Virginia,* 116 F.Supp.2d 694, 708 (W.D. Virginia 2000).

56. *Lewin v. Medical College of Hampton Roads,* 931 F.Supp. 443 (E.D. Virgina 1996).

57. 34 C.F.R. § 99.20(b).

58. 34 C.F.R. § 99.21(a).

59. 34 C.F.R. § 99.22(b).

60. Letter to Parent (August 13, 2004).

61. Id. Quoting from the Joint Statement of Explanation of Buckley/Pell, FPCO has apparently endorsed the view that this hearing may be conducted at either the district or the school level. Id.

62. Id.

63. 34 C.F.R. § 99.22(d).

64. 34 C.F.R. § 99.22(e)–(f).

65. 34 C.F.R. § 99.21(b).

66. 34 C.F.R. § 99.21(c); Letter to Parent (August 13, 2004).

67. Letter to Parent (August 13, 2004).

68. Federal Register Vol. 53 No. 69 11954 (April 11, 1988).

69. 34 C.F.R. § 99.63 & 64.

70. Federal Register Vol. 73, No. 57 15591 (March 24, 2008).

71. 34 C.F.R. § 99.64(c).

72. 34 C.F.R. § 99.64(d). The Department has wrestled with this issue over time, drawing a distinction at one point between a complaint involving complex circumstances and which the complainant has sought to resolve independently, as compared with an alleged violation that occurred "years ago and was never pursued." Federal Register Vol. 53, No. 69 11958 (April 11, 1988).

73. 34 C.F.R. § 99.63. This is a distinction between FERPA and the PPRA (discussed in Chapter IX), where in the case of the later authority to file a complaint is vested only in parents and eligible students.

74. 34 C.F.R. § 99.64(b). Federal Register Vol. 73, No. 237 74841 (December 8, 2008).

75. Federal Register Vol. 73, No. 237 74841–2 (December 8, 2008).

76. 34 C.F.R. 99.62. Previously, the regulation only mentioned "reports," and this change was apparently intended to clarify the full extent of the materials which may be required of the district during the investigation of a complaint. See Federal Register Vol. 73, No. 57 15591 (March 24, 2008).

77. See both Federal Register Vol. 73, No. 57 15591 (March 24, 2008) & Federal Register Vol. 73, No. 237 74841 (December 8, 2008) in this regard.

78. 34 C.F.R. § 99.67. In response to a specific question, the Department acknowledged that it has no authority to withhold any other federal funding a district may receive from any other federal Department, other than the Department of Education. Federal Register Vol. 53, No. 69 11958 (April 11, 1988).

79. Federal Register Vol. 73, No. 57 15592 (March 24, 2008).

80. Gonzaga University v. Doe, 536 U.S. 273, 122 S.Ct. 2268 (2002).

81. Id.

82. Compare *Chisolm v. Tippens,* 289 Ga.App. 757, 658 S.E.2d 147 (Ga.App. 2008)(State statute permitting parents access to child's education records creates no private cause of action) with *Scott v. Minneapolis Public Schools,* Special Dist. No. 1, 2006 WL 997721(Minn.App. 2006) (State Data Practices Act authorized jury verdict and award of damages and fees in excess of $180,000 to parents of student whose special education assessment was inadvertently disclosed to other students).

Chapter 4

Internal School Disclosures without Prior Permission

FERPA's original purposes included protecting student information from unauthorized access—including unauthorized access by other school officials. However, both Congress and the Department realized that requiring school officials to obtain prior written consent before accessing any and all student records would significantly challenge and impair the effective daily operation of educational institutions. Consequently, FERPA contains a number of exceptions permitting educational institutions to access student records without the prior permission of students or parents. The most significant of these is the exception permitting access by those "school officials" possessing a "legitimate educational interest" in so doing; however, FERPA contains a number of similar exceptions permitting internal review and disclosure of a student's educational records. In this chapter, we will also address disclosures to state or federal authorities in connection with an audit or evaluation of an educational program.

THE LEGITIMATE EDUCATIONAL INTEREST EXCEPTION

What is the "legitimate educational interest" exception?

The "legitimate educational interest" (or "LEI") exception permits "school officials" possessing a "legitimate educational interest" to access a student's educational records without prior parent or eligible student authorization; however, an institution may only employ LEI if it has adequately defined (1) who it considers to be a "school official"; (2) what will be regarded as a "legitimate educational interest"; and (3) has given parents or eligible students notice of these definitions.

What is the purpose of the "legitimate educational interest" exception?

FERPA's protections of personally identifiable information contained in educational records are so expansive that—without this particular exception—they would significantly frustrate the effective operation of educational institutions. Imagine a professor unable to conduct a routine "status check" on his or her advisees' progress toward graduation without each advisee's prior, express written permission, or a principal unable to prepare for an IEP meeting by reviewing a student's permanent record without his or her parents' prior written permission. As a result, Congress authorized school officials to access students' educational records without prior parental or eligible student permission where they have a "legitimate educational interest" in so doing.[1] With perhaps the exception of directory information, the "legitimate educational interest" is undoubtedly the most utilized and functionally crucial FERPA exception.

While the "legitimate educational interest" may seem relatively clear, it has been the subject of numerous misunderstandings leading to FPCO complaints and litigation. Although FERPA permits disclosure to "school officials" with a "legitimate educational interest," neither of these terms is expressly defined in FERPA or its regulations. Would, for example, a retired professor whose assistance was sought by a graduate student challenging a grade constitute a "school official" with a "legitimate interest?"[2] Could a chief flight instructor employed by the Federal Aviation Administration (FAA) serving as a college flying instructor report student violations of federal aviation regulations to the FAA?[3] Would the exception permit a college professor charged by a student with sexual harassment to give relevant student records to his personal attorney?[4] All of these situations—addressed specifically in FPCO opinion letters—are discussed below.

What exactly is a "legitimate educational interest which permits the disclosure without consent to other school officials?"

As with many other places in the law, unfortunately FERPA does not expressly define what constitutes a "legitimate educational interest" nor does it present school officials with a guide for determining when such an interest exists. Instead, the Department has seemingly permitted educational institutions wide latitude in establishing criteria for determining such an interest, requiring only that the institution's criteria for making such a determination be included in the annual notification to parents and/or eligible students and consistently applied.[5] The *sole* FPCO guidance is contained in a 2005 letter, in which FPCO commented: "Generally, if a school official is performing an official task for the [institution] that requires access to information in education records, that official has a legitimate educational interest."[6] Consequently, educational institutions have very broad discretion in determining their own criteria.

What steps are necessary for identifying those whom an institution believes to possess a "legitimate educational interest?"

Determining who possesses a legitimate educational interest ("LEI") is both relatively easy and simultaneously complicated by FPCO's seeming refusal to establish any specific criteria—or even guidance—as to when an official has such an interest. In March 2008, the United States Department of Education expressly conceded that the proposed 2008 regulations "do not address what constitutes a legitimate educational interest."[7] Similarly, those FPCO opinions addressing the issue treat it very briefly, with FPCO apparently never overturning the criteria selected by an educational institution to determine LEI.[8]

Practice Pointer—Under FERPA, educational institutions have very broad discretion in determining whom they believe to have a "legitimate educational interest" in accessing a student's educational records without prior permission. However, remember FERPA is a very balanced law—where institutions generally receive the ability to access without permission, it is often accompanied by a requirement that parents or eligible students receive effective prior notice. In the context of the "legitimate educational interest" exception, an institution's failure to promulgate, disseminate, and enforce effective definitions of "school official" and "legitimate educational interest" will effectively bar schools from taking advantage of this very useful exception.

What notice do institutions have to provide parents or eligible students regarding what the institution considers to be a "legitimate educational interest?"

While the LEI exception permits institutions access to student records without prior parent or eligible student permission, to employ the exception, institutions must first annually disclose the criteria on which they will base their decision and make all determinations consistently with these criteria. "An educational agency or institution that discloses information under this exception must specify in its annual notification of FERPA rights . . . the criteria it uses to determine who constitutes a school official and what constitutes a legitimate educational interest."[9] Institutions may specify those personnel by position (for example, teachers, administrators, professors, and support personnel whose access to records is necessary to fulfill an official task) or by criteria (for example, any employee or agent of the institution whose knowledge of information contained in the records is necessary to perform an official task). While either method would seemingly work, it is important that this procedural step be followed—otherwise, the institution cannot use the LEI exception.[10] In the December 2008 regulatory comments, FPCO specifically recommends drafting the criteria broadly enough to include members of an educational institution's law enforcement unit, permitting sharing information with the institution's law enforcement unit in circumstances that may not rise to the level of a "health of safety emergency." [11]

Practice Pointer—As institutions are required to provide an annual FERPA rights notification and directory information "opt out" provision, they should use this opportunity to detail whom they consider to be "school officials" and what constitutes "legitimate educational interests." The language should be categorical and not limited to specific positions ("institutional personnel performing official or related acts, including but not limited to third parties conducting services for the institution," not "instructors and administrators"), and should take advantage of FPCO's expansive interpretation of "legitimate educational interest," identifying a legitimate educational interest as "any action required by the school official's duties or responsibilities."

***An Example*—"Legitimate Educational Interest"**—City County School District considers a faculty or staff member or any other person acting for the school district to possess a legitimate educational interest in a student's educational records if that access is necessary for the individual to perform an authorized task, including, but not limited to, a task required or necessitated by the employee's job description; to provide a benefit or service to the student or his or her family; or for reasons related to school or student safety or security.

Who may be designated as a school official with a legitimate educational interest?

FPCO has taken a very expansive interpretation of who can constitute a "school official" with a "legitimate educational interest." Some categories of "school officials" are very clear—administrators, teachers, and related personnel providing educational services within an institution. In addition, this concept has also grown to include less likely individuals and institutions, such as "outside legal counsel, psychologists[,] collection agents[,]" third-party agencies maintaining educational records on behalf of schools, law enforcement units within schools and institutions, emeritus or retired faculty, and a national "degree verify" services.[12] For example, FPCO has specifically found that the National Student Clearinghouse Degree Verify Service can constitute an "other school official" possessing a "legitimate educational interest," as can an emeritus professor who no longer actively teaches.[13]

Can this include volunteers and other third parties who may not be employed by the institution?

Yes. The December 2008 regulations specifically permit institutions to classify individuals who are not employed by an institution, including "a contractor, consultant, volunteer, or other party to whom an agency or institution has outsourced institutional services or functions" as "other" school officials.[14] Recognizing that individuals who are not employees of institutions often provide institutional services or functions and may, as a result of their job duties, need to access educational records, FERPA permits institutions to identify non-employees acting for the institution as "other school officials." These expressly include:

- [P]arents and other volunteers who assist school in various capacities, such as serving on official committees, serving as teachers' aides, and working in administrative offices;
- "Outside" legal counsel;
- School transportation officials (including bus drivers);
- School nurses;
- Practicum and fieldwork students;
- Unpaid interns;
- Consultants and contractors; and
- Other outside parties providing institutional services and performing institutional functions.[15]

Regardless of the position, the individual so designated must meet the remaining requirements of being designated as an "other school official." These are detailed immediately below.

Are there any conditions attached to the designation of third parties as school officials?

Yes. In order to designate any of the individuals listed above as "school officials," these individuals must satisfy three conditions. First, these individuals must "perform an institutional service or function for which the agency or institution would otherwise use employees." Second, the individual must be "under the direct control of the agency or institution with respect to the use and maintenance of education records." Third, the individual must be subject to the FERPA re-disclosure requirements relating to personally identifiable information.[16] An elaboration on each of these concepts may be found below.

How should institutions handle student record access by volunteers and other non-employees who a school designates as "other school officials?"

While the December 2008 regulations specifically permit institutions to classify volunteers as "other school officials" and permit them to have access to educational records, the regulatory comment specifically cautions institutions to "use good judgment in determining the extent to which volunteers . . . need to have access to education records." Institutions are further cautioned to ensure that volunteers "do not improperly disclose information from students' education records."[17]

As a practical matter, institutions should be *very careful* when permitting volunteers and other individuals over whom a school district may have direct, but consequence-free control, to have access to a student's educational records. Unlike contractors and other third parties that may be contractually bound to adhere to FERPA confidentiality requirements and whose compliance may be guaranteed through specific penalties in the contract, institutions can take few meaningful steps against volunteers who violate confidentiality provisions. At a minimum, if an institution elects to provide volunteers with access to educational records, the institution should develop a process to educate volunteers as to the confidentiality requirements of FERPA and place them on notice that, in the event of a breach of confidentiality, they may not be allowed to volunteer in any future capacity.

Practice Pointer—Institutions should be particularly concerned by parent volunteers who may misuse institutional privileges to access information related to their child. In such instances, parents may believe their child was "mistreated" by the institution when compared to another, leading to a number of complicating and time-consuming challenges.

Why do third parties have to be "acting for" an educational institution in order to be classified as an "other school official?"

In the view of the Department, this limitation is grounded in the very origins of FERPA, when Senator Buckley and Senator Pell "specifically referred to materials that are maintained by a school *or by one of its agents.*"[18] This concept that the outside party is acting as the agent for the institution is crucial in distinguishing between the permissible use of personally identifiable information by the outside party, and the prohibited designation of outside parties as school officials "any time a vendor or other outside party wants to access education records to provide a product or service to schools, parents and students" (such as the institution's insurance company wanting the names of all students taking drivers' education in order to provide parents with information about insurance rate discounts).[19] In the case of the later, the outside party would not be acting within the scope of any agency relationship designated or recognized by the school, and therefore, would not fall within the acceptable scope of a school official for these purposes.

An Example—By state law, City County School District is required to maintain a "student information system," securely and electronically maintaining student data. CCSD contracts with EduKnow, a third-party data information service, to collect and maintain the student information. As part of its service, EduKnow performs routine "paper" audits against its electronic records to verify that grades and other information are being appropriately transferred to the central server. This requires EduKnow personnel to access both a student's electronic record and his or her "paper" record kept at the school district. As this is a service that would ordinarily be performed by school officials and is necessary in CCSD's determination for EduKnow to adequately perform its record-keeping function, EduKnow is acting as an agent of the school district, and could be designated as an "other school official" with LEI—provided CCSD followed appropriate notice requirements.[20]

Practice Pointer—Remember, the third party *must* provide services for which the "agency or institution would otherwise use its own employees" (subject to FERPA's interpretation of this term, which is explained further below). It would not extend to the example above of the school district's insurance company requesting the names of all students completing a drivers' education class in order to inform their parents of potential discounts on their insurance.[21] Under such a scenario, the appropriate response would be to require that the insurance company procure parent or eligible student authorization to disclose the information as a condition of offering the insurance.

What does "direct control" mean in the condition that third parties are under the "direct control" of the institution?

The purpose of this provision is to impose an independent limitation as to those individuals or entities that may be designated as school officials" by the institution, prohibiting an institution from sharing records with a third party "unless it can control the party's maintenance, use, and re-disclosure of education records."[22] For example, the institution could require a contractor to maintain the records in a particular manner as designated or approved by the institution.

The Department's positions on what constitutes direct control have, at times, seemed directly contradictory. The Department has stated that the "direct control" standard does not require institutions to enter into contracts with outside parties guaranteeing that they will not re-disclose educational records provided to them by an institution. However, the Department has also suggested that one manner in which schools may ensure that outside parties understand their duties under FERPA would be "to clearly describe those responsibilities in a written agreement or contract."[23] Nor does the "direct control" standard specifically require that schools verify that outside parties have the resources to comply with FERPA, though of course, schools do remain responsible for "ensuring that outside parties that provide institutional services or functions as 'school officials . . . do not maintain, use, or re-disclose education records except as directed by the agency or institution."[24]

Does the requirement that "an agency or institution would otherwise use its own employees" mean that an institution's employee must ordinarily perform the outsourced service in order for the outside party to be considered a school official?

No. The exception permitting institutions to share educational records with third-party vendors and other non-school employees performing services that the institution "would otherwise use its own employees" does *not* require the institution to have an employee who formerly performed this service, but which the institution now elects to "outsource it." [25] Instead, the requirement appears to distinguish non-employees performing education-related or other functions (such as legal services, speech therapy, accounting, or transportation services) that would—in the absence of the availability of the third party—have to be performed by a school employee because they are necessary to the operation of the institution.

An Example—City County School District Board of Education retains the law firm of Dewey, Piaget, and Hunter to provide legal services to the school district. The district receives a letter from Ms. Plaintiff, alleging that the district has violated her son John's right to special education services under the Individuals with Disabilities Education Act (IDEA), and is requesting a meeting. Dr. Jones, the education officer, sends a copy of John's educational file and relevant special education evaluation records to the law firm, requesting an opinion as to whether John's rights have been violated. Although the district has never employed a lawyer "in house" to provide this service, FERPA permits Dr. Jones to send this information to Dewey, Piaget, and Hunter as it is performing a function—assessing the likelihood of an IDEA violation—that would otherwise have to be performed by a school official.[26]

Are employees who are also parents (employee/parent) considered "other school officials" when using institutional privileges to access the educational records of their own children?

Only if the purpose and scope of the employee/parent's access falls within the institution's definition of "other school officials"—that is, the employee/parent's access is necessitated by his or her job responsibilities and not his or her parental interests. While employee/parents may be more familiar with the nature and location of the educational records of their children, they should have no greater rights of access under FERPA than non-employee parents.

Practice Pointer—As a practical matter, employee/parents present a number of FERPA challenges to school officials. By virtue of their profession and their presumptively greater familiarity with FERPA, they may be much more effective in exercising their FERPA rights than non-employee parents. Additionally, school officials often share information with employee/parents more freely than they would with non-employee parents about their own children—as well as their children's interactions with other students. School officials should remind employee/parents that FERPA does not invest them with special status, nor are they likely to fall within the "other school official" exception when they are proceeding as a parent. Consequently, school officials should treat employee/parents as they would any other parent when they are making inquires about their own (or other) students.

An Example—Vivian is a ninth grade biology teacher at City County High School. Her eleventh grade son, Kyle, is involved in a fight with Trevor, another eleventh grader. Kyle is suspended for a week for violating the school's "zero tolerance" policy on fighting; however, Vivian notices that Trevor continues to attend class. She approaches Danielle, the building principal, and asks why Trevor is still in class. Instead of informing Vivian that she cannot discuss the matter with her, Danielle informs Vivian that Trevor has an emotional/behavioral disorder, is covered by an I.E.P., and his manifestation determination recorded in a written finding by the school concluded that his fight with Kyle was substantially related to his disability. Although Vivian is a teacher at the school, it is highly unlikely that she would fall within the school's definition of "other school official" with a "legitimate educational interest" in this instance as she primarily seeks this information in her role as a parent, not a teacher. As a result, Danielle may well have violated FERPA by disclosing this information to Vivian.

Are FERPA's confidentiality provisions violated when employee/parents use institutional privileges to access the educational records of their own children?

Probably not. While FERPA does not provide employee/parents with greater access, it also does not expressly prohibit employee/parents from using (or abusing) institutional privileges to access their own children's educational records. Assuming a school has adequate institutional protection protocols, an employee/parent who inappropriately accesses only their own child's educational records would not have inappropriately accessed any record to which he or she was not otherwise entitled under FERPA—even if the employee/parent failed to follow appropriate institutional protocols for accessing educational records. However, an employee/parent's "misuse" of institutional privileges or access to a records system might constitute an independent violation of a workplace rule, giving rise to a potential adverse employment action.

Practice Pointer—An institution has an obligation under FERPA to ensure that it maintains a records system that effectively prevents access to educational records by individuals who do not have an appropriate interest in accessing those records (see Chapter VII). A parent/employee's misuse of institutional privileges to access educational records in which he or she has no legitimate educational interest may indicate a lack of overall security in the maintenance of educational records by the institution and be worthy of further investigation.[27]

What are the record access rights of employee/students at post-secondary institutions?

Employee/students are the postsecondary analogue of employee/parents. While these individuals are likely to have greater practical ability to access their own educational records, FERPA does not grant them any greater legal rights. As with employee/parents, an employee misusing institutional privileges to inappropriately access his or her own educational records may create an independent basis for adverse employment action. For a discussion of those records of employee/students that fall outside the definition of an education record under FERPA, see Chapter II.

Can law enforcement personnel be "other school officials?"

Yes. FERPA contains a limited exception permitting institutions to designate law enforcement personnel as "other school officials." However, the ability to make such a designation turns upon whether law enforcement personnel are accessing the records for law enforcement purposes or for educational purposes. If a law enforcement officer is acting for or under the direct control of the school AND has a legitimate educational interest in accessing the records, he or she could qualify as an "other school official" under the LEI exception (provided the school has previously either designated the officer as such a "school official," or the officer falls within the school's functional definition of "school official").[28] If, however, the law enforcement officer's purpose in accessing the records is not related to the student's education—such as locating a student to serve an arrest warrant—then the officer would not be performing a service or responsibility the institution would normally perform itself and is unlikely to qualify as an "other school official."[29]

An Example—A sheriff's deputy enters the registrar's office at Sheldon State Community College in Tuscaloosa, Alabama, requesting a student's current location. The officer informs the registrar that he has a contempt order from a judge's office, representing that it was the equivalent of an "arrest warrant." The College declined to provide the officer with information, noting that he would need a subpoena to access the records. FPCO approved the College's decision, noting that no FERPA exception provided unrestricted access to law enforcement officials for this purpose.[30] However, FPCO did note that if the College included a student's schedule in its designation of "directory information," this information could have been provided to the deputy without prior notice.

Practice Pointer—As discussed in Chapter II, a properly designated law enforcement unit may accumulate some records which are not considered educational records under FERPA and which may be shared with the local police without relying upon specific FERPA exception. However, if an institution develops a sufficiently broad definition of "other school official" and "legitimate educational interest" to include its law enforcement unit (LEU), the LEU will most likely accumulate both educational records (subject to FERPA) and non-educational records. For this reason, it is advisable that the LEU "maintain education records separately from law enforcement unit records."[31]

May parents limit disclosures to other school officials by "opting out" in much the same manner they may do with directory information?

No. FERPA only requires an institution notify parents and eligible students of the definition of school officials with a legitimate educational interest. It does not convey any right to parents or eligible students to remove educational records from within the scope of such disclosures once notice has been provided. Upon the required notice being provided, covered school officials may disclose and discuss (for educational purposes) information obtained from a student's educational records without a parent's knowledge or consent.

An Example—In their annual notification of FERPA rights, Pam's parents receive notice of City County's definition of "other school officials" and "legitimate educational interest." As they traditionally do, they indicate that they do not want her directory information disseminated. This year, they additionally indicate they do not want her school information shared with anyone outside the school. However, City County's definition of "other school officials" includes third-parties "performing data storage or records retrieval for the school district," and, for several years, the district has contracted with DataStore, a company that digitizes and maintains its employee and student records. As DataStore constitutes an "other school official" under the district's definition, Pam's parents' preference regarding dissemination of her student records does not prevent the district from sharing this information with DataStore.

Are school officials with a legitimate educational interest entitled to access to any and all educational records concerning the student?

No. The legitimate educational interest limits school officials' access only to those records that are of genuine educational value in their performance of their official duties for the educational institution.[32] Again, it is the institution's responsibility to determine when such an interest exists and include such a definition in its notice to parents and eligible students.[33] An institution disclosing a student's personally identifiable information to a "school official" without also determining that the individual has a legitimate educational interest in accessing the particular information—or if the institution does not maintain sufficient safeguards to prevent such impermissible access—may well violate FERPA.[34]

Practice Pointer—FERPA generally prohibits the relatively widespread practice of teachers complaining in the teachers' lounge or to their spouses about students and parents when those sessions involve the disclosure of personally identifiable information contained in an educational record. The "other school official" exception *requires* a "legitimate educational interest" before disclosure is permitted, and FPCO has yet to recognize generalized complaining as carrying such an interest. Parents have brought lawsuits and filed ethics complaints against teachers and other educators who publicly, but unwittingly, complained about students in front of educators who were personal friends of the parents of the child about whom the complaint was made. Although some of these conversations may involve information acquired through personal knowledge (as opposed to from an educational record), educators would do well to remember that most states' mandatory codes of ethics for educators contain confidentiality prohibitions that are broader than FERPA, and the disclosure of information shared on the basis of personal knowledge (rather than obtained from inspection of a record) may well be subject to discipline by their state certification agency.

Do educators risk violating FERPA if they disclose personally identifiable information about a student to other students in a class or at the school, such as the contents of a student's IEP?

Absolutely. Educating students with exceptionalities in the "least restrictive environment"—ideally, the classroom in which they would be placed if they lacked any exceptionality—poses unique challenges to educators. Educators frequently ask the degree to which they can "share" information relating to the student's exceptionality with other students or their parents in a genuine attempt to explain why the student "acts the way he does" or to prevent other students from teasing the student. Unfortunately, FERPA generally prohibits such disclosures, regardless of the laudability of the educator's motives in informing other students or their parents. Moreover, an educator doing so risks not only sanction by his or her employing school district, but potentially the state's educator ethics panel or personal litigation from the student's parents for allegedly violating the student's privacy, his or her rights under state laws protecting medical or "confidential" information, and any of a number of other state-law legal claims.

Practice Pointer—Remember, parents and eligible students may always authorize dissemination of educational records or information contained in them. If an educator believes that the educational environment for a student with a disability would improve if other students knew of the disability and the limitations it places on the student's behavior or capacity, the educator may always request permission from the student's parents to discuss it with other students and their parents. Obviously, any such authorization should be given in writing.

Can FERPA apply to conversations about student records as well as disclosure of the written records themselves?

FERPA specifically includes the verbal or oral discussion of information contained with a record as constituting disclosure for purposes of the Act.[35] However, as is frequently the case, information in a student's record can be duplicative of an educator's personal observations or information the educator has from another source—information seemingly not falling within FERPA's definition of an educational record. In several opinion letters considering whether an educator's dissemination of information contained both in educational records and in other, more public, sources constitutes a violation of FERPA, FPCO has offered inconsistent opinions, alternatively requiring the disclosing educator or the student to show that the source of the information either was an educational record (in the case of the student alleging a FERPA violation) or was not (in the case of the educator defending against).[36] Given both the inconsistency of FPCO's interpretations and the difficulty in demonstrating which "source" an educator used in disseminating information, the safer route for educators is to consider dissemination of information contained within a student's educational record—regardless of the source—as falling within FERPA's protections.

Does a school official have a legitimate educational interest in accessing or disclosing educational records without permission when he or she is the subject of *personal* litigation by a student or parents?

Generally, no. While FERPA permits the non-consensual disclosure of information from educational records where a parent or eligible student has taken an "adversarial position" against an institution (for further description of what constitutes an "adversarial position," see Chapter VI), this exception does not apply where a parent or eligible student initiates litigation against an educator personally (as opposed to in his or her official capacity). The legitimate educational interest implies that an institution permits a school official to access information to benefit the student, not for his or her personal benefit.

An Example—A graduate student at the University of New Hampshire filed criminal charges against her former advisor, a professor at the institution. The professor had the student's Graduate Records Examination (GRE) scores in his personal possession, which were given to him by the student prior to her admission to her graduate program. He provided these scores to his criminal defense attorney without the knowledge or consent of any other university official. His attorney used them against the student in the professor's criminal defense.

The student subsequently filed a FPCO complaint, alleging that the University violated her FERPA rights when the professor provided the GRE scores to his attorney. The University argued that the student waived her FERPA rights to the information when she provided her scores to the professor and the professor was an "other school official" with a "legitimate educational interest." FPCO disagreed with both points, noting that the student's providing her records to the professor did not permit him to disseminate them as he pleased as he was still an "agent" of the institution bound by FERPA. Moreover, while the professor could have been a "school official," he did not have a "legitimate educational interest" in disclosing the records to his personal attorney.[37] If the professor wanted his attorney to have the records, the more appropriate step would simply have been to attempt to have them subpoenaed.

What if a school official (who is being sued) is releasing information previously provided to him or her by an eligible student or parent?

While seemingly a better case for the school or university than a faculty member using institutional resources to obtain the records, FPCO's position is that it simply does not matter—when parents or an eligible student provide educational records to a school official, that official is acting as the "agent" of the educational institution and is subject to the re-disclosure provisions of FERPA.[38] "Regardless of how [a student's educational records] came into [an educator's] possession . . . they are the [s]tudent's education records and protected by FERPA against nonconsensual disclosure."[39]

Can a student teacher or graduate student conducting fieldwork be classified as a school official with a legitimate educational interest?

Yes. In the December 2008 regulations, the Department specifically identifies "school transportation officials (including bus drivers), school nurses, practicum and fieldwork students, unpaid interns, consultants, contractors, volunteers, and other outside parties providing institutional services and performing institutional functions" as potential "school officials" for purposes of the legitimate educational interest exception.[40] If the individual is not an employee of the institution, he or she must satisfy the three conditions for "third party" LEI dislosure discussed on pages 75–78.

Must a school district keep a record of these internal disclosures to "school officials?"

No. Unlike most disclosures without parental or eligible student authorization, disclosures made to "school officials" under the "school officials with a legitimate educational interest" exception do not require notation in the student's file.[41] This record-keeping exception—like the "school official" exception itself—is wholly dependent upon the institution specifying both criteria for determining a school official and a legitimate educational interest in its annual FERPA notification. If it fails to do so, the institution's ability to use the LEI is highly questionable.[42]

Practice Pointer—While FERPA does not require institutions to maintain records of access by school officials, one of the major discussions in the 2008 regulatory comments was the importance of securing student records from intrusion by school officials who might not have a legitimate educational interest in so doing.[43] This was largely as a result of the access educators have to electronic recordkeeping systems "in which a user may have access to all records."[44] In its guidance, the Department encouraged educational institutions to implement electronic recordkeeping systems permitting the institution to control and track access by school officials, suggesting that "[a]n agency or institution may wish to restrict or track school officials who obtain access to education records to ensure compliance with [the LEI exception]."[45]

Does FERPA require institutions to provide training to officials handling educational records?

The Individuals with Disabilities Education Act requires that anyone collecting or using a student's personally identifiable information must receive training or instruction in the confidentiality policies under IDEA and FERPA.[46] Beyond this specific requirement, institutions are permitted (but not required) to adopt such practices as requiring annual training for all other school officials (in addition to those already covered above), requiring fingerprint or background investigations of outside parties, and participating in regional training offered by the Department.[47]

Are school officials subject to the Act's limitations upon re-disclosure?

Absolutely. While the legitimate educational interest exception provides school officials with access necessary to perform job duties, it does not allow them to indiscriminately disseminate accessed student records. LEI does not permit a school official to disclose information provided to him or her, nor to use it for purposes other than those giving rise to the original legitimate educational interest for which the records were accessed.

SENDING AND RECEIVING RECORDS FROM OTHER SCHOOLS

Does FERPA permit sharing educational records with another school at which the student seeks to enroll?

Yes. FERPA specifically permits educational entities to share educational records with "officials of another school, school system, or institution of post-secondary education where the student seeks or intends to enroll, or where the student is already enrolled so long as the disclosure is related to the student's enrollment or transfer."[48]

An Example—Johnny Smith enrolls and begins attending school at County High School in Fall 2008. After just a few days, several of his teachers report that Johnny is extremely hyperactive and is already disrupting class repeatedly. Johnny's teachers question Principal Paul as to whether Johnny has ever been identified as a child with a disability and whether he has an I.E.P. or a behavior intervention plan of any kind. When Paul contacts City High School, Johnny's former school in State B, he is told that Johnny's mother has refused to sign a consent for release of records, and that therefore they cannot forward any records to County High School or discuss any information contained in Johnny's records from State B. However, as Johnny has enrolled in County High School, FERPA permits City High School to share records with County High School without Johnny's mother's express consent.

Does the "former school" exception apply only to the school that the student most recently attended, or can any school that the student previously attended provide records without parental consent?

In 2008, the Department clarified that this provision applies to "any school that a student previously attended, not just the school that the student attended most recently."[49] For example, the high school of a student currently seeking to enroll in graduate school may send that student's high school records directly to the graduate program under this provision, even though the student may not have attended the high school for many years.

Are there limitations on what records the previous institution may share with the student's current school?

A student's former school may disclose "any records or information, including health records and information about disciplinary proceedings that it could have disclosed when the student was seeking or intending to enroll."[50] The major (and perhaps singular) limitation on the educational records which one public school may disclose to another is found not in FERPA, but in IDEA. Under IDEA, if a student with a disability seeks to enroll in a private school located within the geographical boundaries of another school district, school officials in the child's original school district cannot share information about the child's disability with officials of the public school district in which the private school is located without the consent of the child's parents.[51]

An Example—Tim Smith enrolls in The Windows School, a private school located within Neighboring School District. Tim is extremely withdrawn and refuses to make eye contact or speak with the other students and staff at the Windows School. Tim's teachers bring this to the attention of Headmaster

Giles, questioning whether Tim has ever been identified as a child with a disability. Dr. Giles reports this to Mr. Winters, the Director of Exceptional Education in Neighboring School District, which provides special education services at The Windows School. Dr. Winters checks Tim's file and sees no special education records. He telephones Tim's former school in City County School District and requests information about Tim's "disability." Even assuming Tim has a disability and City County has files relating to the same, IDEA prohibits City County from disclosing this information without Tim's mother's prior consent to Neighboring School District.

Does that mean a student's former school may disclose a student's treatment records (such as medical or psychological treatment documents) to a student's current school?

This is an interesting question, especially as "bona fide treatment records" are generally not considered educational records in the first instance under FERPA.[52] However, FPCO has authorized the disclosure of treatment records without the consent of the eligible student under any of the non-consensual disclosure provisions, including disclosure "to a school where a student seeks or intends to enroll, or where the student is already enrolled, so long as the disclosure is for purposes related to the student's enrollment or transfer."[53] In addition, treatment records may be disclosed with the consent of the eligible student to "treatment providers at the new school."[54]

Can a college or university refuse to admit a student unless his or her parent authorizes release of the student's special education records?

Public post-secondary institutions should note that Section 504 of the Rehabilitation Act prohibits pre-admission inquiries regarding a student's disability status.[55] In the case of P-12 public institutions, Section 504 also prohibits discrimination against students on the basis of the student's status as a student with a disability.[56] As a result, if an institution admitted non-disabled students without a release of "all" the students educational record, a school's insistence on having "all" records—including special education records—for students with disabilities might appear to be discrimination against this class of students. For a more comprehensive discussion of special education records, please see Chapter VIII. And, of course, we have seen that such a parental release is not generally necessary in order to share records with a school in which the student seeks to enroll.

What about sharing information from educational records—as opposed to sharing the records themselves—with officials from another institution?

As discussed in Chapter II (and previously in this Chapter), the verbal or oral sharing of information contained in educational records may certainly constitute a "disclosure" of educational records for FERPA purposes. However, as long as the other institution is one in which the student is currently enrolled—or in which they are seeking to enroll—FERPA permits sharing information from educational records, as well as forwarding copies of the records themselves.

Practice Pointer—An institution providing educational records to another institution where the student seeks to enroll may—and perhaps should—require documentation or other evidence of a student's intent to enroll prior to providing otherwise confidential student records or information. Educators should remember that while FERPA permits the sharing of certain records without prior parental consent, it is the duty of the institution seeking to exercise the exception—the disclosing institution—to ensure that the records are only being shared consistently with the exception. In other words, the institution providing the information has the burden of ensuring that the student is actually seeking to enroll in the requesting institution.

An Example—Troublesome Timmy shows up with his father, Frank, and seeks to enroll in County Schools in the middle of October. Previously, Timmy was enrolled in City Schools. According to Frank (who is separated from Timmy's mother), Timmy is coming to live with him for the rest of the year since his mother just took a new job preventing her from putting Timmy on the bus in the mornings and supervising him when he gets home in the afternoon. County High Principal Phillip calls his friend, Principal Beverly at City High, to check and make certain that Timmy has been an "okay" student. At this time, Beverly tells Phillip that she just suspended Timmy from City High due to his involvement in a bomb threat that morning. Phillip asks Beverly if she can send him a copy of the disciplinary report on this incident—which FERPA permits.

Does FERPA either prohibit (or require) the forwarding of copies of a student's educational records to another educational institution?

FERPA does not compel institutions to share records, and the exception permitting institutions to share records with other institutions in which the student seeks to enroll should not be read to create such a requirement. The purpose of this exception is to remove concern of a FERPA violation occurring through an institution providing student records to a school in which the student seeks to enroll. This has been a common misperception and troublesome issue for schools attempting to acquire the educational records of newly transferred students, and it is important to note that the Department has specifically provided a "solution" to this problem in the FERPA regulations.

Do other laws require educational institutions to forward a student's educational records to other institutions?

Absolutely. The No Child Left Behind Act contains at least two specific requirements that educational institutions receiving federal funding must forward the educational and/or disciplinary records of a student to any other school in which the student enrolls.[57] Additionally, IDEA requires the district receiving a student with a disability to promptly request a copy of that student's IEP and other related records, and imposes a similar duty upon the student's former district to "take reasonable steps to promptly respond" to this request.[58] Further, state laws, rules, or regulations frequently impose similar obligations on educational institutions to forward at least some of a student's educational records within a given number of days upon request.

Practice Pointer—Under IDEA's regulations, it is the student's new school or district that is initially responsible for originating a request for the student's IEP and other documentation. A practice, for instance, of waiting on a parent to have records forwarded from the previous district without any other action by the district in which the student is currently enrolled risks violation of IDEA's mandate that the new district itself "must take reasonable steps to promptly obtain" the relevant records.[59]

Are there any educational records the district may refuse to forward to another school or district in which the student seeks to enroll?

As noted above, FERPA permits, but does not require, an institution to forward a student's educational records. However, state laws frequently do require a district to forward a number of education records, and both NCLB and IDEA require school districts to forward certain educational records. If the documents at issue are not addressed by state law, NLCB or IDEA, there is no independent FERPA requirement (subject to one cautionary note below) that any records be forwarded to the next school or district.

Does FERPA create an obligation to maintain or forward records created by a non-employee?

In Chapter III, we discuss the right of parents or eligible students to ask for a hearing regarding the accuracy of educational records, and if not satisfied with the hearing result, attach a statement explaining their contentions as related to those records. FERPA requires that any such statement submitted by a parent or eligible student be attached to and maintained with the disputed records themselves, and in the authors view, would also require that if the disputed records are being provided to another school or district, that the statement also be included.

Can educational records be disclosed without consent if the student is attempting to enroll in a private school?

This non-consensual disclosure exception applies only to "educational agencies and institutions" as defined by FERPA. A private school accepting federal funds may qualify as such an institution. If so, the district may rely upon this provision in order to disclose records to the private school.

However, some private schools will not satisfy the FERPA definition of an "educational agency or institution" and, in such instances, a district *may not* rely upon this particular non-consensual provision to disclose educational records of the student.

How should a school determine whether a private school qualifies as an "educational agency or institution" for purposes of FERPA?

According to the Department's 2008 Joint Guidance, the private school must receive funds from a Departmental program in order to become subject to FERPA. Specifically, the Department has stated:

> [A] private school is not made subject to FERPA just because its students and teachers receive services from a local school district or State educational agency that receives funds from the Department. The school itself must receive funds from a program administered by the Department to be subject to FERPA. For example, if a school district places a student with a disability in a private school that is acting on behalf of the school district with regard to providing services to that student, the records of that student are subject to FERPA, but not the records of the other students in the private school. In such cases, the school district remains responsible for complying with FERPA with respect to the education records of the student placed at the private school.[60]

Does that mean a school cannot forward copies of a student's educational records to a private school that does not qualify as an "educational agency or institution"?

No. It simply means that the school cannot do so without parental consent. A school may always disclose records with the specific, written authorization of the parents or eligible student. Of course, the private school may (and frequently does) require the parent of a the student provide a consent for release of all records as a condition of enrolling in the private school.

DISCLOSURE IN CONNECTION WITH AN AUDIT OR EVALUATION

When is disclosure permitted to federal, state, and local educational authorities in connection with an audit or evaluation of educational programs?

FERPA permits disclosure of educational records to authorized representatives of several federal agencies and "state and local educational authorities" in connection with the "audit or evaluation of federal or state supported education programs," or for enforcement or compliance actions related to those programs.[61] The officials specifically identified include:

- The Comptroller General of the United States
- The Attorney General of the United States
- The Secretary [of Education] and
- State and local educational authorities.[62]

This exception requires federal, state, and local agencies collecting information pursuant to this exception to ensure that personal identification of "individuals" is not permitted beyond those specifically authorized above, and that such information is destroyed when no longer needed for the purposes for which it was collected.[63]

Who is considered a state or local educational authority for purposes of program audit or evaluation?

FERPA does not define what constitutes a "state or local educational authority" or what constitute "federal or state supported educational programs." However, FPCO's construction of state or local education authority is expansive, generally including "an agency or other party with educational expertise and experience that is responsible for and authorized under state or local law to regulate, plan, coordinate, advise, supervise or evaluate elementary, secondary, or post-secondary programs education programs, services, agencies, or institutions in the state."[64]

Can a state or local educational agency authorize or designate another agency as its "authorized representative," making that agency a "state or local educational authority?"

Yes. However, that agency must be under the *direct control* of the state educational authority or local educational agency. This issue commonly arises in the context of non-educational state entities wishing to access educational records to match data against state labor records in order to meet the requirements of the Workforce Investment Act and other federal reporting requirements.[65] Prior to 2003, FPCO took a very expansive interpretation of who could constitute an "authorized representative" of a state or local educational authority. However, in 2003, FPCO significantly narrowed its interpretation, requiring "authorized representatives" of state and local educational authorities also be under the *direct control* of the agency.[66] FPCO defined "direct control" as being "an employee, appointed official, or contractor." A "contractor"—which had the potential to be expansively interpreted—was limited to a "third-party" providing services that the state or local educational agency would otherwise provide for itself.[67]

Have there been any further examples of agencies that may qualify as designated representatives under FPCO's more recent, narrower interpretation?

Yes. In 2005, FPCO was asked whether educational records could be provided to the Texas Attorney General's Office in connection with an investigation of a school district's alleged failure to provide educational records under the Texas Public Information Act, which it was charged with enforcing. In its analysis, FPCO considered whether the Texas Attorney General could be construed to be an authorized representative of the state educational authority, assisting the Texas Education Agency with enforcement of FERPA.[68] Concluding that the Texas Attorney General's office did not directly provide legal advice to the Texas Education Agency or act as its "outside" legal counsel, FPCO concluded that the Texas Attorney General was not under the direct control of the state education agency and therefore could not constitute an "authorized representative."[69]

Can a State educational agency re-disclose educational records gathered pursuant to the "state officials" exception to organizations conducting studies for them or on their behalf?

No. While educational agencies and institutions may disclose educational records to organizations conducting studies for them or on their behalf for the improvement of education or instruction, this exception does not extend to state education authorities gathering information pursuant to the "state officials" exception.[70] Should state agencies desire such studies be conducted, they must redact any personal information from student data, rendering it essentially anonymous. It is further worth noting that the study exception itself implies "an education agency or institution has authorized a study. The fact that an outside entity, on its own initiative conducts a study which may benefit an educational agency or institution, does not transform the study into one done "for or on behalf of" the educational agency or institution."[71]

ENDNOTES

1. 34 C.F.R. § 99.31(a)(1).
2. See Letter to Dr. Hunter Rawlings, III (undated but referencing letter dated February 28, 2000).
3. See Letter to Julie Ann Evans, Esq. (August 15, 2005).
4. See Letter to Dr. John R. Leitzel (undated).
5. Letter to Dr. Hunter Rawlings (undated but referencing letter dated February 28, 2000); Letter to Carol Fuller (April 16, 2004).

6. Letter to Julie Evans, Esq. (August 15, 2005).
7. Federal Register Vol. 73 No. 57, 15580 (March 24, 2008)
8. Letter to Dr. Hunter Rawlings (undated but referencing letter dated February 28, 2000); Letter to Carol Fuller (April 16, 2004).
9. 34 C.F.R. § 99.31(a)(1); Letter to Carol Fuller (April 16, 2004); Federal Register Vol. 73 No. 57, 15575, 15578 (March 24, 2008).
10. Letter to Carol Fuller (April 16, 2004).
11. Federal Register Vol. 73, No. 237, 74815 (December 9, 2008). In one case, the school's simple definition of school officials "a person employed by, or under contract to, the school board to perform a special task" was found sufficient by the court to reject a complaint by parents concerning the disclosure of information about disabled student with behavioral issues to a counselor who was jointly employed by the County and the School Board. *Larson v. Independent School District No. 361* 2004 WL 432218 *7 (D. Minn. 2004).
12. Letter to Carol H. Fuller (April 16, 2004); Letter to Judith Bresler, Esq. (February 15, 2006); Letter to Jeanne-Marie Pochert (June 28, 2006); Letter to unidentified "Parent" (September 7, 2004).
13 Letter to Dr. Hunter Rawlings (undated but referencing letter dated February 28, 2000); Letter to Carol Fuller (April 16, 2004).
14. 34 C.F.R. 99.31(a)(1)(i)(B).
15. Federal Register Vol. 73, No. 237, 74814 (December 9, 2008).
16. 34 C.F.R. 99.31(a)(1)(i)(B)(1–3).
17. Federal Register Vol. 73, No. 237 74814 (December 9, 2008).
18. Federal Register Vol. 73 No. 237 78314 (December 9, 2008), quoting from the "Joint Statement in Explanation of Buckley/Pell Amendment." (Joint Statement), 120 Cong. Rec. S21488 (December 13, 1974).
19. Federal Register Vol. 73 No. 237 78314 (December 9, 2008),
20. See Letter to Daniel Boehmer (April 19, 1993).
21. Federal Register Vol. 73 No. 57, 15575, 15580 (March 24, 2008).
22. Federal Register Vol. 73 No. 237 78316 (December 9, 2008).
23. Id.
24. Id.
25. Federal Register Vol. 73 No. 237, 74813–14 (December 9, 2008)
26. Id.
27. In the 2008 Comments, there is some discussion of the District's duty to utilize "reasonable methods" of security which may be read to suggest a fairly individualized approach to determining the particular controls which may be necessary to maintain confidentiality. See Federal Register Vol. 73 No. 237 78317 (December 9, 2008).
28. Federal Register Vol 73, No. 237, 74815 (December 9, 2008).
29. *Id.*
30. Letter to Diane Layton (undated but included under FPCO letter from 1998) and downloaded from http://www.ed.gov/policy/gen/guid/fpco/ferpa/library/shelton_al.html on December 27, 2008).
31. Federal Register Vol. 73 No. 237 78315 (December 9, 2008),

32. 34 C.F.R. 99.31(a)(1)(ii).

33. 34 C.F.R. § 99.31(a)(1)(ii).

34. Federal Register Vol. 73 No. 237 78317 (December 9, 2008).

35. As discussed in Chapter II, however, there are cases wherein the court has recognized that some information about a student which would be confidential if contained within a record, inevitably becomes known to some individuals merely by virtue of their presence within the school. For instance, other students who observe a student going into a self-contained special education classroom setting may come to know of that student's status as a student with a disability. While the ultimate effect may be the same, this reality is distinct from an educator purposefully disclosing the same confidential information (i.e. the student has an IEP) about the same student to others.

36. Letter to Dr. J. Chris Toe (March 11, 2005) (indicating student/employee could not demonstrate that information disclosed by employee was accessed from student's records rather than from employee's "personal knowledge and observations."); Letter to Dr. John Leitzel (undated) (implication that personally identifiable information (GRE scores) provided to professor by student prior to student's admission constituted an "educational record" maintained by the institution).

37. Letter to Dr. John Leitzel (undated).

38. Letter to Dr. John Leitzel (undated but included under FPCO letters from 2001) and downloaded from http://www.ed.gov/policy/gen/guid/fpco/ferpa/library/unh.html on December 27, 2008.

39. *Id.*

40. Federal Register Vol. 73 No. 237 78315 (December 9, 2008).

41. 34 C.F.R. § 99.32(d)(2). See also Federal Register Vol. 73 No. 237 78315 (December 9, 2008).

42. 34 C.F.R. §99.32(d)(2); Letter to Jeanne-Marie Pochert, Esq. (June 28, 2006).

43. Federal Register Vol. 73 No. 57, 15575 15579–80 (March 24, 2008).

44. Federal Register Vol. 73 No. 57, 15575 15580 (March 24, 2008).

45. Id.

46. 34 C.F.R. § 300.623(c); 34 C.F.R. § 300.123.

47. Federal Register Vol. 73 No. 237 78316 (December 9, 2008).

48. 34 C.F.R. §99.31(a)(2). It is notable that the language conditioning such disclosures as being related to the student's enrollment or transfer was added to the text of the regulations in 2008.

49. Federal Register Vol. 73 No. 237 78318 (December 9, 2008).

50. Federal Register Vol. 73 No. 237 78318 (December 9, 2008). For instance, the Department has stated that "any records or information, including health records and information about disciplinary proceedings" may be disclosed. Id.

51. 34 C.F.R. § 300.622(b)(3). See also Chapter VIII for a further discussion of this provision from the IDEA regulations.

52. See Chapter II for discussion of the treatment records exception.

53. Federal Register Vol. 73 No. 237 74818 (December 9, 2008).

54. Id.

55. 34 C.F.R. § 104.42(b)(4) & (c).

56. We have found this issue to occur on several instances when schools are making discretionary decisions about accepting students from outside their attendance zone or outside the school district. While the acceptance of students residing outside the city, county, or attendance zone is often permissive (though of course subject to State or local law or rule), schools which decline to admit out of county students on the basis that "they're special education and cost more" often inadvertently violate Section 504's prohibition on discrimination against students with disabilities.

57. 20 U.S.C. 7165; Federal Register Vol. 73 No. 237 74819 (December 9, 2008).

58. 34 C.F.R. § 300.323(g).

59. Id.

60. Joint Guidance on the Application of FERPA and HIPAA to Student Health Records, published by the Department of Education and the Department of Health and Human Services in November of 2008.

61. 34 C.F.R. § 99.35(a).

62. Id.

63. 34 C.F.R. § 99.35(b).

64. Letter to Deborah Wilkins (July 11, 2005).

65. Letter to Chief State School Officers (January 30, 2003).

66. Letters to California and Pennsylvania Departments of Education (February 18, 2004 and February 25 2004, respectively). It is furthermore notable that the Department's interpretation of direct control expressed in these opinion letters appears to have survived into the 2008 regulations.

67. *Id.*

68. Letter to Katherine Minter Cary (July 25, 2006).

69. Id.

70. Letter to Deborah Wilkins (July 11, 2005).

71. Letter to Amy C. Foerster (February 25, 2004).

Chapter 5

Educational Records: Directory Information

The provisions of the Act relating to directory information offer the District the singular opportunity to determine in advance what information about students can and should be available for public distribution. In contrast with the application of the vast majority of the non-consensual disclosure provisions which are very specific to the facts and circumstances surrounding an individual case (and discussed in Chapters IV and VI), the decision as to whether to designate any student information as directory, and if so, exactly which pieces of information, is a systematic process which District personnel may and should engage consciously and thoughtfully prior to the beginning of each school year. Of course, not all information about students may be designated as directory, and the District's deliberations in this regard must take place within the confines imposed by the definition of personally identifiable information. However, once the process of identifying and notifying parents as to that information which will be considered directory has taken place, and always taking account of those parents who elect not to have their children included in this policy, a directory information policy has the great advantage of removing the administrative burdens associated with obtaining parental permission in individual instances (for example, when the newspaper seeks to publish the names of the award-winning debate team). On the other hand, because any District liability under FERPA is generally predicated upon a "pattern or practice" of violations, and since mistakes in the handling of directory information are more likely to be systematic and pervasive than, for example, an isolated instance of one teacher's breach of confidentiality, directory information is more sensitive in this regard.

OVERVIEW, BASIC CONCEPTS, AND DEFINITIONS

What exactly is directory information?

Directory information is defined as "information contained in an education record of a student that would not generally be considered harmful or an invasion of privacy if disclosed."[1] Within the scope of this definition, however, each District may define directory information differently, or may choose to forego the designation of any directory information at all.

What are some examples of the kind of information that is generally considered to fall within the definition of directory information?

The Department has listed certain types of information which it considers to be directory. This list, which is neither exclusive nor exhaustive, includes the following:

> A student's name, student's address, telephone listing, electronic mail address, photograph, date and place of birth, major field of study, dates of attendance, grade level, enrollment status (undergraduate/graduate; full/part-time), participation in officially recognized activities and sports, weight and height of members of athletic teams, degrees, honors and awards, and the most recent educational agency or institution attended.[2]

Has this list of directory information changed over time?

Yes, most recently the Department added "enrollment status," "electronic mail address" and "photograph" to the list of the "illustrative types of records that would not generally be considered harmful or an invasion of privacy."[3] In discussing email addresses, the Department analogized these to the student mailing addresses, which have already been recognized as an example of directory information, while the Department concluded that photographs generally would not be considered an invasion of privacy.[4]

Are there certain categories of information which the Department has specifically prohibited from being listed as directory information?

Absolutely, though historically this has been done on a case-by-case basis. The fundamental standard which may not be breached is that the District cannot designate as directory information which, if released, would be considered harmful or an invasion of privacy. Some specific categories of information the Department has declared as falling within this prohibition include:

> Race, ethnicity, disability, tuition status, grades, test scores, credit hours attempted, financial aid status, social security number, parents' real estate taxes and property values, an individual's status as registered sex offender, and communicable diseases.[5]

Of course, this list is not exhaustive, and in the case of any District or institution which seeks to designate as directory information not specifically recognized as such within the regulations, and/or information similar or analogous to any of the specifically prohibited categories above, specific consultation with the Department or a knowledgeable education law attorney is highly recommended.

Does FERPA prohibit or limit the District's authority to collect or require social security numbers from students?

No, FERPA does not govern the types of information the District may collect from students, but rather governs parental and student rights in connection with access to records, amendment to records, and consent before the disclosure of personally identifiable information in most circumstances.[6] However, the 2008 FERPA regulations do specifically prohibit the designation of social security numbers as directory information.[7]

Are there any other pieces of information that are specifically prohibited from being listed as directory information in the regulations themselves?

Yes, historically and in the 2008 FERPA regulations the Department has taken the position that a student identification number may not be listed as directory information, unless specific conditions are satisfied.[8]

What are the conditions attached to the designation of student identification numbers as directory?

The 2008 regulations provide that a student identification number may be designated as directory information only "if the identifier cannot be used to gain access to education records except when used in conjunction with one or more factors that authenticate the user's identity, such as a personal identification number (PIN), password, or other factor known or possessed only by the authorized user."[9] In the context of university students accessing their own educational records electronically, the Department has approved a system under which a student must use an authentication system unique to them (such as a PIN or password) in addition to their personal identifier (such as an email address).[10]

Is the use of student identification numbers on I.D. cards permissible under FERPA?

Yes, the Department has stated that student identification numbers may be listed on student I.D. cards (regardless of whether or not the student I.D. numbers are listed as directory information), since merely listing the numbers on the I.D. card alone is not a disclosure for purposes of FERPA.[11] However, if the student identification number is not designated as directory information, the District may not require the student to disclose the number to school officials who do not have a legitimate educational interest in accessing this information (or who fall within another provision allowing for non-consensual disclosure).[12]

Is it permissible for a school to use the student's social security number for purposes of verifying a student's enrollment status?

In the past, FPCO has taken the position that "the confirmation or verification of personally identifiable information such as a SSN in a student's education records in and of itself constitutes a prohibited disclosure of personally identifiable information under FERPA."[13] Consequently, in order to use the student's social security number, the school was required either to have prior written consent, or apply one of the existing and permissible grounds for non-consensual disclosure. However, in 2008 the Department seemingly softened this stance, writing that "there is no statutory authority under FERPA to prohibit an educational agency or institution from using SSNs . . . to search an electronic database, so long as the agency or institution does not disclose the SSN in violation of FERPA."[14]

Do "dates of attendance" under a directory information policy include a student's daily attendance?

No, the Department amended the regulations to specifically clarify that the phrase "dates of attendance" does not refer to or otherwise include "specific daily records of a student's attendance at an educational agency or institution."[15] Instead, this provision would allow the District to designate as directory information, and disclose accordingly, the fact that a student attended City High School from 1985–89.

Practice Pointer—In the past, some Districts have mistakenly confirmed a student's actual attendance or absence from school on a specific day, in response to inquiries from parties who actually sought to locate a student (or their parent) and do them harm. In some cases these individuals claimed to be a parent, while in other instances school officials erroneously treated the student's attendance as directory and thus subject to any disclosure upon request.

May the District share a student's attendance records with local authorities investigating truancy or suspected violations of compulsory attendance laws?

In some cases, these agencies or individuals may be designated as "school officials with a legitimate educational interest" in accessing the student's attendance records. In other cases, such as the juvenile court, these records may be subpoenaed by the judge, which is one of the permissible, non-consensual disclosures under FERPA. In the case of programs which have been in existence since before 1974, (or a program based upon statutes enacted since 1974 and which operate to serve students prior to their adjudication by the juvenile court) FERPA specifically contains an exception which permits the disclosure of educational records.[16] In the absence of any of these situations, or of the existence of a properly designated law enforcement unit (discussed in Chapter II) or a health or safety emergency (discussed in Chapter VI), FERPA does not contain a specific basis which would permit the nonconsensual disclosure of a student's attendance records as described above. Individual parental consent would be necessary, therefore, in order to share such information with local authorities.

May different Districts choose to include different pieces of information in their Directory information policy?

Yes, as long as each item identified as directory is either included on the specific list of directory information included in the regulations, or is consistent with the strict limitation against inclusion of information that would be an invasion of the student's privacy or harmful if disclosed.

An Example—At County High School, Freshman Father notices in his daughter's student handbook at the beginning of the year that the school has a "directory information policy," where the school lists as directory information each student's name, address, telephone listing, electronic mail address, photograph, date and place of birth, major field of study, dates of attendance, grade level, enrollment status (undergraduate/graduate; full/part-time), participation in officially recognized activities and sports, weight and height of members of athletic teams, degrees, honors, and awards. In November, Freshman Father moves and enrolls his daughter in City High School. While enrolling her in the office, Freshman Father sees the City High School Student Handbook lists as directory information only a student's name, photograph, grade level, participation in officially recognized activities and sports, weight and height of members of athletic teams, degrees, honors, and awards. Both City and County High School directory information policies identify permissible pieces of student information to designate as directory.

What about different schools within a District—can each school adopt a distinct set of directory information?

There is no provision in FERPA which would expressly authorize or prohibit a District from designating a particular set of information as directory for the District's elementary schools, for instance, and a different or slightly different body of directory information at the middle or high schools. Of course, it is vitally important that parents at each school be provided with the required notice and opportunity to opt out of the directory information as related to their child.[17]

Is the District required to maintain a record of access as to the release of directory information?

No, the record-keeping requirements of the Act do not apply to disclosures of directory information.[18]

What about the limitations on the re-disclosure of information—do these apply to directory information ?

No, the re-disclosure rules and limitations do not apply to directory information, but only cover certain provisions of the Act governing the non-consensual disclosure of personally identifiable information.[19]

Is it possible that class roster and class schedules can be designated as directory information?

While in the past the Department has advised that this information may be directory, in 2000 the Department stated that it was reevaluating this position in light of concerns expressed that releasing this information "may lead schools to disclose sensitive information."[20] Until this issue is again addressed or clarified, therefore, the conservative approach would be to avoid designating this information as directory.

An Example—A police officer reports to the front office of the school with a warrant for the arrest of a student, and asks the school receptionist where the student may be found. Does FERPA prohibit the release of the student's course schedule to the officer? Yes, according to the Department, unless the District has identified student's schedules as directory information. However, the Department has gone on to say that "FERPA does not prohibit the institution from locating a student for a law enforcement officer or anyone else if a staff member happens to know where the student is and, therefore, does not have to release or retrieve the information from an education record, such as the student's recorded class schedule."[21]

What are some examples of disclosures the District is permitted to make if it does adopt a Directory Information policy?

In the Model Notice of Directory Information, the Department lists five different examples of disclosures which are permissible after such a policy has been adopted. The five examples cited by the Department are: "a playbill, showing your student's role in a drama production; the annual yearbook; honor roll or other recognition lists; graduation programs; and sports activity sheets, such as for wrestling, showing weight and height of team members."[22] Conversely, one may infer that in the absence of such a policy or an executed release by the parent of each student, a District violates the Act by publishing, for example, the name of a student in any of these specific or directly comparable circumstances. The apparently benign and yet widespread publication of each of the five types of documents listed above strongly suggests the benefits to the school of using the directory information policy provision.

An Example—Middling Middle School does not have a directory information policy. In the Spring, the Middling Middle School Yearbook club publishes the school's yearbook, which in addition to each student's name and picture also includes students' participation in clubs, sports, and other extracurricular activities, as well as many honors and awards conferred upon individual students by the school. In the absence of a release from the parents of each student included in the yearbook (and since there is no directory information policy), publication of the yearbook would be considered a FERPA violation by the Department.

PERSONALLY IDENTIFIABLE INFORMATION

What is the definition of personally identifiable information?

According to the Department, personally identifiable information includes (but is not limited to), a student's name, the name of the student's parent or other family member, the address of the student or the student's family, any personal identifier (social security, student number, or biometric record) or other information that, alone or in combination, is linked or linkable to a specific student that would allow a reasonable person in the school community, who does not have personal knowledge of the relevant circumstances, to identify the student with reasonable certainty, or information requested by a person who the educational agency or institution reasonably believes knows the identity of the student to whom the education record relates." [23]

What is the definition of a biometric record?

The concept of a biometric record was added to the regulatory definition of personally identifiable information in 2008, and is defined therein as "a record of one or more measurable biolcgical or behavioral characteristics that can be used for automated recognition of an individual."[24] Examples of biometric records included within the regulations are "fingerprints, retina and iris patterns, voiceprints, DNA sequence, facial characteristics, and handwriting."[25]

How can a student's name and address be both directory and personally identifiable information?

As directory information, a student's name may only be released when done in connection with other pieces of information which are also directory. For instance, if the District has designated student participation in athletic teams, height, and weight as directory information, the District may publish an athletic program containing the name, height, and weight of the members of the football team. In contrasts, the same District would not be permitted to disclose the name, height, and weight of two football players who allegedly got into a fight on the bus trip to an away football game, since this disclosure impermissibly links personally identifiable information about the students (their involvement in a fight, a violation of the code of conduct at the school and presumably subject to disciplinary action) with their directory information.

Our school has a practice of identifying students by their initials (for example, M.D.), and treating the records containing such initials as public records—is this acceptable under FERPA?

Not necessarily. As discussed below, one aspect of the FERPA regulations which has changed recently is the adoption of a "reasonable person in the school community" standard to determine whether any particular disclosure is actually personally identifying. In 2008, the Department stated that "experience has shown . . . that initials, nicknames, and personal characteristics are often sufficiently unique in a school community that a reasonable person can identify the student from this kind of information."[26]

Does FERPA provide a definition of the term "easily traceable" as related to personally identifiable information?

No, though historically the Department's general rule has been to employ as a test "whether a reasonable person in the educational community or a requester who does not have specific knowledge about the student would be able to identify the student to whom the records relate without substantial, additional effort."[27] However, in 2008 the easily traceable standard was significantly revised for several reasons, including the lack of "specificity and clarity," as well as the suggestion (by use of the term "easy") that this standard was "fairly low."[28] Instead, the language was incorporated into the regulations as noted above.[29] By way of further explanation, where a requester asks for a specific student's disciplinary records, then it would be reasonable to conclude the identity of the student would be obvious to the requester such that even the disclosure of fully redacted or scrubbed records would be a violation of FERPA.[30]

What is meant by the reference to the "school community" in the definition of personally identifiable information?

In explaining this term, the Department used the example of the "students, teachers, administrators, parents, coaches, volunteers, or others" at the school.[31]

An Example—Troublesome Tommy was caught bringing a gun to City High School last month, and this fact was known among students and teachers at the school. When the City Gazette requests copies of the redacted reports of punishment imposed for any students caught at City High with a gun at school in the past two months, Principal Paul should decline to do so since "a reasonable person in the high school would be able to identify the student" (Tommy).[32]

In determining whether any particular disclosure will inappropriately identify an individual student's identity, is the District also required to take into consideration the apparent prior knowledge of the requesting party?

Yes, though the standard to determine whether a requesting party has such prior knowledge has changed over time. In the past, the Department clearly took the position that the very first factor a university should consider in responding to a request for information about a student is "whether the party seeking access to the records has prior knowledge of the students listed in the education record."[33] Then in the 2008 regulations the Department included as an alternative definition of the term "personally identifiable information" the following—"information requested by a person who the educational agency or institution reasonably believes knows the identity of the student to whom the education record relates."[34]

How is the school supposed to determine the knowledge of a party requesting access to educational records?

The school is expected to make use of information that would be known to a reasonable person in the school community.[35] The school is not required, however, "to make any special inquiries or otherwise seek information about the person requesting information," and is expected to "use information that is obvious on the face of the request or provided by the requester."

An Example—The County Gazette publishes a newspaper article about basketball players who were expelled after accepting bribes. Thereafter, an individual requests the redacted transcripts of any basketball students expelled for accepting bribes. In this instance, identity of the student is already known by the school community in light of the newspaper story, so redacting the personal information from the student's transcripts would be a "useless formality . . . the subject's identity is already known."[36] Consequently, the School may not release the documents requested.

Does the personally identifiable information limitation generally prohibit the disclosure of any information at the student (as opposed to the aggregate) level?

Not necessarily. The Department has approved the release of student level data when all "personally identifiable information" has been removed—a process described as "de-identified or anonymous data."[37] For example, it has been found acceptable to release standardized test data after removing the name, address, identification number, alphabetical or testing order, and "any other information that would make the student's identify easily traceable."[38] In the case of disciplinary records, the Department has also authorized disclosure after removal of the student's name, identification number, the exact date, and the time of the incident.[39] Most recently, the 2008 regulations set forth the process and rules related to the disclosure of "de-identified" student records.[40]

So the limitation as to disclosing personal characteristics if the identity of the student is ascertainable does not mean, for example, that FERPA requires the District to avoid any disclosure if it is merely possible for someone to identify the student?

This is correct—the essence of this limitation is whether a reasonable person would be able to identify the student, while also taking into account any prior knowledge the requesting party has about the student and of which the District is aware. There mere fact that, eventually, an individual was able to successfully trace the identity of a student by using information obtained from the District and combining this with, for example, prior knowledge of which the District was not aware, and extraordinary investigative efforts on their part, does not mean that the District has violated FERPA in this instance.

What is the concept of "linkage," and how does this relate to the release of directory information under FERPA?

Linkage is the concept that information about a student, even information that has been designated as directory for all students, may not be released in a manner which impermissibly "links" confidential (non-directory) information about a particular student with that individual student's directory information. Consider the following situation: County Middle School has designated a student's name, photograph, and telephone number as directory information. Later that year, a student at County Middle School is involved in an off-campus sexual assault. The County Herald requests the School to release the picture and name of the student, contending that since the school has designated this as directory information for all students they must release this information for individual students. According to the Department, however, the School may not release the requested information, since to do so would impermissibly link information which would be considered "harmful or an invasion of privacy" (the alleged involvement of a minor in a criminal assault) with the student's directory information.[41]

So even if the type of information requested by any outside entity has been designated as directory by the District generally, the District is prohibited under FERPA from disclosing that information if doing so would allow a reasonable person in the school community to identify the individual student with reasonable certainty?

This is correct.[42]

Does the release of information only at the aggregate level always serve as a sufficient protection against release of personally identifiable information?

Not necessarily. The Department has clearly stated that "there are circumstances . . . in which the aggregation of anonymous or de-identified data into various categories could render personal identify easily traceable. In those circumstances, FERPA prohibits disclosure of the information without consent."[43] For a further discussion of the protections and precautions to be taken when releasing aggregate level information, please see Chapter VI.

Does a warrant for a student's arrest fall under the subpoena exception for non-consensual disclosure?

In a 1997 opinion, the Department distinguished between a subpoena directed to the District for the purpose of obtaining information about a student allegedly in the possession of the District (which would fall under the subpoena exception discussed further in Chapter VI), and a warrant for the arrest of the student.[44] The latter is an order issued against the student, and is generally not considered to be a judicial order directing or requiring the compliance of the District or any third party.

If an individual contacts a school and, claiming to be the student's father, asks whether the child is currently enrolled in the school, does FERPA require the school to release this information?

Remember that even if the school has designated enrollment status as directory information, the directory information provisions are permissive, not mandatory disclosure requirements, and are entirely distinct from the rights of parents to access the educational records of their children. For instance, a parent would retain their FERPA access rights even if the District chooses not to designate any information as directory at all. In this particular instance, if this individual is seeking to exercise their FERPA access rights to their student's educational records, FERPA allows the school up to 45 days to respond this request, and requires reasonable measures to authenticate the parental status of the requesting party.

Is a student's United States residency status (for example, as an undocumented child of an illegal alien) considered personally identifiable information?

Yes. Since students in the P–12 setting are entitled to a public education under the Supreme Court's decision in *Plyler v. Doe* regardless of their citizenship status, many Districts will not necessarily require or possess reliable records pertaining to a student's residency status.[45] And while the Act does allow a student's address, as well as the date and place of their birth, to be designated as directory information, the Department has specifically stated that a student's "country of origin" may not be designated as directory information.[46]

May the District disclose personally identifiable information about a student (such as their residency) to the Department of Homeland Security?

Yes, at least in connection with the administration of the Student and Exchange Visitor Information System (SEVIS). The Illegal Immigration Reform and Immigrant Responsibility Act provides that FERPA is inapplicable to aliens to the extent necessary for administration of the SEVIS program, so that the FERPA is not a limitation on the provision of information to the Department of Homeland Security in connection with the administration of this program.[47]

If the District receives a request for the residency status of all students by a local law enforcement agency, what should the District do?

Generally speaking, we believe the District should request that this information be subpoenaed as it is unlikely that any other exception to the nonconsensual disclosure of personally identifiable information (which includes residency status) will be construed by the Department to apply.

Is the fact that a student is absent from school due to their suspension for misconduct considered personally identifiable information?

Yes. In one case, the court recognized a theoretical FERPA claim by a student who alleged that the principal had impermissibly told another student of his suspension.[48] Interestingly, the student in this case also complained about the principal's disclosure to other administrators at the school of his suspension, a claim which the court summarily rejected since such disclosures were "in furtherance of an important governmental objective (school safety and student discipline) and substantially related to that objective."[49]

What if a particular student has a severe food allergy—is this considered a disability, and if so, does FERPA prohibit the school from notifying other students and their parents as to the identity of this student and measures necessary to protect the student from harm?

It is certainly possible that a student's allergies may rise to the level of a disability under Section 504 and the American's with Disabilities Act. In these instances, the school will be required to offer a reasonable accommodation to provide the student with access to public education. The medical condition of the individual student would be considered personally identifiable information, so that the school may well provide notice to the class generically without identifying the particular student— "there is a student in our class with a life-threatening food allergy, so our class is being designated a food free zone." In some instances, the parents of students with such medical conditions also consent to the identification of their child as part of the overall effort to educate all children about the nature and danger of such allergies.

Does FERPA prohibit the observation of a student's classroom by non-school personnel?

Not necessarily. In one case where the issue was whether or not an expert witness could observe several LEP classrooms to determine the quality of instruction provided in these classrooms, a court held that "mere observation of classes will not implicate FERPA's provisions concerning access to educational records and personally identifiable information."[50] However, it should be noted that in this case the court also prohibited the witness from accessing any student records, and even then, also took the step of issuing its order under FERPA's subpoena exception.

If information is publicly available from another source, does the District have any greater flexibility to designate that information as directory?

According to the Department, the answer is no. For instance, at one time the Department took the position that a District could not disclose as directory information the presence of an individual student at particular school who was also a registered sex offender. The Department came to this conclusion even though the State maintained a website which published the picture, name, and address of registered sex offender, finding simply that "there is no exclusion from the definition of 'education records' for information that is available from another source, even if the information is publicly available."[51] In 2008, however, the Department specifically added a regulatory exception authorizing the non-consensual disclosure of information related to registered offenders.[52] (Please see Chapter VI).

What if the parents of a student publicly disclose confidential information about their child; may the District then consider this information no longer protected by FERPA?

Again generally no, unless one of the specific rules relating to the nonconsensual disclosure of information otherwise apply (See Chapters IV and VI). FERPA does not provide that parents may, by publicly disclosing information the District is restricted from publicizing, implicitly waive their confidentiality rights under the Act.[53] This has been the Department's historical position and was reaffirmed in 2008.[54]

What if the parents disclose this information at a public meeting of the Board of Education, or to the newspaper?

Unless a specific, nondisclosure exception applies, the District is still limited by FERPA's confidentiality provisions. Of course, there is nothing which prevents the District from requesting the parents provide written consent to discuss this information, and in the absence of such consent, clarify that the District is unable to discuss the student unless and until such consent has been provided.[55]

An Example—Parent Phyllis attends a meeting of the County Board of Education, and during the public comment section of the meeting she lambasts the Principal of the High School for his excessive, arbitrary, and irrational discipline of her son—Princely Phil, who after all was only experimenting with a "foreign substance" because he was bored with the ridiculously easy academic curriculum. After the meeting, Randy Reporter asks Superintendent Cindy if she has any response to Phyllis' complaints. Cindy responds by saying, "I would be delighted to share with you the full, complete, and accurate information related to the concerns expressed by Parent Phyllis—if she will simply execute this complete and total waiver and release of any and all possible claims relating to this disclosure—including any potential FERPA or privacy claims based upon FERPA. Phyllis—can I get your John Hancock here!"

Does this mean the District has to obtain consent to share personally identifiable information when parents or eligible students file a complaint or lawsuit against the District?

No, the Department has recognized an implied consent doctrine in these instances. (See Chapter VI) for a further discussion of this concept.

DIRECTORY INFORMATION POLICY AND NOTICE

What process must the District follow in designating directory information?

In order to designate and disclose directory information without consent, the District must notify parents and eligible students of the following: (1) the types of personally identifiable information which have been designated as directory, (2) their right to refuse to permit the designation of any or all of this information as directory, and (3) the period of time within which the parent or eligible student must notify the District if they wish to decline to permit some or all of information to be designated as directory.[56]

Does the Act require the District to provide for any particular period or length of time allowed to parents to submit their opt-out decision?

No. The FERPA regulations appear to leave the determination of the actual period of time up to each individual agency or institution. However, the regulations do specifically require that the public notice to parents and eligible student about the directory information policy include the period of time within which the decision to opt out must be submitted.[57]

What about the children of parents who move into the District during the school year—is the new District required to provide them notice and an opportunity to opt of the directory information policy?

Yes. The directory information provision applies to students who are in "attendance" at the agency or institution, so that the parents or eligible students must be given notice and have the opportunity to opt out of the particular District or agency's directory information policy within the actual period of attendance.

If the parents of a child who has moved into the District during the year opted out of the directory information at their previous school, does this decision govern the disclosure of directory information at the new school?

No, since the student was not in attendance at the new District at the time the parent or eligible student responded to the directory information notice and policy of the previous District or agency. Remember, the previous school or District may have designated different information or directory.

What if a parent does not opt out of the Directory Information policy during the designated period, but then attempts to do so later in the school year?

If the District can demonstrate that the Directory Information policy (including the opting out provision) was made available to the parents earlier in the year, and if the District is confident in the integrity of their record-keeping process as to the list of parents who did in fact choose to opt out, then the District may disclose the directory information related to this student even though the parent objects at some later date.[58]

What if a parent initially opts out of the Directory Information policy, but then wishes to withdraw their decision later in the school year?

FERPA itself does not specifically prohibit the District from allowing parents to retract their initial election, though we strongly advise any Districts considering this measure to secure this decision in writing. On the other hand, FERPA does not require the District to waive that initial period of time during which the parent's decision as to Directory Information must be made for that school year. Of course, the parents may also provide written consent for any individual disclosure not permitted in light of their initial decision to opt out.

May the District penalize students who opt out of the directory information policy?

No, students may not be penalized for opting out of a District's directory information policy or otherwise required to waive any of their rights under FERPA.[59]

Is there an exception to the directory information notice requirements for former students?

Yes, FERPA permits the District to disclose directory information about former students without notifying these students (or their parents) of the types of information designated as directory, or of their right (and the time frame within which this right must be exercised) to veto the designation of this information as directory.[60]

Is the District required to honor a request by a former student not to disclose directory information relating to them?

Yes. The exception discussed above applies to the District's duty to specifically notify former students of their rights, and the District is not required to honor a subsequent request by a former student not to disclose directory information. However, if the student did opt out of the District's directory information policy during their last opportunity to do so as a student in attendance, then the District must honor this request until notified otherwise by the student.[61]

What if the District did not have a directory information policy when the student was enrolled?

If the District did not have a directory information policy, then it is highly likely that no parents or eligible students received notice and the opportunity to opt out of any such policy. In this event, the District may not make use of the directory information provision to release directory information about the student.

What if the District is uncertain as to whether or not a parent or eligible student opted out of the directory information policy—for instance, the District has lost the physical copies of the opt-out forms returned by parents (or the District has lost confidence in the record-keeping process used to track such opt outs)?

If the parent or eligible student's current complaint is that the District is not releasing directory information because it is uncertain as to whether the parent or student opted out, FERPA does not require the District to release directory information.[62] In this circumstance, the parent or eligible student does not have a valid FERPA complaint against the District which refuses directory information about the student. On the other hand, if the parent or eligible student's current position is that they did in fact opt out, and the District cannot with confidence dispute this claim, we believe the prudent position for the District to take is to respect the parent or eligible student's current position and request they submit a current, opt out form.

May a parent or eligible student approve the designation of some, but not all, of the information selected by the District as directory?

Absolutely, the FERPA regulations specifically identify the parent or eligible student's "right to refuse to let the agency or institution designate *any or all* of those types of information about the student as directory."[63]

Does this mean that parents could disapprove the release of directory information about their students in certain instances, such as to outside vendors, but permit the use of directory information by the school for athletic programs?

Not necessarily. The regulations appear to contemplate that while parents may pick and choose from among the bits of information to be considered as directory, the rules do not appear to specifically envisage parents having the authority to approve or not the resulting disclosure of this "string" of information to only certain entities. In other words, once the set of directory information for a student is determined, this set of information is now considered directory generally.

Does the District have any discretion to designate different levels of directory information, such as certain information which may be disclosed within the School, and other information which may be disclosed to outside parties?

Yes. In the comments to the 2008 regulations, the Department states that the District's disclosure of information designated as directory within the institution (an example would be in a school-wide student directory) does not, so far as FERPA is concerned, require the District to make this same information available to the public.[64] However, an additional issue may be whether State Sunshine laws would continue to recognize as exempt from public disclosure certain categories of information which the school has designated as directory, but only within the agency or institution.

What is the difference between the notice and designation of directory information specifically, and the District's annual obligation to notify parents and eligible students of their FERPA rights?

The District is only required to notify parents and eligible students of the specific information which has been designated as directory if the District elects to utilize the directory information provisions of the Act. While the designation of certain information as directory may have many practical advantages for the District, the District is not required to recognize and use the directory information provisions of the Act at all. However, the District is required to notify all parents and eligible students annually of their rights under FERPA (access, confidentiality, amendment, and complaint) regardless of whether or not the District seeks to make use of the directory information provisions under the Act. [65]

Is the District actually required to have a directory information policy?

No. A District may choose not to designate any student information as directory, in which case the notice of directory information and opt-out provisions related to directory information would not apply. In this case, the District would be obliged to seek parental consent for each and every individual disclosure of personally identifiable information about a student, with the exception of the military recruiter provisions discussed below (which give military recruiters access to certain student information even in the absence of a directory information policy).

How does the District notify parents and eligible students about the District's directory information policy?

The Department has not specified the procedure District's must use in notifying parents and eligible students about directory information. Certainly, one procedure the District may follow is to include this information with their annual notification of FERPA rights, which may be disseminated "by any means that are reasonably likely to inform the parents or eligible students of their rights."[66] Historically, this notification has been included in the student handbooks distributed early each school year.

Does FERPA require the District to disclose information that has been designated as directory to any party, such as vendor of high school graduation rings, who may request such information?

No, the directory information provision under FERPA is permissive (the District may disclose), but not mandatory in that it does not require the District to disclose directory information to any party. As the Department has stated, "FERPA is not a public open records or freedom of information statute."[67] In the Model Notice of Directory Information, the Department specifically states that "outside organizations include, but are not limited to, companies that manufacture class rings or publish yearbooks."[68] However, in many cases state law may require the release of public records which are not required to be kept confidential under FERPA or any other state law. In these instances, it is important to distinguish between records which must be disclosed under such state laws (which frequently refer only to records which already exist), and the information requested in the particular situation (which often seek a compilation or subset of the student's educational records).

An Example—State University enters into a contract with Big Bank to disclose the name, address, and phone number of students and alumni, in exchange for which State University receives a fee for each student who either opens an account with Big Bank or applies for a credit card with Big Bank. As long as the University has published a directory information notice which notified students that this information may be disclosed, and no such information relating to any students who opted out of the directory information policy is sold to Big Bank, this practice does not violate FERPA.[69]

Does this mean that State law may require the District to disclose directory information about all students, even though FERPA does not require this disclosure?

While this is certainly possible, the answer to this question will depend upon the particular State law at issue. In some cases, State law may recognize privacy rights of students beyond FERPA, may create confidential relationships and records not subject to State disclosure laws, and/or may contain additional exceptions to the disclosure of records under State law that will govern a particular request for records the District may receive. In any case, it is advisable that the school consult with an attorney knowledgeable about the State public records law when addressing this issue.

Does FERPA prohibit the District from collecting recruitment or vendor information from third parties and providing this information to students and parents?

No, FERPA would not prohibit this practice.[70] However, the District which does undertake to forward or distribute information and/or materials from outside parties to student and parents should thoughtfully consider and develop reasonable rules and procedures as to which third parties will be allowed to make use of such a distribution, and how the distribution will actually be handled. Note that similar activity in the opposite direction—the collection of student information for purposes of conveying or selling for marketing purposes—is governed in part by the recent amendments to the Protection of Pupil Rights Amendment. (Please see Chapter IX for a further discussion of these rules).

THE MILITARY RECRUITER PROVISIONS

Is the District required to release any information about students to military recruiters?[71]

Yes. The No Child Left Behind Act included an amendment to FERPA, which requires the District to release particular information about a certain group of students to military recruiters, as long as the parents of students have not opted out of this process.

An Example—The principal of City High School, Sissy Sixties, is no fan of the military or of students from the school being recruited to serve in the military. In the High School Handbook, Sissy notifies parents that the school will release their children's contact information to military recruiters only if they affirmatively choose to allow the school to so, and by returning a signed form authorizing the school to release this information. This notice is accompanied by list of this year's military casualties from Iraq and Afghanistan. However, the practice of establishing an "opt-in" system under which the District does not release information to military recruiters unless the parents or eligible student have affirmatively elected to permit such release has been specifically prohibited by the Department.[72]

Exactly what information is the District required to release to military recruiters?

Under the NCLB amendment, the District is required to release a student's name, address, and telephone number to a military recruiter unless their parent (or the eligible student) has affirmatively opted out of such disclosure. Notably, this requirement applies even if the District has chosen not to designate any directory information for students generally.

What if the District has not designated some or any of this information (name, telephone number, or address) as directory information?

The District must still notify parents that this information will be released to military recruiters upon request, unless parents opt out of these disclosures.[73]

Are all students at the high school subject to the military recruiter access rule?

No, only juniors and seniors are covered by the military recruiter access provisions.[74]

What if a military recruiter wishes to obtain additional information about a student, for example, a copy of their high school transcript or disciplinary record—does the NCLB amendment authorize the District to share this information with a recruiter?

No. In order to permit inspection of any educational records and/or provide information from such records about a student beyond their name, address, and phone number to a military (or college) recruiter, the District must obtain the specific, written consent of the parents or the eligible student.

Is the District required to notify parents about the District's obligations under NCLB in this regard, and their option to opt out of providing this information to military recruiters?

Yes, the District is independently required to notify parents of the requirement that a student's name, telephone number, and address will be released to military recruiters upon request, and of the parent's right to opt out of this disclosure.

May the Board of Education adopt a policy prohibiting entirely the release of this information to military recruiters?

While there is an instance in federal education law which authorizes a local Board to establish a policy, by majority vote, of denying access by military recruiters to directory information of students, this law has been superseded by the No Child Left Behind Act.[75] Under NCLB, the District is required to release directory information to military recruiters regardless of any local policy or vote of the Board of Education unless the parents of those students have opted out of this provision.

May parents opt out of providing information to military recruiters, while permitting the District to disclose directory information without further consent in any or all other instances?

While neither the statute nor FPCO specifically address this point, it is our interpretation that this would be permissible. Of course, in order to be effective an individual parent must specifically elect to opt out of disclosing their child's information to a military recruiter, and then make no (or only a partial) objection to otherwise disclosing directory information about the their child. One precedent in support of permitting parents this flexibility may be found in the pre-existing manner in which parents may opt out of allowing "any or all" directory information to be provided by the District.[76] Since parents may choose to opt out of the specific military recruiter provisions entirely, and have always been permitted to opt of permitting the release of any particular piece of information the District has identified as directory, this result is consistent with the continued recognition of parental choice and control in this regard.

If parents opt out of the District's Directory Information policy, does this also mean that the student's name, address, and telephone number may not be provided to military recruiters?

Assuming the District's Directory Information Policy does include name, address, and phone number, then the parent's decision to opt out of the Directory Information policy also serves to remove their child from the list of students about whom information will be released to military recruiters without their consent.[77]

Are private schools subject to the military recruiter requirements?

Yes, if they receive certain federal funds. Private secondary schools that receive funds under the Elementary and Secondary Education Act are subject to 10 U.S.C. § 503. However, a religious objection to service in the Armed Forces by a private school that is verifiable through the corporate or other organizational documents or materials of that school will exempt the school from the requirements of this provision under the law.[78]

Does NCLB mandate any other form of access to students be provided to military recruiters?

Yes, in addition to the contact information which must be released upon request (and unless the parent/eligible student has opted out), the District must also provide military recruiters with the same access to students as the District allows to post-secondary institutions and prospective employers. For example, if the District permits colleges and/or employers to set up tables and distribute literate at "career fairs," then the District must permit military recruiters to do the same.

Does this mean the District may be required to provide information to students about the military as a career option?

Yes. For instance, if the District maintains a bulletin board or program stand where advertisement or brochures for colleges and universities are made available for students to sample, then the District must allow the military to distribute similar programs and brochures.

How is the military recruiter access provision enforced?

The expectation is that a District will work with State and public officials to resolve any problems under this section. However, if necessary, a senior military officer (e.g., Colonel or Navy Captain) may visit the District within 120 days. If the access problem is not resolved with the District at this stage, the Department of Defense is to notify the Governor of the State within 60 days. If problems remain after a year, they are reported to Congress upon the determination by the Secretary of Defense that a District denies recruiting access to at least two of the armed forces (Army, Navy, Marine Corps, etc.).

ENDNOTES

1. 34 C.F.R. § 99.3.
2. Id.
3. Federal Register Vol. 65 No. 130, 41855 July 6, 2000.
4. Id. It is worth noting the Department's method of analysis in this and other instances of considering whether some additional or different piece of information about a student may be listed as directory. First, is the information "analogous to" information already recognized as directory? Secondly, would release of the information be considered "harmful or an invasion of privacy" generally? And third, will this information allow access to other, sensitive information? Id.
5. Letter to Dr. Pascal Forgione, Jr. (March 2, 2005); Letter to Ms. Ardith Lynch, (May 23, 2005); Letter to W. Joseph Hatley (March 8, 2005); Letter to Melanie Baise (November 29, 2004); Letter to Dr. Thomas Henry (August 23, 1999). It is always

important to keep in mind the context-specific function of the "easily traceable" limitation. For instance, in a case involving a small community, the Department found that disclosing a student's first name and tribal affiliation would be prohibited in the absence of consent. See Letter to Michael Riley (October 11, 2005).

6. Letter to University Student (July 1, 2004). However, State laws may give parents the right to refuse to provide social security numbers of their minor children to the District, and the Social Security Act (42 U.S.C. § 405) continues to govern the collection, use, and required disclosure of social security numbers by most governmental agencies.

7. 34 C.F.R. § 99.3(b)(1).

8. 34 C.F.R. § 99.3(b)(2).

9. 34 C.F.R. § 99.3(c).

10. Id.

11. Federal Register Vol. 73 No. 237 74808 (December 9, 2008.

12. Id.

13. Letter to Carol H. Fuller (April 16, 2004).

14. Federal Register Vol. 73 No. 237 74808 (December 9, 2008). In these Comments, the Department also said that "FERPA does not prohibit using a student's SSN, without consent, to search records in order to confirm directory information. Id.

15. Federal Register Vol. 65 No. 130, 41852 (July 6, 2000); 34 C.F.R. § 99.3.

16. 34 C.F.R. § 99.31(a)(5)..

17. On the one hand, there would appear to be some rational basis to distinguish between elementary and secondary school students in this area. However, FERPA is a statute of which rules apply by virtue of a District or Institution's receipt of federal funding, and this decision is not often made at the school level. From an administrative and perhaps an enforcement perspective, a uniform directory information policy may well present certain conveniences.

18. Letter to Dr. Thomas Henry (August 23, 1999).

19. Id.

20. Federal Register Vol. 65 No. 130, 41855 (July 6, 2000). In particular, the Department's concern here seems to have been focused upon the issue of whether class roster information permits access to, or releases, other sensitive information. For instance, the Department noted that class schedules might indicate that a student is enrolled in a special education class, and that some class rosters include social security numbers.

21. Letter to Ms. Diane Layton, undated but responding to an inquiry dated February 10, 1997.

22. Family Educational Rights and Privacy Act "Model Notice for Directory Information," accessed from http://www.ed.gov/policy/gen/guid/fpco/ferpa/mndirectoryinfo.html on January 2, 2009.

23. 34 C.F.R. § 99.3.

24. Id.

25. Id.

26. Federal Register Vol. 73, No. 237 (December 9, 2008).

27. Letter to Mr. Thomas D. Watkins (August 13, 2003).

28. Federal Register Vol. 73, No. 237 (December 9, 2008).

29. 34 C.F.R. § 99.3.

30. Letter to Diane Walker (September 27, 2002).

31. Federal Register Vol. 73, No. 237 74832 (December 8, 2008). Whether the precise language used by the Department will be given literal effect is unclear, though the use of the conjunctive "or" in this exemplary sentence is potentially of great importance. For instance, it may often be well known among the school's administrators what disciplinary consequence is assigned to students—will this literally be interpreted to mean that disclosure of redacted reports concerning offenses and consequences at the school are now impermissible? We suspect not, though the potential for confusion or concern certainly exists.

32. Federal Register Vol. 73, No. 237 74832 (December 8, 2008).

33. Letter to Lee Tyner, Jr. (February 12, 2002).

34. 34 C.F.R. § 99.3.

35. Federal Register Vol. 73, No. 237 74832 (December 8, 2008).

36. Id.

37. Letter to Ms. Corlis Cummings (September 25, 2003).

38. See *Bowie v. Evanston Community Consolidated School District #65,* 522 N.E.2d 669 (Ill. App. I Dist. 1988), aff'd 538 N.E.2d 557 (Ill. 1989) and *Kryston v. Board of Education, East Ramapo Central School District,* 77 A.D. 896, 430 N.Y.S.2d 688 (App.Div 2nd Dept. 1980).

39. Letter to Ms. Corlis Cummings (September 25, 2003).

40. 34 C.F.R. § 99.31(b). See also Chapter VI for further discussion of this regulatory section.

41. Letter to Dr. Pascal Forgione, Jr. (March 2, 2005).

42. Letter to Ms. Robin Parker (October 19, 2004).

43. Letter to Ms. Corlis Cummings (September 25, 2003).

44. Id.

45. *Plyler v. Doe*, 457 U.S. 202 (1982).

46. Letter to Mr. Thomas McElvain (March 12, 1999); Letter to Mr. Van Johnson (December 1998). In addition, some State enrollment statutes, regulations, or policies may specifically prohibit the District from inquiring or gathering information related to the student's citizenship, legal, or illegal alien status.

47. Letter to Jerome Sullivan (August 27, 2004). SEVIS actually requires the maintenance of a fairly detailed list of information concerning aliens or those who are applying for nonimmigrant status under the Immigration Act.

48. 466 F.Supp.2d 434, 442 (D. Conn. 2006). However, after examining the record in this case the court rejected the student's claims after finding "no evidence of disclosure of any potentially private information."

49. Id.

50. *Santamaria v. Dallas* Independent *School District* (2006 WL 1343604)(N.D. Texas 2006)(Civil Action No. 3:06-CV-692-L).

51. Letter W. W. Joseph Hatley (March 8, 2005). The Department's position on this issue may have been overly literal and given insufficient weight to the fact that

State laws may permit or require the publication of this information, which arguably undercuts an individual's legitimate expectation of privacy in this information. In our view and experience, the court will often weigh the reasonableness of the individual's expectation of privacy in particular information, including whether the individual has voluntarily disclosed this information or the State requires or permits this publication, and is sometimes less likely to find a reasonable expectation of privacy than the Department has historically recognized. Also, this position pre-dates the 2008 amendments which specifically recognize the added, non-consensual disclosure provision related to sex offenders and information provided to the agency or institutions in the higher education setting pursuant to 42 U.S.C. 14071; 34 C.F.R. § 99 31(a)(16).

52. 34 C.F.R. § 99.31(a)(16).

53. While we believe this continues to be the position of the Department, certainly some courts will view a claimed violation by parents with less sympathy in those instances where the parents have, for their own reasons or perceived benefit, publicly disclosed information about their child.

54. Specifically, the Department stated that "we have not found and do not believe that parents and students generally waive their privacy rights under FERPA by sharing information with the media or other members of the general public." Federal Register Vol. 73, No. 237 74831 (December 9, 2008).

55. Letter to Dr. Robert Wagoner (March 10, 1999).

56. 34 C.F.R. § 99.37(a).

57. 34 C.F.R. § 99. 37(a)(3).

58. Of course, it is often the case that the District will acquiesce in the parent's demands at this point and decline to disclose the information. Depending upon the particular context, this response may not give rise to any controversy and may well appease the most likely contestant in any dispute likely to emerge. For example, if the issue concerns publication of their child's name on the honor roll and the District agrees not to do so upon parental insistence, it is unlikely that a complaint from any other party will be received in connection with this decision. However, we do caution Districts to be mindful of the cumulative difficulty which may be encountered in creating and maintaining the list of parents who have opted out of the Directory Information policy when any specifically defined period of election is, essentially, abandoned.

59. Federal Register Vol. 73 No. 237 74808 (December 9, 2008).

60. 34 C.F.R. § 99.37(b).

61. 34 C.F.R. § 99.37(b); Federal Register Vol. 73 No. 237 74808 (December 9, 2008); Letter to Anonymous (March 10, 1999).

62. Federal Register Vol. 73 No. 237 74809 (December 9, 2008).

63. Id.

64. Federal Register Vol. 73 No. 237 74808 (December 9, 2008).

65. 34 C.F.R. § 99.7(a)(1); 34 C.F.R. 99.37(a).

66. 34 C.F.R. § 99.7(b).

67. Federal Register Vol. 69 No. 77 21672 (April 21, 2004).

68. Family Educational Rights and Privacy Act "Model Notice for Directory Information," accessed from http://www.ed.gov/policy/gen/guid/fpco/ferpa/mndirectoryinfo.html on January 2, 2009.

69. For an interesting discussion of this practice, as well as the financial arrangements sometimes involved, see New York Times Section B1 "Extra Credit: Colleges Profit as Banks Market to Students" (January 1, 2009).

70. Letter to Dr. Pascal Forgione, Jr. (March 2, 2005).

71. See generally "Policy Guidance—Access to High School Students and Information on Students by Military Recruiters" (October 9, 2002).

72. Colleague Letter from Deputy Secretary Hanson (July 2, 2003).

73. Policy Guidance "Access to High School Students and information on Students by Military Recruiters" (October 9, 2002).

74. Joint Letter from Secretary Paige and Secretary Rumsfeld, October 9, 2002.

75. 10 U.S.C. § 503; Dear Colleague Letter from Deputy Secretary Hanson July 2, 2003; 20 U.S.C. § 7908.

76. 34 C.F.R. § 99.37(a)(3). We recognize that this is a slightly different question than whether parents may opt to allow directory information about the children to be disclosed to certain, identified outside entities, while refusing to permit release of this same information to other parties (beyond the military recruiter).

77. Policy Guidance "Access to High School Students and information on Students by Military Recruiters" (October 9, 2002).

78. Id.

Chapter 6

External Disclosure without Permission

In drafting FERPA, Congress recognized that schools could not effectively operate if all disclosures of educational records to individuals beyond the educational institution required prior, express, and written release by parents and/or eligible students. As a result, FERPA permits the release of educational records without prior parent or student permission in certain circumstances. Historically, these exceptions have been strictly construed by FPCO and sometimes the courts, and both institutions and educators have frequently violated the confidentiality provisions of FERPA. However, in the wake of the events at Virginia Polytechnic Institute and State University ("Virginia Tech") on April 16, 2007, FPCO has clarified—and seemingly loosened—the parameters on what information may be shared with external agencies in particular situations. In this chapter, readers will examine the situations in which records may be disclosed to agencies or individuals outside the educational institution without prior written authorization of parents or eligible students, and will examine FPCO and court interpretations of those exceptions.

OVERVIEW OF NON-CONSENSUAL DISCLOSURE RULES

Can educational records be disclosed to individuals who are not employees of the educational institution where the student is enrolled without parent or eligible student permission?

Generally, FERPA provides that educational records—or more specifically personally identifiable information from such records—may not be disclosed to "third parties" without the prior written consent of a student's parent or guardian, or if the student has reached the age of 18 or is attending an institution of post-secondary education, the student himself or herself.[1] This is, of course, subject to numerous exceptions explained in further detail in this chapter.

Are there any exceptions to this limitation?

Yes. FERPA currently contains approximately seventeen (17) explicit exceptions to what the Family Policy Compliance Office calls the "prior written consent rule," and one instance of implied consent authorizing disclosure. The December 2008 regulations recognized an additional two (2) exceptions to the previous list of fifteen (15)."[2] These disclosures may be generally divided into "internal" and "external" disclosures, depending upon whether the disclosure is within the institution ("internal") or to third parties beyond the school ("external"). Internal disclosures are generally addressed in Chapter IV of this work; however, the complete list of regulatory exceptions to prior authorized disclosure is included below. Each of these is specifically addressed in either Chapter IV or this chapter.

What are the authorized exceptions to the prior written consent rule?

Below are listed all seventeen (17) of the exceptions to the prior written consent rule authorized through issuance of the December 9, 2008, final regulations. While many of these exceptions seem relatively clear, these exceptions have been the subject of considerable debate and clarification by the courts and the Family Policy Compliance Office since 1974.

The exceptions are:

- Disclosure to school officials (including teachers) within the institution whom the institution has determined to have "legitimate educational interests." (See Chapter IV.)
- Disclosure is to another school, school system, or institution of post-secondary education where the student intends to enroll. (See Chapter IV.)
- Disclosure is to certain federal, state, or local education authorities in connection with the audit or evaluation of federal or state supported educational programs. (Chapter IV.)
- Disclosure in connection with the student's application for financial aid if the information is necessary to determine eligibility for aid, determine amount of aid, determine the conditions for aid, or enforce the terms and conditions of the aid.
- Disclosure to state and local juvenile justice officials under certain state laws.
- Subject to limitations; disclosure to certain organizations to develop, validate or administer predictive tests; administer student aid programs; or to "improve instruction."
- Disclosure to accrediting organizations to carry out accrediting functions.

- Disclosure to parents of "dependent" students, even if the student is above eighteen (18) years of age.
- Disclosure pursuant to a judicial order or lawfully issued subpoena.
- Disclosure in connection with a health or safety emergency.
- Disclosure of directory information after proper designation, notice, and the opportunity to opt out of the Institutions directory information policy (See Chapter V.)
- Disclosure to a parent of a student who is not eighteen (18) or enrolled in post-secondary study, or to the eligible student himself or herself. (See also Chapter III.)
- Subject to limitation, disclosures of post-secondary disciplinary actions taken against perpetrators of certain violent offenses to their victims.
- Disclosure to a parent of a minor student enrolled in an institution of post-secondary education regarding the student's violation of any federal, state, or local law, or any rule or policy of the institution, governing the use or possession of alcohol or a controlled substance.
- Disclosure concerns sex offenders and other required to register under the Violent Crime Control and Law Enforcement Act of 1994.
- Disclosure of de-identified records after removing all personally identifiable information and determining that a student's identity is not otherwise personally identifiable.[3]

It is important to recognize that, in the absence of one of the above listed exceptions, FERPA prohibits virtually all disclosures without the prior written authorization of a parent and/or an eligible student. In the absence of an exception, a high school could not publish a yearbook nor could a student's current math teacher research a student's historic school performance access educational records from the previous year without obtaining the specific written consent of a parent or eligible student. A college could not send grades home to the parents of a nineteen-year-old student, despite the fact that the parents were paying the student's tuition and he remained a dependent. Faced with a judicial subpoena, a school district would have to choose between disclosing the records sought and violating FERPA or not disclosing the information and risking a contempt of court charge.

APPLICATIONS FOR FINANCIAL AID

What information may be disclosed to third parties in connection with a student's application for financial aid?

Under FERPA, information may be disclosed when it is necessary in order to determine the student's eligibility for financial aid, the amount or conditions of any such financial aid, or to enforce the terms and conditions of financial aid.[4] This might include inquiries to banks and other third parties seeking to verify information provided by the eligible student or his or her parents on the financial aid application, inquiries related to financial aid disbursement or inquiries from a financial aid provider seeking the location of a graduate who has defaulted on his or her student loan. Notably, the Department has specifically approved the release of information contained in student records to a student loan "clearinghouse" for the purpose of reporting and monitoring the enrollment status of borrowers.[5]

Is there a definition of financial aid under FERPA?

Yes. Under FERPA, the term financial aid means "a payment of funds provided to an individual (or a payment in kind of tangible or intangible property to the individual that is conditioned on the individual's attendance at an educational agency or institution."[6]

Practice Pointer. Under the Taxpayer Relief Act of 1997 (and the Hope Scholarship Credit and Lifetime Learning Credit provisions, specifically), Congress authorized the Department of the Treasury obtain certain student information (including name, address, Taxpayer Identification Number, as well as course or credits completed) from post-secondary institutions. Although FERPA does not contain an express exception for the release of this information, the Department concluded that since the Taxpayer Relief Act was the "later enacted and more specific statute," this Act did authorize the disclosure of this otherwise personally identifiable information.[7]

JUVENILE JUSTICE OFFICIALS

When may an institution disclose educational records to state and local juvenile justice officials?

One of FERPA's original exceptions addresses institutions providing information about a student to state or local juvenile justice authorities. Prior to FERPA's adoption, a number of states had laws permitting institutions to provide student information to juvenile justice authorities without the prior express consent of parents or an eligible student. In 1974, when FERPA was enacted, it "grandfathered" in pre-existing state laws allowing for broader disclosure of information to juvenile justice authorities; however, for state laws enacted after FERPA's adoption, a much stricter standard applies.

If a state law allowing disclosure was enacted prior to November 19, 1974, an institution may—without prior parental authorization—disclose student information if the information requested "concerns the juvenile justice system and the system's ability to effectively serve the student whose records are released."[8] However, for state laws enacted after November 19, 1974, institutions may only disclose information without prior consent if the "reporting or disclosure allowed by State statute concerns the juvenile justice system and the system's ability to effectively serve, prior to adjudication, the student whose records are released, an educational agency or institution may disclose education records."[9]

What is the distinction between statutes enacted before or after November 19, 1974?

In the case of a statute pre-dating the enactment of FERPA, the disclosure need only be for the purpose of a juvenile justice system "serving" the student, and it is not limited by the condition that such service must be delivered prior to the "adjudication" of the student—thus a much broader authorization of disclosure. If the statute upon which disclosure is based was enacted after November 19, 1974, the disclosure must be for the more limited purpose of effectively serving the student "prior to adjudication."

An Example—On November 13, 1974, the State of Blackacre adopted a law requiring secondary and post-secondary state educational institutions to provide "any and all" information requested "within thirty (30) days" to state juvenile justice authorities "regarding any public school student in the state who is currently or has formerly received services through the state's juvenile justice system." This law specifically authorizes Blackacre juvenile justice authorities to request student records of students formerly incarcerated in the state's juvenile justice system, permitting them to "follow up" on the careers of former detainees. As this law was enacted prior to November 19, 1974, FERPA permits disclosure of this information without prior parental or eligible student authorization. However, if the law was enacted a week later—November 20, 1974—this disclosure would violate FERPA as it permits disclosure to state juvenile justice authorities *after* the adjudication of a student's case.[10]

Are there any additional requirements for disclosures made under state laws enacted after November 19, 1974?

Yes. The regulations specifically provide that "the officials and authorities to whom the records are disclosed shall certify in writing to the educational agency or institution that the information will not be disclosed to any other party, except as provided under State law, without the prior written consent of the parent of the student."[11] For disclosures under state laws enacted prior to November 19, 1974, FERPA contains no such certification requirement.

Is it possible for a local law, policy, or ordinance to serve as the basis for either of the disclosures mentioned above?

No. While this exception contemplates that permissible disclosures may be made to local officials, the authority upon which these disclosures is based must be grounded in state law, not a local law, policy, or ordinance.

Practice Pointer—While the regulation does not specifically address who makes the determination as to whether the information is necessary for the juvenile justice system to effectively serve the student, remember that FERPA applies only to disclosing—not requesting—institutions. Any request that an institution disclose student records falling within FERPA's protections without prior written consent requires the disclosing institution to determine whether the request (and the information provided in support of it) is sufficient to satisfy the requested exception.

RESEARCH & ACCREDITATION PURPOSES

When may an institution disclose educational records "to develop, validate, or administer predictive tests, administer student aid programs, or improve instruction?"

FERPA generally permits educational agencies to disclose information without prior written consent "to organizations conducting studies for, or on behalf of . . . institutions" for certain purposes related to education evaluation generally. These include:

- To develop, validate or administer predictive tests;
- To administer student aid, or
- To improve instruction.[12]

These exceptions appear to provide institutions with significant latitude to release otherwise restricted student data; however, this exception is, in fact, severely limited. As will be explained further below, information released under this exception cannot be disclosed in such a way that it would allow for the personal identification of parents or students other than by representatives of the organization conducting the study—which is, in practice, a fairly significant limitation. Recognizing that state educational agencies are the parties most likely to request information under this exception, the Department suggests "it may not be necessary or even advantageous for state educational authorities to use the studies exception in order to conduct or authorize educational research because of [its] limitations."[13] Instead, the Department offers that state educational agencies may wish to take advantage of the broader authorization permitting local educational agencies to disclose information to state agencies under 34 C.F.R. § 99.31(a)(3)(iv), which permits the disclosure of personally identifiable information without prior consent to "audit and evaluate" educational programs.[14]

The two conditions that make this exception so limited relate to the method in which the information is released and the requirement that it is destroyed when it is no longer needed. Specifically, in using this exception, FERPA requires that:

- The study be conducted in a manner that does not permit personal identification of parents and students by individuals other than representatives of the organization; and
- The information be destroyed when no longer needed for the purposes for which it was provided.[15]

Is this the provision under which a university researcher unaffiliated with the institution would request data?

No. In the 2008 regulatory changes, the Department specifically notes that this exception would not permit an educational institution to disclose data to an "independent" researcher, or one not working on or for a project for an educational institution.[16] However, it does allow disclosure to an otherwise independent researcher if he or she "may propose or initiate research projects for consideration and approval by the state educational authority . . . either before or after the parties have negotiated a research agreement."[17] In such an instance, it would seemingly be left to the institution's discretion to determine whether it had an interest in pursuing such a project and providing the researcher with the data he or she needed.

Is there any penalty under the Act for a researcher that does not adhere to either of the conditions described above?

Yes, but only for a violation in connection with the failure to destroy records that are no longer needed. In this event, the district may not allow that entity to receive any personally identifiable information for a minimum of five years.[18]

When may educational records be disclosed to accrediting organizations?

FERPA permits the disclosure of educational records to accrediting organizations, for the purpose of carrying out their accrediting functions. For example, if the Southern Association of Colleges and Schools (SACS) conducts an investigation into the accuracy of a school district's student attendance records related to the district's adherence to SACS standards, individual student attendance records may be disclosed to SACS investigators.

THE SUBPOENA EXCEPTION

When can an educational entity disclose educational records pursuant to a judicial order or lawfully issued subpoena?

FERPA permits educational entities to disclose educational records without consent when required to do so by a judicial order or lawfully issued subpoena.[19] However, prior to disclosure, an educational entity must first make a "reasonable attempt to notify" the parent or eligible student of the subpoena and the date by which the institution will have to comply.[20] This requirement does not apply to subpoenas issued by a federal grand jury in which the court has ordered that the contents of the subpoena or information furnished in response to the subpoena be kept confidential.[21]

Who is responsible for notifying the parent or eligible student of the subpoena?

Prior to December 2008, confusion and disagreement existed as to who had the burden of notifying the parent or eligible student regarding the issuance of the subpoena—the requesting party or the institution receiving the subpoena. In the December 2008 regulations, the Department resolved the issue by clarifying that "party that receives a court order or lawfully issued subpoena"—usually the school—". . . must provide the notification."[22]

What constitutes a judicial order or lawfully issued subpoena?

In the majority cases, this will be a question of state law governing the court from which the order or subpoena has been issued.[23] Generally, the authority of an entity to "lawfully issue" a subpoena is a matter of state law—is the individual executing the subpoena authorized by state law to do so, has the subpoena been properly delivered, does the subpoena allow an appropriate time period between service and the date that the records are requested, and similar questions. This is particularly an important question as states greatly differ in granting authority to various entities—and not just courts—to issue subpoenas, and failure to properly respond to a lawfully-issued subpoena may subject an educator *individually* to significant penalties. An institution receiving a subpoena requesting disclosure of protected student records would do well to consult with legal counsel regarding the sufficiency of any such subpoena.

An Example—City County High School receives what purports to be a subpoena for educational records from the Blackacre State Juvenile Justice Authority. The subpoena is issued to Principal Paul as custodian of the school's records. Principal Paul recalls that during a FERPA training, he was informed that the State of Blackacre did not have a law—either prior to November 19, 1974 or after—permitting schools to disclose educational records to juvenile justice authorities without prior consent, and he ignores the subpoena. While he was correct in that Blackacre did not have a law permitting non-consensual disclosures to juvenile justice authorities, unfortunately Blackacre does have a law authorizing the state's juvenile justice authority to subpoena documents. As a result, the ability of the school to disclose the requested documents turned upon the "lawfully issued subpoena" exception and not the "juvenile justice exception." This is appropriately explained to Paul by the judge at his subsequently ordered contempt hearing.

What is a "reasonable attempt to notify" a parent or eligible student of a subpoena?

As noted above, prior to producing documents in response to a lawfully-issued subpoena, institutions generally have an obligation to notify parents or eligible students of the requested subpoena, providing them an opportunity to intervene in the case and quash the subpoena if they do not want the records produced. In determining what constitutes a "reasonable attempt to notify" a parent or eligible student of the existence of a subpoena prior to disclosure, FPCO looks at the "totality of the circumstances" in each individual case. In so doing, FPCO considers:

- The time period that an educational agency or institution was given to comply with the subpoena from the date the subpoena was served;
- Whether this time period for compliance was reasonable, considering the urgency of the issuer's need for the subpoenaed documents and the educational agency's obligation under FERPA to attempt to notify the parent or eligible student;
- Whether the educational agency has made a good faith effort under FERPA in its attempt to notify the eligible student or parent of the subpoena in advance of compliance with; and
- When and how the educational agency attempted to notify the eligible student or parent of the subpoena, and whether the parent or eligible student was given sufficient time to move for an order to quash the subpoena.[24]

If, for example, the subpoena requires production of documents within twenty-four (24) hours, FPCO would likely determine several telephone calls to constitute a "reasonable attempt to notify." If the institution received a subpoena to produce documents in another state in seven (7) days, a certified letter mailed the following day to the student notifying him or her of the institution's intention to comply with the subpoena would probably be sufficient.[25] However, when the window for compliance is narrow, FPCO encourages educational entities to attempt notification by a variety of methods, including "certified mail, telephone, or facsimile."[26]

What should a notice to parents that their child's educational records have been subpoenaed contain?

The notice should contain a copy of the subpoena, along with a letter indicating whether the institution intends to comply, and the date of compliance. For example, a notice might include the following:

> On February 13, 2009, City County School District received a subpoena for any and all of your educational records held by City County, a copy of which is enclosed. We intend to comply with this subpoena by February 20, 2009. If you wish to object to the release of your records, you or your attorney must file a motion to that effect in the court from which the subpoena was issued. If you do intend to file any such objection, we do request that you or your attorney please send a copy of any such notice to my attention at the address on this letter as soon as possible.

Are there any situations in which an institution should *not* notify parents or an eligible student of the existence and contents of a subpoena for educational records?

Yes. If federal grand subpoena has specifically prohibited notice to a parent or student of the subpoena's existence, or any other court or issuing agency has ordered either the existence or the contents of the subpoena for law enforcement purposes not to be disclosed, the institution should not disclose this information to parents or eligible students.[27] This provision has also been specifically extended to certain *ex parte* orders obtained under the Patriot Act.[28] It does not, however, extend to other types of subpoenas issued for non-law enforcement purposes.

An Example—In the State of Blackacre, the Teacher Certification Commission has the authority to issue subpoenas in connection with the investigation of complaints involving the certificates of educators that have been granted by the Commission. In a case involving a suspected, consensual relationship between a teacher at City High School and a student at the school, the Commission subpoenas the educational records of the student suspected of involvement with the teacher, further ordering that the existence of the subpoena not be disclosed to the student or her parents. However, since the subpoena is issued in connection with the ethical rules governing the license of a teacher, and *not* for a law enforcement purpose, the institution will be required to notify the parents about the subpoena as set for above.[29]

Are any additional new and specific rules concerning the disclosure of *ex parte* orders under the Patriot Act?

Yes. The Department has stated that an agency or institution that notifies a parent or eligible student of a request for disclosure of documents in violation of The Patriot Act may violate the terms of the court order (risking a contempt citation) and may also fail to meet the "good faith" requirements of the USA Patriot Act for avoiding liability for the disclosure.[30]

Practice Pointer—The requirements of The Patriot Act are simultaneously controversial and complicated. In attempting to reconcile the non-disclosure provisions of The Patriot Act and the notice provisions of FERPA, the Department expressly recommends that institutions consult with legal counsel when responding to non-disclosure orders under the Patriot Act.

If neither the parents nor an eligible student objects to the subpoena, what should the institution do?

After ensuring that all of the documents requested in the subpoena are, in fact, responsive to the subpoena, and ensuring that no personally identifying information of other students is included in the documents, the institution (or more frequently, the institution's counsel) may comply with the terms of the subpoena.

Practice Pointer—Institutions uncertain as to whether records fall within the scope of a subpoena and reluctant to "over-include" information may directly contact the court issuing the subpoena and request permission to provide the records to the presiding judge for an "in camera" inspection of the records. This permits the *judge*—and not the institution—to determine what records are relevant to the subpoena.

May the institution receive a subpoena for documents that are not "educational records" under FERPA?

Yes. For example, it is common in divorce or contested domestic litigation for attorneys for one parent to subpoena school counseling records of a child when seeking information related to the determination of child custody. A counselor's notes typically fall within the "sole possession" exception to FERPA and therefore are not "educational records." As these are not "education records," FERPA does not require institutions to provide parents with the same type of notice when counseling notes (and other non-educational records) are requested.

What should an institution do if it is concerned about the confidentiality of information contained within the documents subpoenaed, but no parent or eligible student objects to their production?

Generally speaking, an institution may produce documents without fear of consequence upon complying with the notice provisions of FERPA. However, for a variety of reasons, institutions are sometimes reluctant to provide records containing information they regard as "highly sensitive"—particularly to attorneys representing parties either adversarial to the student or in cases in which the student has no direct involvement. In such instances, the institution may instruct their counsel to approach the court issuing the subpoena and request an "in camera" inspection (described above) of the records by the court prior to their disclosure.

What if instead of a subpoena for records, an administrator or teacher is personally subpoenaed directly to testify about a student in a judicial proceeding?

An often-attempted tactic by attorneys familiar with FERPA is to subpoena educators (instead of documents), attempting to compel them to testify to information that would normally be contained in educational records. It is initially important to recall that the definition of "disclosure" for purposes of FERPA specifically includes the oral communication of personally identifiable information from a student's educational records.[31] In many cases, counsel for the institution is able to discuss the anticipated subject of the educator's likely testimony with the party requesting the subpoena. Sometimes it is possible to clarify that the individual educator does not actually possess relevant or helpful information, and so the subpoenaed may be withdrawn. In other cases, the teacher's testimony may continue to be sought and is expected or likely to involve the disclosure of personally identifiable information about one or more students. In these cases, the authors recommend notifying the parents of the students involved as soon as practicable, and that individual witnesses (perhaps accompanied by legal counsel) specifically request the judge to rule on whether or not they may answer any question which seems to call for the disclosure of confidential information.

HEALTH AND SAFETY EMERGENCIES

What is the "health or safety emergency exception"?

The "health of safety emergency" exception allows an institution to "disclose personally identifiable information from the educational records of a student to appropriate parties in connection with an emergency if the knowledge of the information is necessary to protect the health or safety of the student or other individuals."[32] However, Congress recognized that "a blanket exception for 'health or safety' could lead to unnecessary dissemination of personal information," and originally intended the "health or safety emergency" exception to apply in "exceptional circumstances," such as "the outbreak of an epidemic."[33] Since 1974, FPCO has consistently interpreted the "health or safety emergency" provision to only be applicable to "specific situation[s]" presenting an "imminent danger" to students or other members of the community, or requiring an "immediate need" for information in order to avert or diffuse "serious threats to the safety or health of a student or other individuals."[34]

In the aftermath of the tragic shootings at Virginia Tech, the Department subsequently revised its position and no longer "strictly construes" the health or safety emergency exception. In the December 2008 regulations, the Department revised the interpretation of a health or safety emergency, granting educational institutions far more latitude in determining when such circumstances exist (discussed further below).

What are some examples of the types of situations which have been interpreted to fall within the health and safety exception?

Historically, FPCO consistently interpreted this exception to apply to medically challenging situations, such as "outbreak[s] of diseases such as measles, rubella, mumps, and polio," and other diseases posing "threat of permanent disability or death for the individual" that are also "epidemic in nature."[35] After 9/11, the Department released FERPA guidance relating to "anti-terrorism activities," wherein the Department noted: "[T]he health or safety exception would apply to non-consensual disclosures to appropriate persons in the case of a smallpox, anthrax, or other bioterrorism attack"—an elaboration consistent with the Departmental "epidemic" interpretation and application of the "health and safety" emergency provision.[36]

An Example—County Health Department requests City Elementary School to provide a list of students who have not obtained immunizations as required under State law. Under FERPA, and in the absence of any extenuating circumstance, a school would generally be unable to provide this information. In comments to the 2008 regulations, the Department specifically makes clear that FERPA "does not allow disclosures on a routine, non-emergency basis such as . . . routine, nonemergency disclosures of student's immunization data to public health authorities.[37]

However, in the event of an outbreak of a highly contagious disease, an institution might determine that providing this information to the health department was essential in preventing the spread of the disease and therefore constituted a "health or safety emergency." For example, in the attendance zone of City Elementary School, an exceptionally high number of parents have chosen not to have their children immunized for fear that the immunizations themselves may expose their children to increased risk of certain medical conditions, such as autism. At the beginning of the year, the student population at City Elementary School suffers a sudden outbreak of rubella (which is included on the State list of required immunizations prior to enrollment in public school). In response to this outbreak, the County Health Departments requests a list of the students who have not been immunized against rubella. In this instance, it is most likely that this disclosure is permissible under the health/safety emergency exception.[38]

Does the "health or safety" exception permit disclosure in the case of students who exhibit threatening behavior?

Yes. Following the Virginia Tech shootings in April 2007—in which the "failure" of various educational institutions to "share" information related to the shooter was much discussed in the media—President George Bush directed the Department to investigate issues relating to the shootings, including sharing information. These discussions revealed significant misunderstandings regarding when and what information could be shared under FERPA.[39] "It was almost universally observed that these fears and misunderstandings likely limit the transfer of information in more significant ways than is required by law."[40] The "health and safety emergency" exception was particularly misunderstood, and the Department was concerned that the law prior to 2007—with its admonition that the regulation should be "strictly construed"—did not provide educators and institutions with effective guidance in applying the exception. As a result, the exception was rewritten in 2008 to provide that schools may disclose information under the "health and safety" exception where the failure to do so "pose[s] a significant risk to the safety or well-being of [a] student, other students, or members of the school community" based on the "totality of the circumstances pertaining to a threat."[41] In the December 2008 regulations, the Department clarifies that should an educational agency have a "rational basis" for determining that a health or safety emergency exists, "the Department will not substitute its judgment for that of the educational agency or institution[.]"[42] .

What constitutes a "significant and articulable threat" for purpose of the health or safety emergency exception?

The Department has explained that this simply requires that "a school official be able to express in words what leads him or her to conclude that a student poses a threat," and that the threat itself is "significant," meaning "of a noticeably or measurably large amount."[43] By way of further explanation, the Department stated that "if a school official can explain why, based on all the information then available, the official reasonably believes that a student poses a significant threat, such as a threat of substantial bodily harm, to any person, including the student, the school official may disclose education records."[44]

What is a "rational basis" for determining a threat to health or safety?

At present, FPCO has not offered guidance as to what constitutes a "rational basis" for concluding that a "significant risk to the safety or well being of [a] student" or others exist. However, the Department has stated that it "will not substitute its judgment for that of the agency or institution if, based on the information available at the time of the determination, there is a rational basis for the agency's or institution's determination that a health or safety emergency exists and that the disclosure was made to appropriate parties." [45]

An Example—Bob is principal at City County High School. A student approaches him and informs him that Jim Jones, a twelfth-grade student who has a documented "emotional/behavioral disorder," has been bragging to other students that he is going to "shoot up the school" tomorrow. The student tells Bob that Jim went into great detail about what he was going to do, and told the student that he should "skip school tomorrow." Acting under the "school official with a legitimate educational interest" exception, Bob pulls Jim's student records, particularly considering his counseling evaluations. In those evaluations, Bob does not see that Jim has a history of making idle threats or threatening violence. Bob then holds a conference with Jim's counselor and special education coordinator, discussing the threat with them. Both are concerned about it, noting Jim's attitude has significantly worsened lately. The counselor reveals (under the "school official" exception) that Jim's parents divorced a month ago, about the time his mood began to darken. Also proceeding under the "school official" exception, Jim's special education coordinator reveals that she is aware from Jim's writings that Jim has multiple weapons in his home to which he has unrestricted access. Bob is satisfied that he now has a credible threat, and calls his school security officers into the conference. Proceeding under the "health or safety emergency" exception, Bob informs them of the threat, and directs them to intercept Jim when he comes into school the next morning.

May school officials share their observations of students with others when those observations give school officials concern for the safety of either that or other students?

In Departmental guidance after the tragedy at Virginia Tech, FPCO stated that "nothing in FERPA prohibits a school official from sharing with parents information about a student that is based on that official's personal knowledge or observation and that is not based on information contained in an education record. Therefore, FERPA would not prohibit a teacher or other school official from letting a parent know of the concern about their son or daughter that is based on their personal knowledge or observation."[46] Although written to address the situation of eligible students at post-secondary institutions, this same rationale appears to apply in the P-12 setting.

May a student's suicidal threats or ideations rise to the level of a health or safety emergency?

Prior to 2008, FPCO concluded that a student's repeated suicide threats, coupled with unsafe conduct and threats toward another student, constituted a "health of safety emergency."[47] FPCO has also noted that the circumstances of this particular case were not equivalent or so broad as to necessarily encompass every suicidal statement a student might make.[48] However, in the comments to the 2008 regulations, the Department also mentions that an emergency might be "a situation in which a student gives sufficient, cumulative warning signs that lead an educational agency or institution to believe the student may harm themselves or others at any moment."[49]

What about a student's at-risk behavior involving, for instance, sexual activity?

It is important to remember that FERPA only applies to information obtained from or contained in educational records. If a school official is revealing or acting upon a non-recorded conversation with the student or with other students, he or she is not revealing information contained in an educational record, and therefore is not subject to any FERPA limitations related to their disclosure (though it is possible that state ethical codes may limit disclosure made to any educator in confidence). However, assuming that information related to ongoing or potential sexual conduct of the student was contained in an educational record, each specific instance would have to be examined to determine whether or not a significant risk to the safety or well being of the student is actually present.

If the knowledge does come from an educational record, may this be disclosed to appropriate parties—such as the Public Health Service—under the health or safety exception (assuming it otherwise qualifies for the exception)?

In the vast majority of cases, we believe the answer to this question is yes. Initially, as long as the student is under 18 years of age and not themselves an "eligible student," the institution may always disclose information from educational records to the parents of the students. In many cases (though with perhaps some variation based upon the age of the students involved) sexual activity between or involving minors may constitute child abuse under state law (discussed further below), or sexual offenses under state law, and is frequently subject to state mandatory reporting requirements in either or both these circumstances. This would certainly contribute to an institution having a "rational basis" for determining a health or safety emergency exists, warranting disclosure.

An Example—In the spring of 1996, public health officials in Rockdale County, Georgia—an affluent county east of Atlanta—discovered what they considered to be a massive outbreak of venereal disease among teenagers. In investigating the outbreak, health officials learned of a sub-culture of sex, drugs, and alcohol among many county students, in which students between the ages of thirteen (13) and seventeen (17) had, quite literally, dozens of sexual partners and were being provided with ready access to drugs and alcohol by adults. County (and later, state) health officials shared this information with school authorities, and school authorities empanelled a county-wide intervention across multiple agencies. This necessitated sharing school district information not only with parents, but with law enforcement and health officials as well, in an attempt to halt both the "epidemic" spread of venereal disease and the illegal acquisition and consumption of illegal drugs and alcohol by minors. While some parents were understandably reluctant to have information about their child shared in the context of such an investigation, this situation appears to epitomize a "health or safety emergency" warranting disclosure without prior parental consent.

In the event of a health or safety emergency, who may receive personally identifiable information from the institution?

Under the "health or safety emergency" exception, information may be disclosed to those individuals whose knowledge of the information is "necessary to protect against the threat."[50] Historically, FPCO has envisaged disclosures being narrowly limited to "law enforcement officials, public health officials, and trained medical personnel."[51] After the shootings at Virginia Tech, the Department expanded its position in the case of "eligible" (most likely postsecondary) students, permitting parental disclosure after FERPA rights have transferred to the student. "[T]he Department has interpreted FERPA to permit schools to disclose information from education records to parents if a health or safety emergency involves their son or daughter."[52]

Has the scope of individuals to whom health or safety information may be disclosed been expanded under the 2008 regulations?

Yes. While the regulatory language itself has not changed, the Department's comments provide authority for the conclusion that the scope of individuals to whom information may be disclosed under this provision has been extended. For instance, the Department's comments include "any person who has information that would be necessary to provide the requisite protection," including by way of example "current or prior peers of the student or mental health professionals who can provide the institution with appropriate protection from the threat," and also, "a potential victim and the parents of a potential victim." By way of further explanation, the Department also stated that a student's current school may share and receive information about a student from the student's former school in order to determine how to address a threat. Interestingly, a former school is not required to make an independent assessment of the threat in this instance, and may instead rely upon the current school's determination.[53]

What information may be disclosed in the event of a qualifying health or safety emergency?

Historically, both Congress and FPCO consistently cautioned that the "health and safety exception" is temporary, and must be "narrowly tailored" to only release that information appropriate in light of the magnitude and immediacy of the emergency.[54] For example, in 2004, FPCO considered whether the State of Alabama could use the "health and safety emergency" exception to permit school districts to share students' immunization information with the Alabama Department of Public Health. After consideration, FPCO determined that such disclosure was inconsistent with the purposes of the "health and safety" exception. Such a release would not be in response to a "health or safety emergency," was not "narrowly tailored" to the emergency or presented only to those individuals capable of addressing the emergency. Instead, it would be an ongoing, "blanket" release of personally identifiable information. Consequently, the information could not be released.

May an institution disclose information about a student to a "threat assessment team"?

Yes.[55] However, in the event the institution intends to include as members of the assessment team individuals who are not employees, the Department recommends that the institution craft its "school official with a legitimate educational interest" exception sufficiently broadly to incorporate these individuals (for a deeper discussion of this exception, please see Chapter IV).[56] Under the "other school officials" exception, recall that any third-parties so designated are under the "direct control" of the educational agency in regard to their use or re-disclosure of personally identifiable information. Of course, once the team determines a health or safety emergency does exist, then the necessary information may be disclosed as set forth above.

Are there specific record-keeping requirements uniquely associated with the use and determination of the health or safety emergency exception?

Yes. In 2008, the Department stated that educational agencies utilizing this exception should record "the articulable and significant threat to the health or safety" so as to be able to demonstrate "what circumstances led them to determine that a health or safety emergency exception existed and how they justified the disclosure."[57] The December 2008 regulations specifically require that the educational agency record both the "significant threat to the health or safety of a student or other individuals that formed the basis for the disclosure" as well as "the parties to whom the agency or institution disclosed the information."[58]

Under what conditions may an educational entity report suspected abuse or neglect to a state agency tasked with investigating the same?

Most states have laws requiring educators to report suspected abuse or neglect to a state division of family and children's services (or an equivalent agency). While information contained in these reports would constitute "educational records" requiring an educational entity to consider whether disclosure was permissible (and most likely, whether the student's situation rose to the level of a "health or safety emergency"), Congress greatly assisted states through enacting federal laws creating an "unlisted" FERPA exception and requiring disclosure in certain cases. Institutions should determine whether their state's mandatory reporting requirement was adopted pursuant to the 1988 amendments to the Federal Child Abuse Prevention, Adoption and Family Services Act (CAPTA), which required states to enact laws requiring reporting of child abuse and neglect.[59] As this law was amended after FERPA's passage in 1974, FPCO takes the position that Congress was aware of FERPA's confidentiality provisions, and, in enacting a subsequent federal law requiring mandatory reporting of suspected child abuse and neglect, intended that these provisions should supersede FERPA's confidentiality provisions. As a result, CAPTA permits the reporting of suspected child abuse, including disclosure of personally identifiable information, without parental consent.[60]

What about requests for information about a child who has previously been referred to protective services—is an institution permitted to continue to make these disclosures under FERPA?

In many cases, family and protective services may monitor or seek further information about the status of a child (for example, whether they are attending school) who has previously been identified as a possible or actual victim of abuse. In general, FERPA does not contain a continuing exception to the confidentiality of such information after the "health or safety emergency" no longer exists.

Practice Pointer—A good practice for both schools and family and children's service organizations is for the organization to obtain authorization from the parents allowing a school to share educational information with the organization. This greatly facilitates a smooth working relationship between the school and protective services. When necessary, the agreement and execution of such a release may also be addressed with the court or judge having initial jurisdiction over the child's case. For example, the court may allow the child to return to the home of the parents only upon a number of conditions, one of which includes the parents consent to an appropriate release of information by the school to protective services.[61]

What about reports relating not to the physical or sexual abuse of a child, but reports or referrals that a child may be neglected by their parent or guardian—do these fall within the scope of FERPA health or safety emergency exception?

In some cases, allegations of child neglect also may rise to the level of a health or safety emergency. For instance, certain instances in which the absence or lack of supervision of the child exposes the child to abuse by other adults (or other children) may very well fall within the Department's expanded interpretation of a health or safety emergency.[62]

Practice Pointer—Remember, FERPA only governs the disclosure of information obtained from educational records about a child—a teacher or counselor's report of information that is personally observed (or about which the student verbally advises them) will often fall outside of FERPA. In many cases, State child abuse and neglect reporting requirements will apply to any covered individual who has a reasonable (or sometimes referred to as "good faith") belief that the child is being abused or neglected. These abuse reporting statutes are generally NOT limited to information contained within educational records.

PARENTS OF STUDENTS OVER 18 YEARS OF AGE

May educational records be disclosed to a student's parent(s) after he or she reaches the age of eighteen (18) or enrolls in post-secondary education?

When a student reaches the age of eighteen (18) or enrolls in an institution of post-secondary education, he or she is deemed "eligible," and all of the FERPA rights previously held by his or her parents transfer to the student.[63] However, as discussed throughout this chapter, there are a number of instances in which educational entities can still disclose educational records to an "eligible" student's parents without his or her consent.

Does the fact that a parent pays all or part of student's tuition and other expenses while the student is enrolled in a post-secondary institution entitle them to inspect their child's education records?

No. As discussed below, the key factor in authorizing a parent to inspect their child's education records while enrolled in a post-secondary institution is not the payment of tuition or other expenses, but the separate (though sometimes related) event of claiming the student as a dependent for federal income tax purposes. FERPA defines a "dependent" consistently with the

Internal Revenue Code, noting that a student remains a dependent so long as his or her parents can claim the student to be on their federal tax return.[64] One manner which the College or University may utilize in determining a student's dependent status is to rely upon the eligible student's own certification to this effect. The Department has published a model form for this purpose.[65]

May a post-secondary institution require students who are not dependents to execute a release of their educational records to their parents?

No. The position of the Department is that the student's enrollment in the institution may not be conditioned upon their execution of any such release.[66]

In the case of parents who are separated or divorced, may only the parent who claims the students as a dependent on their tax return that year receive information from their child's education record?

No. The Department has taken the position that the parent's status as a custodial parent is not relevant for this purpose—"if a student is claimed as a dependent by either parent for tax purposes, then either parent may have access under this provision."[67] This interpretation—that so long as the student is a dependent of a parent, then the institution may release educational records to either parent—should relieve the institution from tracking the common arrangement in divorce or separation agreements. This helps to avoid the child's dependent exemption alternating between the parents, or one parent's access to records hinging upon the payment of child support.

SPECIAL RULES FOR PARENTS OF POST-SECONDARY STUDENTS

What information may the College or University disclose to parents of a dependent student?

In such instances, a student's grades and other educational records may be disclosed to his or her parents. And in the most recent guidance in response to the tragedy at Virginia Tech, FPCO clearly stated that "under FERPA, schools may release any and all information to parents, without the consent of the eligible student, if the student is a dependent for tax purposes under the IRS rules."[68]

Do parents of dependent student continue to hold additional FERPA rights, such as the right to seek a hearing regarding the accuracy of information contained within such records?

No. In fact, the disclosure to parents of dependent student is not properly construed as continuation or even limited extension of parental access and inspection rights generally. Rather, the disclosure by the institution to parents of dependent student is permissive in the same manner as any other non-consensual disclosure provision discussed in this Chapter (or Chapter IV). All other FERPA rights continue to vest with the now eligible student.

Does FERPA give parents of dependent students the right to discuss their child's education with the faculty or staff of a post-secondary institution?

No. FERPA only recognizes the institution's authority to permit inspection of records. FERPA clearly does not require faculty or staff at the institution to discuss the contents of any such records with parents of dependent students. On the other hand, FERPA itself does not prohibit faculty or staff from discussing information contained within the educational records of an eligible (but tax dependent) student with his or her parents. The institution, in turn, may authorize or prohibit such discussion or disclosures on the part of faculty or staff, the breach of which is an employment matter (for example, insubordination or neglect of duty).

Is there any information contained with a student's educational records that the post-secondary institution is prohibited from sharing with the parent of a dependent student?

Generally no. In the case of an 18-year-old male student who remained a dependent on his parent's tax returns and was reprimanded by the Office of Campus Life for being in the room of a female student after hours, this information—and all related records—could (but are not required to) be conveyed to his parents consistently with FERPA.

An Example—Chastity Community College has a rule that whenever a student is suspended or reprimanded for reason, the parent or guardian of the student is notified in writing. Nancy Notsonice is reprimanded by her resident supervisor for having the men's baseball team (at least the starting infield) in her dorm room after visiting hours. However, Nancy is not a dependent on her parent's income taxes (Nancy is a relatively successful entrepreneur paying her own way through Chastity College), and the offense for which she is reprimanded does not fall within any of the alcohol, controlled substance, violent, or non-forcible sex offenses discussed below. In this instance, Chastity College will be in violation of FERPA if and when the resident supervisor sends Nancy's parents the written notice of her rule violation.[69]

Does this mean that parents of dependent students have a FERPA right of access to this information?

No. This provision does not create an equivalent to FERPA access rights in P-12 education. It only removes FERPA confidentiality requirements by the post-secondary institution that would otherwise limit the disclosure of information to the parents of eligible students. Essentially, FERPA allows the post-secondary institution discretion to disclose such information, but does not require that the institution to do so.

Are there any other instances (beyond the tax dependent eligible student) where information may be disclosed to parents of a student 18 years old or older?

If a student enrolled in any post-secondary institution is under the age of twenty-one (21) and violates federal, state, or local law, or any rule of the institution, governing the use or possession of alcohol or a controlled substance, this information may be conveyed to the student's parent, *regardless* of whether the student is a dependent.[70] However, prior to such disclosure, the institution must make a determination that the student has committed the infraction, and the disclosure to the parent(s) must take place before the student turns 21 years old.

Practice Pointer—While the original scope of this provision encompasses federal, state, or local laws (as well as institutional rules) relating to alcohol or controlled substances, it is notable that the institution's authority to disclose this information is triggered by the determination of a "disciplinary violation," which the authors interpret to mean a violation of the institution's own rules. Of course, in the case of the tax dependent, eligible student, the institution may disclose any educational record to either parent regardless of whether the student is over or under 21 years of age, or whether the institution has found a violation of its own rules to have taken place.[71]

What if the student is enrolled in post-secondary classes at a local or community college, even though he or she is still in high school and under the age of 18?

The Department has taken the position that "if a student is attending a post-secondary institution—at any age—the rights under FERPA have transferred to the student.[72]" However, if the student is *simultaneously* enrolled in a high school and a post-secondary institution, "the two schools may exchange information on that student" and "parents still retain the rights under FERPA at the high school and may inspect and review any records sent by the post-secondary institution to the high school" until the student reaches the age of 18.[73]

Does FERPA allow for the disclosure of the results of student disciplinary matters to victims or other parties?

In the P-12 setting, FERPA historically recognized no such exception.[74] At the post-secondary level, FERPA contains two different provisions allowing for disclosure under certain conditions. One provision address disclosure of victims of the final results of disciplinary proceedings against students alleged to have committed certain offenses; the other provision relates to the more widespread disclosure allowed when and if the Institution actually determines that the student actually committed the offense.[75]

When may an institution disclosure the final results of disciplinary proceedings to the victims of certain violent or non-forcible sexual offenses on campus?

Under this provision, the post-secondary institution may disclose to the victim "the final results of disciplinary proceedings conducted by the institution . . . regardless of whether the institution concluded a violation was committed."[76] The term "final results" is defined to include only the name of the student, the violation committed, and any sanction imposed by the Institution. The sanction, in turn, is a description of the action taken as well as the date of imposition and duration of the sanction." However, it is noteworthy that FERPA re-disclosure limitations do apply at this point, and the Institution is expected to notify the alleged victim of this limitation concurrent with providing the information discussed above.[77]

What types of offenses are included in the list of "crimes of violence"?

The offenses which are subject to this reporting exception include the following:

- Arson
- Assault
- Burglary
- Criminal homicide-manslaughter by negligence
- Criminal homicide-murder and non-negligent manslaughter
- Manslaughter
- Destruction/damage/vandalism of property
- Kidnapping/abduction
- Robbery
- Forcible sex offense.[78]

The regulations include several subcategories of a "forcible sex offense," including forcible rape, forcible sodomy, sexual assault with an object, or forcible fondling.[79] The term non-forcible sex offense, in turn, is defined as "statutory rape or incest."[80]

When may a post-secondary institution disclose information in connection with a student alleged to have committed such an offense to someone other than the victim?

A post-secondary institution may not disclose information about students alleged to have committed such offenses to parties other than the possible victim of the offense until and unless it determines that the student did, in fact, violate institutions rules or policies in commission of the offense.[81] The final result contemplated under this provision is a decision by "an honor court or council, committee, commission, or other entity authorized to resolve disciplinary matters within the institution."[82]

Are there any limitations on disclosures in connection with students determined to have committed a covered violation of college or university rules or policies?

Yes. Even after the institution has determined a violation of institutional rules or policies, the name of any other student, including a victim(s) or witness, may not be disclosed without their consent, and the disciplinary proceeding involved must have been finalized "on or after October 7, 1998.[83]" However, once the institution has in fact reached this final result these results may be disclosed to parties other than and in addition to the victim(s) of the offense. Moreover, the re-disclosure limitations of the Act do not apply at this point.[84]

Practice Pointer—It is important to remember that the institution's authority to publicly disclose the results of proceedings against a student found to have committed any of the offense discussed above must be based upon the Institution's finding of a violation of its own rules or policies. A student, for example, who may enter a plea to a related or similar criminal offense but who is not prosecuted (or not prosecuted successfully) under the institution's own disciplinary system is not subject to this provision.

STUDENTS & SEX OFFENDER STATUS

Can institutions disclose information regarding a student's status as a sex offender?

Yes, but only if the information was provided to the institution under the Violent Crime Control and Law Enforcement Act of 1994 (commonly known as the Wetterling Act).[85] The federal Campus Sex Crimes Prevention Act specifically amended FERPA to permit educational agencies and institutions to share information provided to them under the Wetterling Act, which requires a number of law-enforcement agencies to provide relevant information about sex offenders to state institutions—including colleges and schools.

What information about a student may be disclosed under the exception for registered sex offenders?

The Department has explained that this provision allows the Institution to disclose "any information provided to it under the Wetterling Act . . . to also include any additional information about the student that is relevant to the purpose for which the information was provided to the educational agency or institution—protecting the public."[86] By way of example, the Department has allowed that this may include "the school or campus at which the student was enrolled."

Practice Pointer—While it is possible that state sex offender registration requirements vary, it is generally unlikely that sex offender registration will be required prior to adjudication. Therefore, there will almost certainly be instances when a student has been charged with an offense which would be covered under the registration requirements in the event the student is convicted (or perhaps there is a belief among some parents or students that charges have been filed or an arrest made), but where this provision will probably not allow the public disclosure of information about the student involved at this early stage. As always, specific consultation with an attorney who is knowledgeable about the sex offender registration rules of the state is recommended.

DE-IDENTIFIED RECORDS AND DISCLOSURE

Can student records be produced without consent if personally identifiable information is removed?

One of the major challenges under FERPA is balancing a student's individual privacy rights against society's need to evaluate and improve publicly-funded educational programs. To balance these competing interests, the Department permits that individual student data be released without prior disclosure *if* all the personally identifiable information has been removed—so called "de-identified records and information."[87]

The Department declined—and declines—to provide definitive guidance as to a procedure to de-identify student data, placing instead this burden on the institution that wishes to release the data. "The releasing party is responsible for conducting its own analysis and identifying the best methods to protect the confidentiality of information from education records it wishes to release."[88] The Department advises that institutions should consider *at a minimum* whether the "cell size" of any grouping is sufficient to protect the individual identities of students. For example, if there are only three (3) African-American male students in a particular class of 30 students and SAT scores are released without student names, but disaggregated by race and gender, it is possible to determine with a relatively high probability the SAT scores of the three male students).

The Department particularly warns institutions to consider the effects of multiple releases of information containing different types of "de-identified" data, noting technological advances make it much easier for individuals to "re-identify" students when sifting through multiple types of "de-identified" data.[89] For example, if an institution releases de-identified SAT scores of all twelfth graders disaggregated by race in March, by disability in April, by gender in May, and by national origin in June, it becomes increasingly likely that the individual score of a Hispanic male student with a disability could be determined by analyzing all four (4) supposedly anonymous data releases—particularly by someone in the school community who has some level of personal familiarity with the students whose data is supposedly "de-identified." The risk increases if the student is in a relatively discreet student population (assume that the senior class only has three (3) Hispanic males who receive special education services). As a result, the Department requires institutions to consider the possible cumulative effect of *all* previous "de-identified" data releases—not just the data previously received by the current recipient of the newly de-identified data.[90] While this is certainly a daunting task for most institutions, the Department suggests that institutions may minimize their risk by requiring institutions that receive de-identified data to agree that the data will not be further re-disclosed, and the data will be destroyed when it is no longer needed of the study for which it is requested.[91]

Does the exception for release of de-identified student records and information allow for the release of student level data that may be matched to the same source (i.e. student)?

The institution may not release de-identified data that would allow the recipient to identify any individual student. However, the institution may code student-level data in such a way that a recipient can confirm or match data with the same student who is the source of the data.[92] No information regarding how the code is generated may be disclosed, the records involved may only be used for educational research, and the code or record code may not be based upon the student's social security number or any other personally identifiable information from the educational records of the student.[93]

THE IMPLIED WAIVER EXCEPTION

Other than the exceptions discussed above, has FPCO recognized any other exceptions permitting an institution to disclose personally identifiable information without the consent of parents or eligible students?

Yes. FPCO has stated that if a parent or eligible student has taken an "adversarial position" against an educational institution, then parental or eligible student permission is not required prior to disclosure of those confidential educational records necessary for the institution to defend itself. In such instances, FPCO permits institutions to infer an "implied waiver" to consent and release educational records without the authorization of a parent or eligible student.[94] "The rationale for this policy is based on the belief that a student or parent should not be permitted to use rights afforded them under FERPA to prevent an educational agency or institution from defending itself in a court of law when the parent or student has initiated legal action . . . against the agency or institution."[95]

What constitutes an "adversarial position" taken against the institution?

To constitute an adversarial position sufficient to support an implied waiver, a parent or qualifying student must:

- Take an adversarial position against the educational agency or institution;
- Initiate the involvement of a third party by contacting that party in writing and, in so doing, set forth specific allegations against the agency AND request that action be taken against the educational agency or institution, or that the third party assist the student in circumventing decisions made about the student by the institution;
- The third party's special relationship with the educational agency or institution gives the third party authority to take specific action against the educational agency or institution; OR reasonably could be significantly affected if the educational agency or institution cannot refute the allegations; AND
- The disclosure is as limited as is necessary for the educational agency or institution adequately to defend itself from the student's charges or complaint.

The epitome of an "implied waiver" is, of course, that the parent or eligible student initiates a lawsuit or files a complaint against the institution with a state or federal agency with authority over the district. However, this is not the only situation in which an "implied waiver" may be inferred.

May an institution disclose information about a student that is already a "public record" or a matter of public controversy?

Generally, no. A parent or student's public disclosure of what would otherwise be a confidential educational record does not affect an educational institution's responsibility to keep that information confidential.[96] "FERPA prohibits the disclosure of personally identifiable information derived from educational records, whether or not that information is available from another source."[97] This includes both public record filings (such as court papers) and comments to mass media.

Does the implied waiver concept allow public disclosure when parents or an eligible student take their complaints to the press?

Generally no, since the media lacks the "special relationship" (discussed above) with the institution sufficient to allow that specific action be taken against the institution. For example, in 1997 a student at Towson State University (Maryland) made a number of complaints about the university and its faculty to a local newspaper.[98] In response, the university's attorney provided information from the student's educational and medical records to a reporter, refuting the student's allegations. The student filed a complaint with FPCO, alleging the university violated her rights under FERPA. The university argued that the student had a long and involved dispute with the university, in which she previously sought the involvement of numerous state officials and media, and the numerosity and gravity of her allegations necessitated the university's response: "Clearly, [the student] cannot be permitted to charge the University in a public forum with serious misconduct and then, knowingly and intentionally, seek to deprive the University from using the very information it needs to defend itself." FPCO disagreed, noting that while the student did make a number of allegations regarding the university, the university and the newspaper lacked a "special relationship" permitting the newspaper to take action against the university. Additionally, FPCO noted that disclosure to the newspaper permitted no "effective limitation" on the more widespread dissemination of information from the student's educational records.

If the student's lawsuit refers to other students, is it permissible to disclose these students' educational records?

No. The implied waiver only extends to the educational records of the student initiating the lawsuit. "There is no exception in FERPA, or previous interpretations by this Office, that would allow [disclosures] of the education records of other students who have been named in a lawsuit without the other students' prior written consent."[99] However, an entity may disclose the educational records of another student if it removes any and all personally identifiable information, including information that would make the students' identities "easily traceable." If this is not an option because the student names another student specifically, the educational entity may request that the parents of the other student (or the eligible student himself or herself) authorize disclosure. Alternatively, the entity may subpoena the records, notify the student or parents accordingly and, in the absence of motion or order to quash the subpoena, make use of the identified records accordingly.

What should an educational institution do when false allegations are made by parents or a qualifying student about an educator or institution to the media?

In those instances where the institution is confident that the individual or entity has been exonerated from wrongdoing, it is often possible to communicate clearly and specifically about the results of any inquiry into the conduct of these individuals or entities, without discussing or identifying any student who may have been involved in the investigation itself. However, in cases where the allegations directly involve the conduct or behavior of individual students, FPCO has repeatedly encouraged educational institutions to respond to the media by informing them that FERPA prohibits the disclosure of information from the student's education record.[100]

Practice Pointer—Educators and institutions can certainly inform reporters that the parent or eligible student may, in writing, authorize the educational agency to release relevant educational records, after which point the institution would be free to fully and openly discuss the matter. Additionally, should a parent or eligible student make remarks about an institution or educator rising to the level of slander or libel, nothing in FERPA precludes an educator or institution from suing a parent or an eligible student for defamation under state law.

Can educational records be disclosed to a newspaper if a parent or eligible student sues?

No. The "implied waiver" resulting from a parent or eligible student suing an educational institution only permits disclosure to the court or other institution with a "special relationship" with the educational agency. An "educational agency or institution may disclose to the court . . . the student's educational records that are relevant for the educational agency or institution to defend itself."[101] It does not convert educational records into public records.

Does the implied consent exception apply at all if the school sues a parent or eligible student?

If a school sues a parent or student and needs to use educational records in any of its legal filings, the school may use and share with legal counsel any such educational records, provided it first notifies the parent or eligible student of its intentions in this regard.[102] Additionally, the Department has specifically recognized that an institution's legal counsel may qualify as an "other school official" with a "legitimate educational interest" in reviewing a student's educational record.[103]

Are written communications concerning a student between an educational institution and its legal counsel "educational records" subject to disclosure under FERPA?

Under FERPA, letters, emails, and other communications exchanged between an educational institution or educators and legal counsel may contain personally identifiable information about a student and are maintained by an institution, arguably resulting in their being "educational records."[104] However, FPCO recognizes that in incidents where a student has or threatens to file a complaint or legal action against an educational entity, the entity needs to communicate with its legal counsel in a confidential and candid fashion permitted by the attorney/client privilege. In making such a determination, it is likely that FPCO would be guided by relevant state and federal law interpreting the attorney/client privilege in the educational entity's jurisdiction.

Practice Pointer—During or prior to litigation, law firms may create or request that institutions create certain investigatory documents related to the lawsuit or potential lawsuit or conduct depositions of student witnesses. While it could be argued that the law firm is acting "on behalf of" the school district and "maintaining" these investigatory files, this is not an argument likely to be successful. In the single case considering such a situation, the United States District Court for the Middle District of North Carolina concluded that that transcripts of students' depositions in a sexual harassment case against a coach that were contained in the law office of the university's counsel were not "maintained" by the college, and thus were not educational records under FERPA.[105]

May an educational institution release records to a student's attorney?

Educational records may be released to an attorney representing parents or an eligible student if this individual is acting as the legal representative of the student. However, FPCO recommends—and it is an excellent policy—to require either the parent or the eligible student to designate the attorney as his or her legal representative in writing and authorize the disclosure of educational records to the attorney.[106] Additionally, is important to remember that even when a parent or student has retained an attorney and executed a proper release on their attorney's behalf, FERPA does not generally require that the institution provide copies of records at this point—only that the attorney has a right to inspect the records. (See Chapter III for a further discussion of the right to inspect records under FERPA, and when copies may be required.)

ENDNOTES

1. 20 U.S.C. § 1232g(b)(1); 34 C.F.R. § 99.30; Family Policy Compliance Office (FPCO) Opinion Letter, November 15, 1997.
2. 34 C.F.R. § 99.31(a)(1)–(16) & (b). See also FPCO Opinion Letter, November 25, 1997. A number of these provisions are discussed elsewhere, such as disclosures to parents of students, disclosure to other schools or school officials, and the disclosure of directory information. Please see Chapters III, IV, and V, respectively.
3. 34 C.F.R. § 99.31.
4. 34 C.F.R. § 99.31(a)(4)(i).
5. Letter to Mr. Daniel Boehmer (April 19, 1993).
6. 34 C.F.R. § 99.31(a)(4)(ii).
7. Letter to Mr. Jonathan Talisman & Mr. Stuart Brown (November 25, 1997).

8. 34 C.F.R. § 99.31(a)(5)(A).

9. 34 C.F.R. § 99.31(a)(5)(i) (B); 34 C.F.R. § 99.38(a).

10. To some extent, this particular regulatory provision (and the distinctions within the provision) may be less relevant today. Frequently, when students are adjudicated they are assigned to agencies or institutions which themselves constitute separate school systems within the State. Consequently, the disclosure to school officials in another school or school system in which the student enrolled (discussed in Chapter IV) will generally permit the disclosure of any and all educational records to the agency or institution currently serving the student.

11. 34 C.F.R. § 99.38(b).

12. 34 C.F.R. § 99.31(a)(6)(i).

13. Federal Register Vo. 73 No. 237, 74825 (December 9, 2008).

14. Id.

15. 34 C.F.R. § 99.31(a)(6)(ii)(A).

16. Federal Register Vol. 73 No. 237, 74825 (December 9, 2008).

17. Id.

18. 34 C.F.R. § 99.31(a)(6)(iii).

19. 34 C.F.R. § 99.31(9)(i).

20. 34 C.F.R. §99.31(9)(ii).

21. 34.C.F.R. §99.31(9)(ii)(A).

22. 34 C.F.R. § 99.33(b)(2).

23. Letter to Ms. Linda Simlick (June 22, 1998); Letter to Edward Opton (September 17, 1999).

24. Letter to Dr. Leslie Cochran (February 16, 1999).

25. Letter to Dr. Leslie Cochran (February 16, 1999).

26. *Id.*

27. 34 C.F.R. § 99.31(a)(9)(ii).

28. 34 C.F.R. § 99.31(a)(9)(ii)(c).

29. Note that the subpoena is still presumably a valid, lawfully issued subpoena under State law generally, but that it is not included in the specific provision under FERPA which permits disclosure pursuant to the subpoena in the absence of notice to the parents (or eligible student) and the provision does not apply to the subpoena in this example.

30. Federal Register Vol. 73 No. 237, 74819 (December 9, 2008).

31. 34 C.F.R. § 99.3

32. 34 C.F.R. 99.36(a).

33. *Joint Statement in Explanation of Buckley/Pell Amendment*, 120 Cong. Rec. S21489, Dec. 12, 1974 (quoted in Letter to Martha Holloway (February 25, 2004)).

34. *Id.*

35. *Id.*

36. Department of Education Guidance on "Recent Amendments to Family Educational Rights and Privacy Act Relating to Anti-Terrorism Activities (April 12, 2002) quoted in Letter to Martha Holloway (February 25, 2004)); *See also Doe v. Woodford County Board of Education*, 213 F.3d 921 (6th 2000)(Principal's suggestion

to basketball coach that you might want to check the medical records of student w/ hemophilia and Hepatitis B did not violate FERPA).

37. Federal Register Vol. 73 No. 237 (December 9, 2008). However, and depending upon the mechanism utilized in the State or the school to manage the immunization process, it may be possible for the School to designate County Health officials as "other school officials" with a legitimate, educational interest to access student immunization records. See Chapter IV for a further discussion of the process and limitations for designation other school officials.

38. See again Letter to Martha Holloway (February 25, 2004).

39. Federal Register Vol. 73 No. 57, 15575, 15589 (March 24, 2008).

40. *Id.*

41. 34 C.F.R. 99.36(c). See also Federal Register Vol. 73 No. 57, 15575, 15589 (March 24, 2008).

42. Federal Register Vol. 73 No. 57, 15575, 15589 (March 24, 2008).

43. Federal Register Vol. 73 No. 237, 74838 (December 9, 2008).

44. Id.

45. Federal Register Vol. 73 No. 237, 74837 (December 9, 2008).

46. "Disclosure of Information from Educational Records to Parents of Students Attending Post-secondary Institutions," Family Policy Compliance Office at http://.www.ed.gov/policy/gen/guid/fpco/hottopics/ht-parents-postsecstudents.html· accessed on January 19, 2009.

47. Letter to Melanie Baise (November 29, 2004).

48. Id.

49. Federal Register Vol. 73 No. 237, 74838 (December 9, 2008).

50. Federal Register Vol. 73 No. 57, 15575, 15589 (March 24, 2008).

51. Letter to Martha Holloway (February 25, 2004).

52. "Disclosure of Information from Educational Records to Parents of Students Attending Post-secondary Institutions," Family Policy Compliance Office at http://.www.ed.gov/policy/gen/guid/fpco/hottopics/ht-parents-postsecstudents.html· accessed on January 19, 2009.

53. Federal Register Vol. 73 No. 237 (December 9, 2008).

54. *Joint Statement in Explanation of Buckley/Pell Amendment*, 120 Cong. Rec. S21489, Dec. 12, 1974 (quoted in Letter to Martha Holloway (February 25, 2004)).

55. Id. See also Chapter IV for a further discussion of the establishing and managing the "other school officials" exception under FERPA.

56. Federal Register Vol. 73 No. 237, 74839 (December 9, 2008).

57. Federal Register Vol. 73 No. 237, 74837 (December 9, 2008).

58. 34 C.F.R. § 99.32(a)(5).

59. 42 U.S.C. § 5106a(b)(1)(A).

60. Letter to Melanie Baise (November 29, 2004).

61. In the event that no such release has been or can be obtained, and no other exception exists, family and protective services may always seek to subpoena the educational records at issue. In some cases, we have found that merely communicating this intention to the parents (along with their failure to cooperate in the exchange

of information about the child by agreement) has convinced some parents to agree to execute the release.

62. In the view of the authors, the area of child abuse or neglect reporting is one in which the Department or the courts are more likely to afford school officials the benefit of the doubt, especially in cases where the suspected misconduct appears to be based upon reasonable information.

63. 20 U.S.C. § 1232g(d); Letter to Doris Dixon (October 22, 1998).

64. Letter to Doris Dixon (October 22, 1998).

65. See "Model Form for Disclosure to Parents of Dependent Students" at http://www.ed.gov/policy/gen/guid/fpco/ferpa/safeschools/modelform.html· accessed on July 3, 2008. In addition, the Department has also published a model form for college or university students to execute, permitting the college or university to disclose their educational records to their parents even if their parents do not claim them as dependents for tax purposes. This form may be accessed at http://www.ed.gov/policy/gen/guid/fpco/ferpa/safeschools/modelform2.html.

66. See again the Model consent form referenced above.

67. See the Department's "Frequently Asked Questions 5" posted at http://www.ed.gov/policy/gen/guid/fpco/faq.html, and accessed on July 3, 2008.

68. "Disclosure of Information from Educational Records to Parents of Students Attending Post-secondary Institutions," Family Policy Compliance Office at http://.www.ed.gov/policy/gen/guid/fpco/hottopics/ht-parents-postsecstudents.html, accessed on January 19, 2009.

69. Letter to Dr. Omero Suarez (January 16, 2004). It is possible that the institution may be able to argue that this disclosure is permissible under the expanded definition of a health or safety emergency. However, application of the health/safety emergency provision will always be a case-by-case determination and, we suspect, less defensible if the disclosure at issue comes significantly after the fact.

70. 34 C.F.R. § 99.31(15)(i).

71. See the Department's Frequently Asked Questions #8 posted at http://www.ed.gov/policy/gen/guid/fpco/faq.html, and accessed on July 3, 2008.

72. Id at "Frequently Asked Questions 7."

73. Id.

74. Please see Chapter II for a discussion of the view current view of the Department that some cases under the revised health and safety emergency provision may allow for disclosure to student victims or their parents.

75. 34 C.F.R. 31(a)(13) & (14).

76. 34 C.F.R. § 99.31(a)(13).

77. Letter to S. Daniel Carter (March 10, 2003).

78. 34 C.F.R. § 99.39.

79. Appendix A to 34 C.F.R. § 99.

80. Id. These criminal law provisions, of necessity, incorporate the criminal law of the State and thus allow for some variations from institution to institution. For example, statutory rape is defined as "non-forcible sexual intercourse with a person

who is under the statutory age of consent." Appendix A to 34 C.F.R. § 99. The age of consent, in turn, will vary from State to State.

81. 34 C.F.R. § 99.31(14)

82. 34 C.F.R. § 99.39.

83. 34 C.F.R. § 99.31(14).

84. Letter to S. Daniel Carter (March 10, 2003).

85. 34 C.F.R. § 99.31(a)(16). This exception represents the regulatory codification of a non-enforcement position previously taken by the Department as to an institution that did release such information, in recognition of the fact that previously the regulatory text itself did not include a specific exception authorizing this disclosure. Letter to W. Joseph Hatley (March 8, 2005).

86. Federal Register Vol. 73 No. 237, 74820 (December 9, 2008).

87. 34 C.F.R. § 99.31(b)(1).

88. Federal Register Vol. 73 No. 237, 74835 (December 9, 2008).

89. 34 C.F.R. § 99.31(b)(1); Federal Register Vol.73 No. 237, 74835 (December 9, 2008).

90. Federal Register Vol.73 No. 237, 74835 (December 9, 2008).

91. Id.

92. 34 C.F.R. § 99.31(b)(2).

93. 34 C.F.R. § 99.31(b)(2)(i)–(iii).

94. *Id.*; Letter to Dr. Hoke Smith (June 22, 1998); Letter to Doris Dixon (October 22, 1998). See also 34 C.F.R. 99.31(a)(9)(iii).

95. *Id.*

96. Letter to Dr. Hunter Rawlings (Date).

97. *Id.*

98. Letter to Dr. Hoke Smith (June 22, 1998).

99. Letter to Doris Dixon (October 22, 1998).

100. Letter to Dr. Hoke Smith (June 22, 1998).

101. 34 C.F.R. § 99.31(9)(iii)(B).

102. 34 C.F.R. § 99.31(9)(iii)(A); Letter to Dr. Hoke Smith (June 22, 1998).

103. Federal Register, Vol. 73 No. 237, 74814 (December 9, 2008).

104. Letter to Dr. Tana Hasart (June 1, 1999).

105. *Jennings v. University of North Carolina at Chapel Hill*, 340 F.Supp.2d 679, 683–84 (M.D.N.C. 2004)

106. Letter to Doris Dixon (October 22, 1998).

Chapter 7

Electronic Instruction and Records

The development and proliferation of the use of electronic records among educational institutions regulated by the Family Educational Rights and Privacy Act readily demonstrates the much faster pace at which technology evolves than the law governing it. When FERPA was originally enacted in 1974, very few—if any—schools and universities maintained educational records in electronic format. However, beginning in the 1990s, the Family Policy Compliance Office began receiving opinion requests concerning FERPA's application to electronic records. The law responded, albeit slowly. It was not until 2000 that student "e-mail addresses" were expressly added to federal regulations as permissible categories of directory information. This trend continued, and, in both 2004 and 2008, significant regulatory changes were made to address in whole or part challenges posed by electronic records and FERPA.

The challenges posed by electronic recordkeeping and disclosure are not minor, and a law primarily envisaging paper documents being physically kept in "locked" filing cabinets contains numerous compliance issues in a decade in which an entire metropolitan school district's student record repository can be carried in a palm-sized hard disk drive. In 2008, in increasing regulatory security measures required by FERPA, the United States Department of Education identified six (6) examples of incidents in which the safety of students' educational records were compromised. All six (6)—from stolen laptops to compromise of a large post-secondary institution's record bank—concerned electronic records.[1]

The proliferation of electronic records has led to particular records challenges when state and federal agencies—many with missions seemingly unrelated to education—have requested electronic educational records to conduct research (such as unemployment insurance or immunization records). This situation would be unlikely if the records request were to produce thousands of pages of paper that had to be mailed at considerable cost rather than a single file that could be electronically transmitted instantaneously.

OVERVIEW, BASIC CONCEPTS, AND DEFINITIONS

What is an "electronic record"?

Under FERPA, there is no distinction between an electronic student record and its more conventionally maintained counterpart (whether paper or audio recording).[2] Any "record"—whether in paper or a computer database—containing personally identifiable information about a student that is maintained by an educational institution may be an "educational record" subject to FERPA's protections.

When is a record electronically "maintained"?

FERPA contains no specification as to when electronic (or other) records are "maintained." In *Owasso,* the Supreme Court defined "maintained" by referencing a common dictionary definition of "to keep in existence or continuance; preserve; retain."[3] Specifically in the context of educational records and FERPA, the Court observed that "maintained" "suggests FERPA records will be kept in a filing cabinet in a records room at the school or on a permanent secure database, perhaps even after the student is no longer enrolled."[4] Under such an interpretation, a record would seemingly only be electronically "maintained" if it were purposefully contained in a permanent database (the electronic equivalent of a "central repository"). However, subsequent court interpretations have declined to limit "educational records" to a central repository.[5] Consequently, the safer interpretation may be to treat records as "maintained" if the school or institution *preserves* the record—whether physically or in an e-mail or on a database.

Does "maintained" mean permanently so, or on a similarly long-term basis?

Probably not. Again, the definition of "maintains" is fairly fluid, and lacks statutory or regulatory expansion. An institution could be "preserving" a record if it were kept for two or three weeks, losing its protection when no longer serving the purpose for which it was maintained and discarded. However, with the ease in which electronic records are preserved—a small hard drive can preserve the equivalent of a building full of paper records—encourages retention of records that might not ordinarily be maintained by an institution.

For example, many educators and others routinely save copies of e-mail messages of marginal importance—messages that would be readily discarded if they were delivered in a paper format. Should these e-mail messages contain personally identifiable information relating to a student, an excellent argument could be made that a teacher not deleting these from his or her hard drive is intentionally "maintaining" them on behalf of the school, suggesting that the e-mails are electronic records subject to FERPA's protections and disclosure.

How does the institution's record retention policy impact this definition?

Many educational institutions have a specific record retention policy, setting forth the length of time the institution will retain certain records. The policies often provide that some records (like transcripts) will be permanently retained; however, others (like the end-of-semester grading sheets submitted by instructors) may only be retained until "final" grades are entered.

A records retention policy appears to authoritatively address whether an institution intends to "maintain" a record. The institution has affirmatively stated that it believes certain records should be kept in some type of repository—it would be difficult for an institution to argue that a record was not "maintained" if the institution's internal policies required it to be. However, while inclusion in a record retention policy certainly implies that the record is "maintained," institutions should not assume that only those records addressed in records retention policies are "maintained" for FERPA purposes.

Does "maintain" require an intention to maintain? If, for example, my email automatically saves a copy of all e-mails to parents, am I "maintaining" those records?

Again, the answer is somewhat unclear, and we have disagreement between the few courts considering the issue. In the context of electronic records, the concept of "maintained" may pose a significant challenge to school districts. "Maintaining" paper records generally requires an affirmative act—one has to intentionally select and store the records in a particular place. By contrast, electronic records are customarily automatically preserved (think of the automatic "recovery" system located on virtually every computer), and require an affirmative act to *delete* the records. Demonstrative of the disconnection between industry and education is the common perception the average user *wants* to preserve as many of his or her electronic messages and communications as possible—the advertising slogan for a popular online email system is "Never delete another email again!"—and computer systems are developed to automatically store records.

While there is little case authority or FPCO guidance on this, a school district could certainly argue under the guidance of *Owasso* that "maintain" requires an intent to maintain and that a teacher's email system automatically recording all of her messages to parents and storing them on the school's database is not the type of "maintain" that FERPA envisages. However, a parent could certainly argue that most—if not all—email programs possess both the ability to deselect automatically saving a copy of "sent" messages and possess a "delete" button.

Are teacher emails concerning students "educational records" under FERPA?

The law—again—is unclear whether teacher emails to parents or eligible students that personally identify students, contain information related to the student's educational career, and are "maintained" on an institution's computer system are electronic records. The few courts considering the issue are divided, with at least one court considering teacher emails as electronic records and another not.[6] The answer appears to depend upon both the jurisdiction and the contents of the email. In *Bates* (where disclosure was required), the emails in question were authored by individual college students, sought the university's intervention in a matter related to an individual "acting for" the college in regard to the students, and were "maintained" by the institution. In *B.F.* (where unidentified emails were determined not be "educational records"), the court considered a request from adversarial special education parents for what appeared to be virtually every document in the school district that personally referenced their child, including "thousands" of emails. In both cases, the court's decision appeared to be guided by what the court viewed as a "reasonableness" of the characterization of the emails as educational records.

What about teacher emails to other teachers, but which identify and discuss a particular student—are these educational records?

Again, the answer is likely to depend upon the substance of the communication (does it discuss the educational career of an individual student?) and how the correspondence is "maintained." If an instructor takes an affirmative step to retain the document (such as moving it to an "achieve" or archived file within his or her email system), it is difficult to argue the record has not been maintained by the institution or a person acting for it. However, if the email is saved solely as a result of an instructor not deleting it (the email system at the institution automatically saves all emails), then the issue becomes less clear.

***Practice Pointer*—**Instructor emails pose perhaps a unique challenge to educational institutions under FERPA. As noted above, unlike many of the paper communications they replace that would ordinarily be discarded, these documents are frequently maintained by educational institutions (whether they should be or not) and contained personally identifiable information about a student, and relate to his or educational career—and seemingly thus meet the broadest definition of educational record. While FPCO has not provided authoritative guidance on how such communications should be classified, institutions should strategically consider how long they retain emails and other electronic communications, setting up a process by which emails are deleted after a certain time period unless action is taken to preserve them. Presumably, a stronger case would exist that remaining emails affirmatively retained by educators would constitute educational records; however, it is equally likely that less "formal" emails—those containing information that institutions typically could or should discard if provided in a traditional "paper-based" format—would not be present in the system and subject to inspection under FERPA.

Does FERPA require individual teachers or school officials to respond to parent emails?

No. While FERPA entitles parents and eligible students to access their educational records, FERPA does not require that school-parent communication take place in any particular format (teacher-parent meetings, phone calls, emails). However, should teachers choose to respond to communicate with parents electronically, the communications might well constitute an educational record for the reasons identified above. Of course, parents may retain copies of such communications in any event.

Our college uses employee identification numbers and passwords for employees who are also enrolled in classes. Are these numbers now educational records?

Yes. If a college or university uses the same identification number for a former student who becomes an employee or an employee who is taking classes, that number remains subject to FERPA as long as the university maintains a record of it as a student identification number.[7] Employee identification numbers are excluded from FERPA only if they "relate exclusively" to that individual in his or her capacity as an employee.[8]

Are students in "on-line" classes "attending" classes for purposes of FERPA?

Yes. In 2008, FERPA's regulations were amended to specifically address the status of students "attending" schools "through the use of new technology methods that do not require a physical presence in the classroom."[9] This includes participation through videoconferencing, on the Internet, and other "non-traditional" or "non-physical" formats. The December 2008 regulations provide specifically:

Attendance includes, but is not limited to –
(a) Attendance in person or by paper correspondence, videoconference, satellite, Internet, or other electronic information and telecommunications technologies for students who are not physically present in the classroom[.][10]

Our on-line registration system requires students to use their identification number to register for classes. Does FERPA apply to identification numbers?

Generally, yes. However, the full answer requires an inquiry into the purpose for which the registration numbers are used and the duration for which this information is maintained. FERPA applies to any identification number that a school or university creates, assigns, and maintains on any individual who is or who has attended as a student.[11] These identification numbers (and the information relating to them) are typically preserved by the educational institution and used for the duration of the student's attendance at the institution. FERPA's protections typically do not apply to identification numbers given to visitors to campus or applicants creating a temporary identification or password for purposes of completing an online school application or related purposes.[12]

Is a student's participation on a blog or wiki an "educational record"?

Potentially. Again, under FERPA, it matters less what something is called than what is done with it. Under FERPA, an education record remains any record "directly related to a student" that is "maintained by an educational agency or institution or party acting for the agency or institution."[13] Under this broad definition, interaction in an electronic format that is reduced to writing—such as responding in a "chat" room or posting to a blog or wiki—might meet the definition of an educational record, whereas the oral classroom interaction that it is designed to replace would not. However, the Department does not consider a student's required participation in an on-line format to constitute an educational record if it is analogous to a teacher calling on a student in a traditional classroom to answer a question. At most, it might be directory information. A student or parent's declination to disclose directory information "does not include a right to remain anonymous in class [or] impede routine classroom communications and interactions."[14]

The answer becomes somewhat less clear with an increased degree of teacher interaction with the student—particularly as it changes from instruction to assessment. The greater the degree to which a teacher assesses a student's online submission for grading purposes, the more likely it is to become a protected educational record instead of "routine" classroom communication and interaction. Of course, many of the electronic pieces of information created during the conduct an online class are not preserved very long (if at all) after the entering of final grades for the course.

Practice Pointer—Unquestionably, teaching in an electronic medium poses unique problems under FERPA. FERPA does not classify online activity that is the electronic equivalent of in-class discussion (the electronic version of "calling on" students in a classroom) as an educational record, and instructors engaging in online instruction may interact with students in a public, online format without inherently violating FERPA. However, a question may arise if an assignment is "graded" and whether that grade is "recorded" under FERPA—both of which greatly increase the likelihood that the posting is now an educational record.[15] Should instructors wish to ensure that their online communications are not educational records under FERPA, they should limit their interactions to those analogous to traditional classroom interactions with students. This can include commenting on the sufficiency (or insufficiency) of a response; however, the greater a teacher's comments sound like public assessment (such as including a grade at the end of a public "post"), the more likely an educational record is being created.

SECURITY, MAINTENANCE, AND ELECTRONIC RECORDS

What is "adequate security" for electronic records?

The Department recognizes that the security of electronic records—whether physical (stealing of a laptop) or electronic ("cracking" into a college's database)—provides significant compliance challenges for educational institutions. This is particularly true given that electronic records lend themselves to "triangulation of data," in which users can analyze multiple sources of de-identified or directory information and discern personally identifiable records through the cumulative release of non-confidential data.[16] As with traditional records, FERPA does not clearly define what security measures are "adequate" to protect electronic records, leaving such determinations to the judgment of school officials to make "case by case" determinations—"[Schools] themselves are in the best position to analyze and identify the best methods to use to protect the confidentiality of their own data."[17]

FPCO does identify specific practices meeting acceptable levels of security. They include (and are detailed further below) adequate measures to ensure that only school officials with a "legitimate educational interest" access student records, acceptable steps for verifying the authenticity of "electronic signatures" and allowing online access, and appropriate procedures for establishing parent or student personal identification numbers. However, ultimately, the burden is on the recordkeeping institution to meet the electronic equivalent of making certain the filing cabinet is kept locked.

If someone breaks into the school computer systems or steals a teacher's laptop and accesses confidential information about students, has the school violated FERPA?

Probably not; however, it depends on the measures the school takes to protect student data. The Department noted in 2008 that "[N]o system for maintaining and transmitting education records, whether in paper or electronic form, can be guaranteed safe from every hacker and thief, electronic failure, violation of administrative rules, and other causes of unauthorized access and disclosure."[18] The Department expects institutions to take reasonable steps to protect student data it chooses to maintain—precautions that are appropriate both to the format in which the data is stored and its sensitivity, as well as the "size, complexity, and resources available to the institution[.]"[19]

The degree of precautions must increase based upon the potential effect of disclosure: "The greater the harm that would result from unauthorized access or disclosure and the greater the likelihood that unauthorized access or disclosure will be attempted, the more protections an agency or institution should consider using to ensure that its methods are reasonable."[20] While the Department would not necessarily consider either of the questions posed above as violations of FERPA, a security system for student records that could be easily "hacked" might well raise concerns that the institution did not take adequate precautions to safeguard educational records, as might a laptop computer that could be easily accessed without a password.

What should an institution do in either of the situations identified above?

The Department identifies a number of steps institutions should take if their student information systems have been compromised or their electronic records (or devices containing them) are stolen.[21] These include:

- Reporting the incident to law enforcement authorities;
- Determining precisely what information was compromised;
- Take steps immediately to retrieve data and prevent further disclosures;
- Identify all affected records and students;
- Determining how the incident occurred, including identifying responsible school officials;
- Determining whether institutional policies and procedures were breached, allowing the inappropriate disclosures;
- Determining whether the incident occurred because of a lack of monitoring or oversight;

- Conducting a risk assessment and identify appropriate physical, technological, and administrative measures to prevent similar incidents in the future; and
- Notifying parents or eligible students that the Department of Education's Office of Inspector General maintains a Web site describing steps students can take if they are the victim of identity theft. This Web site (as of December 2008) is: www.ed.gov/about/offices/list/oig/misused/idtheft.html.

How does FERPA relate to electronic records and communications maintained by a "third party," such as a national transcript clearinghouse?

FERPA recognizes that educational institutions often use third parties for storing and disseminating educational records. The Department's addresses third-party storage by placing a non-delegable duty on educational institutions to verify that providers are capable of and do comply with FERPA's requirements—"Educational agencies and institutions are responsible for their outside service providers' failures to comply with applicable FERPA requirements."[22] As a result, educational institutions should ensure that third parties maintaining educational records for the institution have both a clear understanding of security obligations under FERPA and procedures in place to ensure that inadvertent disclosure to unauthorized parties is not permitted.[23]

Practice Pointer—Educational institutions are increasingly making use of third parties to maintain educational records, permitting outsourcing of many administrative functions traditionally performed by educational institutions (such as mailing out transcripts). Institutions so doing should make certain they have a contract with the provider detailing the security precautions and access protocols guaranteed by the provider. A true "best practice" would be to include an indemnification clause in such contracts, ensuring that the provider will completely reimburse the institution for any legal costs and other damages arising from a FERPA violation or complaint stemming from the provider's maintenance of the records.

Maintaining records electronically seemingly permits greater access by school officials—including those who do not have a "legitimate educational interest"—to student records. Does FERPA address this?

Yes. While FERPA permits school officials with a "legitimate educational interest" to inspect student records without a parent or eligible student's prior authorization, the electronic maintenance of records poses unique challenges to FERPA compliance. Maintaining records electronically allows educators to have access to a far greater number of student records from a far more private location, such as their desk or home.[24] Owing to this increased risk, institutions permitting electronic access by faculty or staff (and particularly off-campus access or access on computers not controlled by the institution) must ensure that the method permitting access comports with FERPA's privacy protections.[25] Schools maintaining records electronically must use "physical or technological access controls" or, if incapable of maintaining such controls, ensure that its administrative policies and practices are sufficient for limiting access only to school officials with a legitimate educational interest.[26] This may include appropriate training.[27]

To ensure that access granted to school officials is not overly-broad, the Department suggests "role-based" security features. "Role-based" security features permit educators to view only the records of students currently enrolled in their classes, requiring to request access to other records "as needed" from a school administrator.[28] "A school would generally first determine when a school official has a legitimate educational interest in education records and then determine which physical or technological access controls are necessary to ensure that the official can access only those records [which he or she is authorized to access]."[29] The Department also suggests examining security controls used by the National Institute of Standard and Technology (800-53), Recommended Security Controls for Federal Information Systems (December 2007), which can be found at http://csrc.nist.gov/publications/PubsSPs.html.

For institutions unwilling or incapable of adopting physical or technological controls limiting access to only those school officials with a legitimate educational interest, schools must adopt and enforce an administrative policy prohibiting unauthorized disclosures. In the event of a parent or student's challenge, the policy must be one under which the institution can justify any school official's access as legitimate. In such instances, the Department recommends: "Any agency or institution may wish to . . . track school officials who obtain access[.]"[30] Such tracking is normally not required under FERPA for school officials possessing a legitimate educational interest in accessing the records, and would, if created, constitute an *independent* educational record inviting parent or eligible student questions when records were accessed by teachers and administrators other than those with whom the parent or student was familiar.

Can schools share computer network, hardware, software, and personnel resources with other governmental entities?

Again, FERPA contains no discrete prohibition against sharing network, hardware, software, database, or other resources with organizations and agencies beyond the recordkeeping institution *provided* the system contains sufficient safeguard to ensure that unauthorized individuals cannot access restricted educational records.[31]

An Example—City County's Board of Commissioners proposes a plan under which all of the county's offices—including the school district—will share computer and network resources, permitting county officials to quickly and easily share data between departments. While the plan expressly forbids county employees from accessing school district records without prior permission and requires annual training on the same, the school district's technology director discovers that the computer system allows county law enforcement personnel to access student disciplinary files without prior permission from the school district. As a result, this plan would seem to have inadequate safeguards to comply with FERPA.[32]

Can schools outsource the electronic maintenance of student records without a parent or eligible student's written consent?

Yes. Nothing in FERPA precludes an educational institution from contracting with "outside service providers" to maintain records or provide grade verification services that educational institutions would ordinarily do themselves, provided those institutions complied with FERPA non-disclosure and privacy requirements.[33] To the contrary, FERPA envisages parties other than educational institutions maintaining educational records—"Educational records are defined as records that are directly related to a student and maintained by an educational agency or institution *or by a party acting for the agency or institution.*"[34] However, these third-party institutions must be under the "direct control" of the institution (as that term is used in 34 C.F.R. § 99.31(a)(1)(i)(B)(2)) creating or maintaining the educational records. Additionally, institutions are responsible for ensuring that their third-party providers do not use or allow anyone to obtain access to personally identifiable information from educational records except as permitted by FERPA.[35]

DIRECTORY, PERSONALLY IDENTIFIABLE INFORMATION, AND ELECTRONIC RECORDS

May a student's ID number be designated as "directory information"?

Yes, under very limited conditions. While the Department of Education's position on this had, at times, seemed contradictory,[36] the December 2008 regulations make clear that a student's identification number or electronic identifier can be designated as "directory information" "only if the electronic identifier cannot be used to gain access to educational records except when used in conjunction with one or more factors that authenticate a student's identity."[37]

The distinction stems from Department of Education concerns that student identification numbers are "typically used" to establish accounts, gain access or confirm private information, obtain services, and request records.[38] As a result, obtaining such a number may permit someone other than the student to impersonate the student and obtain information and services by fraud.[39] However, if the identifier is not used for such purposes—if it is only used by the student to communicate in an online format or to gain initial access to the online system AND the identifier cannot be used to gain access to educational records without supplemental information known only to the student (such as a personal identification number (PIN) or password)—then the identifier may be designated as directory information.[40] "[FERPA] permit[s] disclosure of a student's ID or other electronic identifier as directory information, but only if the identifier functions essentially as a name; that is, the identifier is not used by itself to authenticate identity and cannot be used by itself to gain access to education records."[41] Consequently, the answer depends upon the underlying purpose served by the number and what it permits a user to do.

Can schools and colleges make student email addresses and other information "directory" only within the school, and not have the information as "directory" outside the institution?

Colleges and schools often want to have certain information—like student email addresses—made available as directory information within the institution, but do not want to have to provide this information to those outside the institution (such as third-party vendors who sell email addresses to electronic advertisers). These institutions often inquire whether FERPA allows different "levels" of directory information, permitting institutions to designate it as "directory" solely for institutional use. While FERPA itself does not recognize "levels" of directory information, the Department of Education reiterated in 2008 the permissive nature of directory information: "[A]n agency or institution is not required to make student directories and other directory information available to the general public just because the information is shared within the institution."[42]

Practice Pointer—Remember that FERPA interacts with numerous state laws—including state open records laws. While "[e]ducational agencies and institutions are not required *under FERPA* to disclose directory information to any party,"[43] many states have open records acts (or "sunshine" laws) that require *public* institutions to provide information to the public that federal law does not expressly require to be kept confidential. Consequently, institutions designating information as directory "for internal use only" are advised to check with legal counsel in determining whether this designation may result in the institution having to disclose such information to any member of the general public upon request and under their applicable state laws.

Can school officials have access to a student's personal identification number (PIN), permitting access to school records?

Yes, but only if the school takes precautions to ensure that the school official has a legitimate educational interest to access that information.[44] Allowing school officials to access a student- or parent-established PIN has significant consequences. Allowing anyone other than a parent or eligible student access to a parent- or student-established PIN erodes the likelihood that the PIN contains adequate privacy protection under FERPA to constitute an "electronic signature."[45] Schools would be better advised to have alternative methods by which school officials with a legitimate educational interest may access student records.

May e-mail addresses be designated as directory information?

Yes. In 2000, FERPA was amended to specifically permit institutions to designate student e-mail addresses as directory information.[46] Again, however, how something is used is far more important than what it is called. Institutions designating student e-mail addresses as directory information should make certain that a student's e-mail address alone would not permit access to educational records. If it does, the e-mail address would be more analogous to a student identification number which—in such instance—may not be designated as directory information.[47] E-mail addresses may be used as identifiers for records systems if they serve essentially the same purpose as a student's name or user name, permitting access only after a parent or eligible student enters a password or other supplemental identifier ensuring that personally identifiable information is not disclosed to unauthorized parties.

Can student web sites be categorized as directory information?

As noted in Chapter V, both the statutory and regulatory definitions of directory information give schools latitude to expand the definition of directory information to include information similar to that information identified. This might include the Web sites that students create at the school. However, recall that very little in FERPA strictly addresses the format in which information is maintained or disclosed (giving schools the flexibility to maintain electronic records systems), instead requiring schools to protect certain types of information (such as educational records containing non-directory personally identifiable information). As a result, if an institution required students to maintain online portfolios of graded work, providing the Web addresses of these pages might be analogous to providing online access to a teacher's gradebook, and would be an impermissible disclosure of educational records. By contrast, if the students' web pages contained only directory information, with any graded work maintained in a confidential location on the site, disclosing the address of these web pages would not appear to violate FERPA.

Practice Pointer—Many college and university students maintain Facebook and other social networking Web pages. Some institutions are using these sites to build cohort or class cohesion. Without considering whether this information could be considered "directory" (and a question arises as to whether a "Facebook" page address constitutes an educational record protected by FERPA), institutions could easily avoid this potential entanglement by offering to publish this information *if the student consent and chooses to do so.* Again, remember that FERPA rights transfer to students attending post-secondary institutions, and they can authorize the institution to disseminate any information they like.

Can a student "opt out" if an institution identifies e-mail or on-line identification as directory information?

Yes. As with all directory information, a parent or eligible student can refuse to permit dissemination of any "directory information" by "opting out" during the appropriate response period. However, nothing in FERPA requires such an "opt out" to be consequence free. The United States Department of Education recognizes that public disclosure of an individual student's identifier may be required for electronic collaboration by students and teachers within and among schools, and a parent's or student's decision may result in the student not being able to take advantage of online portals for class registration, electronic access of class records and information systems, and perhaps certain online classes if access to these services is provided solely through electronic communications or software requiring public disclosure of the student's e-mail address or other personally identifiable electronic identifier.[48] In addressing this point specifically, the Department advised: "The Secretary believes . . . that the right to opt out of directory information and disclosures does not include a right to remain anonymous in class and, therefore, may not be used to impede routine classroom communications . . . by preventing a teacher from identifying a student by name in class, whether class is held in a specified physical location or on-line through electronic communications."[49] As a result, a student may utilize FERPA's "opt out" provisions to prevent disclosure—but such action does not insulate him or her from the instructional consequences of this action.

ELECTRONIC SIGNATURES

Can institutions accept electronic signatures for disclosure of educational records?

Yes and no. FERPA permits schools to accept electronic signatures for disclosure of electronic records and other purposes; however, FERPA recognizes that the acceptance of electronic signatures poses compliance challenges not present with traditional verification methods—"Identification presents unique challenges in an electronic or telephonic environment, where personal recognition and photo identification cards are irrelevant."[50] Consequently, FERPA requires that any electronic signatures contain safeguards to ensure that consent is authentic—that is, verification that the parent or eligible student is the person actually giving consent.

How can schools authenticate electronic signatures?

> The 2008 regulatory amendments to FERPA require:
> (c)An educational agency or institution must use reasonable methods to identify and authenticate the identity of parents, students, school officials, and any other parties to whom the agency or institution discloses personally identifiable information from educational records.[51]

The Department declined to provide all definitive ways to ensure the validity of electronic signatures, noting that such a definition would be an attempt to hit the proverbial moving target: "Authentication of identity is a complex subject that continues to advance as new methods and technologies are developed to meet evolving standards for safeguarding financial, health, and other types of electronic records."[52] Consequently, FPCO will accept any method selected provided it ensures that information is only disclosed to the intended or authorized recipient of the information that is appropriate to the circumstances in which the information or records are maintained.[53]

The most commonly used methods require that schools accepting electronic signatures inspect and disclose electronic records to adopt an information system permitting a parent or eligible student to establish their own personal identification number (PIN) that cannot be used by school officials to access records.[54] The Department recognizes that certain information of a highly private nature—such as social security numbers, credit card numbers, medical records, and other information "that could be used for identity theft or financial fraud"—may require multiple factors to authenticate identity.[55]

An Example—City County School District adopted a new electronic records system permitting online inspection of a student's records, authorization of record disclosures, and filling transcript requests. Any parent or eligible student wishing to use this system is required at the beginning of the school year to use a school-provided unique password to establish an account. Once the account is established, the parent or eligible student is prompted to create a user name and password known only to the student or the parent. Any access to the account requires that the student enter both of these factors to access the record database and authorize disclosures. This electronic signature authorization would seemingly comply with the Department's standards.

The most certain way is to adopt the same standards approved by the federal government for student loan transactions (FSA Standards).[56] In 2004, the Department approved these standards as a "safe harbor" for any institution accepting electronic signatures for FERPA purposes.[57] These standards are fairly rigorous, and can (as of December 2008) be found at: http://www.ifap.ed.gov/dpcletters/attachments/gen0106Arevised.pdf.

Can any portion of a student's Social Security Number—such as the last four digits—be used in a student's online identifier or for grade postings?

No. For years, a common practice at schools and institutions was for faculty to post mid-term and final examination grades by the last four digits of a student's social security number. FERPA defines "personally identifiable information" requiring prior permission for disclosure as including "personal identifier[s], such as a student's social security number or student number," forbidding designation of SSNs as directory information.[58] FPCO interprets this provision to prohibit the disclosure of *any portion* of a student's social security number, regarding such information "by definition" as "personally identifiable information."[59] FPCO is particularly careful regarding Social Security Numbers "because of the relative ease with which [SSNs] can be used to access other information about the student that would be considered harmful or an invasion of privacy if disclosed."[60]

An Example—A computer science professor posted student's mid-term and final grades on a Web site only accessible to members of his class, identifying students by a portion of their Social Security Numbers. The professor argued that this practice did not mention student names, and permitted students to "easily identify their own grades, yet remain unable to identify any other student's identities." Determining that revealing any portion of a student's Social Security Number was prohibited, FPCO concluded that this was a violation of FERPA. However, FERPA would have permitted the professor to assign each student a personally identifying number that only he and the student knew.[61]

DISCLOSURE AND TRANSMISSION OF ELECTRONIC RECORDS

We frequently have requests for student electronic records from universities and institutes conducting research. Can electronic records be disclosed for research purposes? If so, what steps—if any—must be taken to protect the information?

Schools and universities often receive information requests from researchers for student-level electronic records. While Congress recognizes that student-level data can provide parents, educators, students, researchers, policymakers, and the general public with "reliable information about educational practices that improve academic achievement," this interest does not outweigh the interest of parents and eligible students in the privacy of their educational records. Consequently, while FERPA permits disclosure of student-level data for educational research, such data can only be released where it has been de-identified through removal of all personally identifiable information.[62]

FPCO will not pursue an action against a school or institution releasing student-level data for the purposes of educational research if the following requirements are met:

1. The records do not contain a personal identifier, and any non-personal identifier –
   a. Is not a scrambled social security number or student number, unless such identifiers are protected by written agreements reflecting generally accepted confidentiality standards within the research community; and
   b. Cannot be liked to an individual student by anyone who does not have access to the linking key;
2. The anonymous data file is populated by data from educational records in a manner that ensures the identity of any student cannot be determined, including assurances of sufficient cell and subgroup size; AND
3. The linking key that connects the non-personal identifier to student information is itself an educational record subject to the privacy provisions of FERPA. The linking key must be kept with the school or university and cannot be shared with the requesting entity.[63]

When may records be electronically transmitted or maintained?

FERPA contains no distinct requirements or prohibitions on the maintenance or transmission of electronic records. Under FERPA, a record maintained electronically is the equivalent of any other educational record—and subject to the same protections and disclosure requirements.[64] A school could maintain all of its records electronically and comply with FERPA—provided the records had equivalent security as "traditional" records, and parents and eligible students still had the same rights of access and challenge.[65] As discussed previously, this may be somewhat challenging from a confidentiality standpoint since electronic records are generally more readily accessible and subject to more (and easier) widespread dissemination than their paper counterparts. However, just as a school could not permit teachers to place all of their report cards on a table and allow students or parents to search through them until reaching their own, "a school district may not maintain a system [for electronic recordkeeping] that provides for access to education records by parties that are not parents, students, or authorized 'school officials.'"[66] Consequently, schools have the obligation to maintain adequate security for electronic records.

ENDNOTES

1. Federal Register Vol. 73 No. 57, 15598 (March 24, 2008).
2. Letter to Alan McGraw, Esq. (October 7, 2005).
3. *Owasso Independent Sch. Dist. No. I-011 v. Falvo,* 534 U.S. 426, 433 (2002).
4. *Id.*
5. *See,* for example, *Unincorporated Operating Division of Indiana Newspapers, Inc, v. Trustees of Indiana University*, 787 N.E.2d 893, 905 (Ind.App. 2003).
6. *See Bates College v. Congregation Beth Abraham* (Sup. Ct. Me. Feb. 18, 2001) (*Cited in* M. O'Donnell "FERPA Turns Thirty: A New Look at an Old Friend." Presented at the IAPP 2005 National Summit (March 9, 2005)); *See also B.F. v. Fulton County School District,* 2008 WL 42224802 (September 9, 2008) (determining that a school district's failure to disclose "certain emails" did not violate FERPA as "the school district was not required to turn those types of documents over.").
7. Letter to Marya Ryan (November 26, 2004).
8. *Id.*
9. Federal Register Vol. 73 No. 237, 74806–07 (December 9, 2008).
10. 34 C.F.R. § 99.3; Federal Register Vol. 73 No. 237, 74806, 74807 (December 9, 2008).
11. Letter to Marya Ryan (November 26, 2004).
12. *Id.*
13. 34 C.F.R. § 99.3.
14. Federal Register Vol. 73 No. 57, 15590 (March 24, 2008).
15. Federal Register Vol. 73 No. 237, 74811–12 (December 9, 2008).
16. Federal Register Vol. 73 No. 57, 15584 (March 24, 2008).
17. Letter to Alan McGraw, Esq. (October 7, 2005); Federal Register Vol. 73 No. 57, 15575, 15584 (March 24, 2008).

18. Federal Register Vol. 73 No. 237, 74844 (December 9, 2008) (quoting Federal Register Vol. 73 No. 57, 15598–99) (March 24, 2008).
19. *Id.*
20. *Id.*
21. Federal Register Vol. 73 No. 237, 74844 (December 9, 2008).
22. Federal Register Vol. 73 No. 57, 15579 (March 24, 2008); Federal Register Vol. 73 No. 237, 74816 (December 9, 2008).
23. Federal Register Vol. 73 No. 237, 74816 (December 9, 2008).
24. 34 C.F.R. § 99.31(a); Federal Register Vol. 73 No. 57, 15580 (March 24, 2008).
25. 34 C.F.R. § 99.31(a)(1)(ii)
26. 34 C.F.R. § 99.31(a)(1)(ii).
27. Letter to Alan McGraw (October 7, 2005).
28. Federal Register Vol. 73 No. 57, 15580 (March 24, 2008).
29. Federal Register Vol. 73 No. 237, 74817 (December 9, 2008).
30. Federal Register Vol. 73 No. 57, 15580 (March 24, 2008).
31. Letter to Alan McGraw (October 7, 2005).
32. Letter to Alan McGraw (October 7, 2005).
33. Letter to Carol Fuller (April 16, 2004); Letter to Jean-Marie Pochert (June 28, 2006).
34. 34 C.F.R. § 99.3 (*emphasis added*).
35. Letter to Jean-Marie Pochert, Esq. (June 28, 2006). For a more detailed analysis of when third-party providers are under the "direct control" of educational institutions, see Chapter IV.
36. 34 C.F.R. § 99.3; Federal Register Vol. 73 No. 237, 74806, 74807 (December 9, 2008); Letter to Judy George (November 5, 2004) (acknowledging that FPCO's prohibition of designation of student ID numbers as directory information related more to the purposes for which the number was used than nomenclature). See also Letter to Marya Ryan (November 26, 2004); Federal Register Vol. 73 No. 57, 15575 (March 24, 2008).
37. 34 C.F.R. § 99.3.
38. Federal Register Vol. 73 No. 57, 15575 (March 24, 2008); Federal Register Vol. 73 No. 237, 74806, 74807–08 (December 9, 2008).
39. *Id.*
40. *Id.*
41. Federal Register Vol. 73 No. 57, 15575–76 (March 24, 2008).
42. Federal Register Vol. 73 No. 237, 74808 (December 9, 2008).
43. Federal Register Vol. 73 No. 237, 73809 (December 9, 2008).
44. 34 C.F.R. § 99.31(a); Letter to Judy George (November 5, 2004).
45. *Id.* at 15575–76.
46. 65 FR 41852, 41855 (July 6, 2000).
47. Federal Register Vol. 73 No. 57, 15575 (March 24, 2008).
48. Federal Register Vol. 73 No. 57, 15576 (March 24, 2008).
49. Federal Register Vol. 73 No. 57, 15590 (March 24, 2008).

50. Federal Register Vol. 73 No. 57, 15585 (March 24, 2008).

51. 34 C.F.R. § 99.31(c).

52. Federal Register Vol. 73 No. 57, 15585 (March 24, 2008).

53. Letter to Alan McGraw, Esq. (October 7, 2005).

54. Federal Register Vol. 73 No. 57, 15585 (March 24, 2008).

55. Id.

56. It should be noted that not all FSA Standards apply to FERPA. For example, the FSA Standards require that paper copies of all transactions be kept and provided to student financial aid borrowers at no cost. In 2004, the Department noted, "We agree that some circumstances within the FSA Standards do not relate directly to FERPA." Federal Register Vol. 69 No. 77 (April 21, 2004).

57. Federal Register Vol. 69 No. 77 (April 21, 2004).

58. 34 C.F.R. § 99.3.

59. Letter to Dr. Evangelos Gizis (undated).

60. Letter to Daniel Boehmer (August 2, 1999).

61. Letter to Dr. Evangelos Gizis (undated).

62. Federal Register Vol. 73 No. 57, 15580 (March 24, 2008); Letter to Matthew Pepper (November 18, 2004).

63. Letter to Matthew Pepper (November 18, 2004).

64. Letter to Alan McGraw, Esq. (October 7, 2005).

65. Id.

66. Id.

Chapter 8

Educational Records: Special Education Records

Issues surrounding the educational records of student with disabilities, like many of the issues arising in connection with disabled students, are among the most emotional and contentious disputes that arise at the school level. To a significant degree, this may be attributed to the reality that there are additional Federal educational statutes that overlap with FERPA in this area, statutes which in some cases enhance the rights of parents and students in this regard, while in other instances these statutes may provide an additional, adversarial forum in which these disputes may be litigated. Furthermore, the District's files for student with disabilities, especially those with IEPs, often contain vastly more information and documentation related to the student, providing in effect many additional documents subject to potential dispute between parents and schools. Finally, parents of students with disabilities are often (and rightly so) especially concerned about the privacy and confidentiality of information contained within the District's records.

IDEA AND FERPA RECORDS PROVISIONS: OVERVIEW

In addition to FERPA, what are the most significant Federal and State sources of rules relating to the educational records of disabled students?

The Individuals with Disabilities in Education Act (IDEA) provides parents of disabled students with numerous, additional substantive rights in connection with the records of special education students. Individual state special education rules and regulations may replicate these federal requirements, or in some instances, they may expand upon and convey additional rights.[1] Also, the Rehabilitation Act of 1974 (Section 504) and the Americans with Disabilities Act (ADA) protect disabled students and their parents from discrimination and retaliation.

Does IDEA use the same definition of "educational record" as FERPA?

Yes, the IDEA specifically adopts the FERPA regulatory definition of education records—"education records means the type of records covered under [FERPA]"[2]

Are there different rules under IDEA for the educational records of special education students?

Absolutely, and in a number of areas, such as access rights, confidentiality, record retention, and destruction, FERPA and the Individuals with Disabilities Act treat the records of special education students differently than those of regular education students. In addition, most states have state-level special education regulations or rules which further define the rights of special education students and which may extend the rights contained in the Individuals with Disabilities in Education Act. For the most part, these additional rules serve to increase the duties of the District in matters such as maintaining the confidentiality of educational records, while also vesting greater authority in parents and eligible students in regards to record retention and disposal issues, as well as access to educational records themselves. However, in this area there is simply no substitute for the careful review of the individual State special education regulations or rules.

CONFIDENTIALITY AND SPECIAL EDUCATION RECORDS

How are the confidentiality rights of disabled students different from the confidentiality provisions of FERPA generally?

Perhaps most importantly, a student's very status as a student with a disability is considered personally identifiable information under FERPA, and therefore may not be disclosed by school personnel in the absence of a controlling exception (See Chapter IV and VI), or consent by the parents of the student. As a result, the intentional disclosure of a student's disability, 504 plan, or IEP outside of any permissible reason to do so can easily form the basis for complaints of harassment or retaliation, in addition to a breach under the State ethical codes for certificated or licensed personnel. Each of the above are in addition to the underlying FERPA violation.

Does IDEA set forth any specific rules regarding the confidentiality requirements of special education records?

Yes, in at least one instance there are specific, additional rules relating to the confidentiality of special education records. This is in the case of a disabled student who enrolls or seeks to enroll in a private school which is outside the District of the parent's residence—in this instance, the District must obtain parental consent before disclosing any educational records of the student to school officials in the LEA where the school is located.[3]

Practice Pointer—In addition, there are many practical and sometimes emotional consequences associated with a breach of confidentiality in connection with special education records which parents frequently react to with much greater concern than may be the case in other areas. In some cases, a breach of confidentiality by a school employee has permanently fractured the relationship between the school and that parent, leading in some instances of years of multiple due process hearings and hundreds of thousands of dollars in legal fees.

When a child is enrolled in a private school in another District (ex. District B), what is the reason for requiring consent before disclosing personally identifiable information from the District (District A) in which the child's parents reside to school officials in District B?

In one of the more interesting changes to emerge from the IDEA reauthorization and regulatory process, the Department ultimately took the position that the privacy interest of the child and their family outweighed any interest in facilitating the implementation of child find on the part of District B. Recall also that after IDEA 2004, the District where the private school is located (District B), rather than the District where the parents reside (District A), is now responsible for identifying the student with a disability.[4]

May the transcripts of elementary and secondary school students include information about whether the students received special education or related services due to a disability?

No, they may not, according to the Office of Civil Rights (OCR). Admitting that neither Section 504 nor IDEA contain specific provisions addressing transcripts or report cards, the Office of Civil Rights nonetheless concluded in 2008 that "it would be a violation of Section 504 and Title II (ADA) for a student's transcript to indicate that a student has received special education or a related service or that the student has a disability."[5] Fundamental to this conclusion appears to be the adoption by OCR (without any reference or authority) of a definition of a transcript as "intended to inform post-secondary institutions or prospective employers of a student's academic credentials and achievements." This position is in contrast the Department's approach to report cards which, since they are primarily used to communicate student progress to parents, may identify the fact that a student is a student with a disability.[6]

Can an impermissible disclosure of information from a special education student's records by school officials constitute a form of retaliation under either IDEA or Section 504?

Absolutely. In response to one Section 504 Complaint, the Office of Civil Rights found a high school Spanish teacher's posting of a student's 504 plan on his bulletin board after her mother complained about the his failure to implement the plan could be an impermissible act of retaliation.[7] However, it is important to remember that in order for such a disclosure to constitute impermissible retaliation, the parent must also be able to demonstrate that the inappropriate disclosure was caused by or directly related to their participation in a protected activity under either IDEA or Section 504. For example, in this case the parent successfully argued that her actions in advocating on behalf her child (which is certainly a protected activity) led to the teacher's decision to post her daughter's 504 plan.

Does FERPA permit or prohibit the District from videotaping a special education classroom, or even an individual disabled student within a regular classroom?

Generally speaking, FERPA neither mandates nor prohibits the nature of information that the District may collect about students (including video images, for instance); rather, FERPA sets forth those rules the District must follow regarding that information which is actually collected. In reference to videotapes specifically, FERPA itself would not prohibit the District from videotaping a classroom of regular or special education students. However, FERPA would apply to the District's process of providing access to (and maintaining confidentiality of) these records in the event that the video tapes are determined to be educational records.

If the District does videotape a special education class or a classroom with a special education student in attendance, is the parent of that student entitled to inspect or obtain a copy of the tape?

First, the District must determine whether the videotape constitutes an education record of this student (See Chapter II and the discussion of videotapes therein), and if so, whether the District may provide access to the video without disclosing personally identifiable information about other students. One additional issue in addressing this question, we believe, is whether or not the tape captures any additional information beyond what a parent, volunteer or visitor (to the extent this is permitted at the School) would personally observe by their presence in the room. Answering this question, in turn, depends to some extent on the actual policy or practice of the District in permitting access to classrooms by volunteers or visitors. In some schools, for instance, the widespread use and presence of parent volunteers is a relatively common practice in elementary school settings, but much less so in the classrooms of older students.[8]

An Example—Argumentative Andy (a fifth grader) has been diagnosed with ADHD by Doctor Crock, a physician well known in the County for diagnosing anyone who may be referred to him and covered by insurance. The School did develop an IEP and BIP for Andy, but in numerous meetings with Andy's mother (Daisy Denial), the parties are not able to get past Andy and Daisy's insistence that Andy is not doing anything wrong in the class, that his teacher is "stupid," and that everyone else at the school is just "mean." Without consulting with the Central Office, Principal Paula has a video recorder tape Andy's classroom one day for the purpose of gathering additional information about his behavior, to convince Daisy that the behavior problems are real (by showing her the good parts), and to revise Andy's BIP in conjunction with the behavior specialist and the IEP team. That particular school day is relatively calm, and the video tape does not capture any images of any other students engaging in discipline-worthy behavior. When Daisy finds out about the tape, she demands to inspect the video footage of the entire day—is this required or permitted under FERPA? In light of the purported use of the video tape record, and in the absence of any other educationally relevant student images, we believe the stronger position in this particular case is that the tape is an educational record under FERPA to which Daisy should have access.

Are there any categorical instances when school videos are not educational records?

Possibly. If the District has designated a law enforcement unit which creates and maintains (perhaps only briefly) videotapes of classrooms, hallways, and other areas around the school for security purposes, these videotapes (as law enforcement records) may not fall within the definition of education records. Please see Chapter II for a further discussion of law enforcement records.

How does FERPA apply to disclosing information about disabled students to other students in the school, especially when these disabled students are being served in the regular educational setting?

While any disclosure of personally identifiable information about a student with a disability to other students (outside of a specific exception) is a FERPA violation in the equivalent manner in which public disclosure of that same information would be a violation of FERPA's confidentiality provisions, the courts have recognized that information of which students (and parents) become aware of simply by virtue of their physical presence in the classroom or the school (and not from educational records per se) does not implicate FERPA.[9]

An Example—Regular Education Ronnie is sitting in the back of his 9th grade math class when a teacher's aide and another student, Learning Disabled Lenny, join him on the back row of seats in the class. Note that this is not Lenny's preferential seating arrangement. Throughout math class, the aide goes over each problem with Lenny, who slowly but gradually seems to understand more and more of the material. The fact that Ronnie may reasonably conclude that Lenny is a student with a disability is not a violation of FERPA in such an instance, since this information is not disclosed to Ronnie from any educational record at all, but rather, is merely information of which he becomes aware due to his physical presence in the classroom with Lenny.

What about disclosing information about a student's disability when explaining the behavior of a particular child?

This is generally prohibited, as it involves the disclosure to others (parents, teachers, or other students) of confidential information about a student. In one case the principal told several other parents that a child "was neither on the same cognitive or social/emotional level as the other student," and a federal complaint officer did find this to be a FERPA violation. Central to the complaint officer's rationale, it appears, was his rejection of the claim that the principal was only sharing information of which he was generally aware rather than information specifically obtained from a review of the student's special education records.[10]

So if a student with a disability engages in misconduct with a regular education student, the District may not share any information about the disabled student (including their status as a student with a disability) with the parent of the regular education student in order, for example, to explain the different punishments that may be imposed?

Yes, this is correct, though it is sometimes helpful to remind both parents that the handling of each individual child's school and disciplinary proceeding is confidential, and there are many variables within such proceedings that may account for different outcomes.[11]

Do parents of disabled students have a right to obtain information about the number of IEPs developed for students in a particular disability area?

No, a federal court specifically cited FERPA in denying a parent's claim for information about IEPs for students with disabilities similar to their daughters, citing both that these records were not relevant and that this information was protected by FERPA.[12] The information about other students with IEPs (including their presence in the class), of course, is highly unlikely to be considered to be a part of the educational records of any other, individual student and thus not within the scope of access rights afforded to the parents of the individual student.

What about information related to the services provided to other students in the District with similar disabilities—may parents subpoena records related to other students in order to contest the District's denial of services to their child?

As discussed in Chapter VI, the disclosure of educational records a subpoena pursuant to is an exception under FERPA which permits the disclosure of personally identifiable information about a student without the consent of the parent or eligible student. In the case of any subpoena contested by either the school or the parents of other students, the court must make an individual determination as to whether the records sought should be disclosed. As indicated in the previous question, some courts will be very skeptical of any claim that another student's records are relevant to the due process hearing of an individual student. However, each of these cases must be resolved on a case-by-case basis by the judge.

Can a school be held responsible for the harassment of disabled students by other students?

Absolutely, and especially when information about the disabled student has been impermissibly disclosed or negligently maintained by school officials, resulting in the inappropriate disclosure of information about the disabled student. [13] In one case, a regular education student obtained the test results of a student with a disability, and proceeded to harass the disabled student by calling him "dumb," "stupid," and "retarded." Ultimately, the school was held responsible and the parent of the disabled student awarded damages in excess of $180,000.[14]

If other students are bullying or harassing a student with a disability, may the District share information about the individual, disabled student in an effort to educate other students and hopefully prevent future attacks upon the disabled child?

In some cases, the parents of individual disabled students may provide their consent to share personally identifiable information about their child with other students in an effort to further educate others about their child's disability area. In other cases, schools have provided all students in the class with awareness or sensitivity training about, for example, students with epilepsy. However, in the absence of parental consent, we believe the school must be very sensitive to the reality that a general awareness program on "students with epilepsy" may quite evidently disclose to the classroom that the named, individual student who recently suffered a seizure in class does suffer from a diagnosed, medical condition. Of course, any individual student's diagnosis is generally considered to be personally identifiable information.[15]

In the event a student with a disability is suspected of committing a crime, does FERPA limit the information which may be shared by the school with the police?

Actually, IDEA requires that "an agency reporting a crime committed by a child with a disability must ensure that copies of the special education and disciplinary records of the child are transmitted for consideration by the appropriate authorities to whom the agency reports the crime."[16] At the same time, IDEA also requires that this transmittal be authorized "only to the extent that the transmission is permitted" by FERPA.[17] Notably, this requirement arises when the school reports a crime committed by the student—not at the point of any subsequent and tentative occasion of the student's actual arrest or final determination of guilt.

An Example—In one case, a 16-year-old student with various disabilities was detained by local authorities for several weeks after his arrest for an off-campus altercation with another student. The student ultimately remained in a juvenile detention facility for 14 school days without any special education services. The District apparently provided copies of the student's records to the parents, but not directly to the authorities who were holding him in custody. After finding the District in violation of IDEA for failing to provide the relevant records directly to the juvenile detention facility, the hearing officer went on to impose a "reasonable time period for insuring transmittal . . . ordinarily . . . no later than the tenth consecutive school day . . . following the student's detention."[18]

Practice Pointer—In the case mentioned above, the State hearing officer further opined that the proper course of action for a District to take once a student has been reported to police "will be to attempt to contact the parent immediately and seek consent for the records release; absent consent, promptly notify the parent of the intended disclosure; and transmit copies of the student's discipline and current special education records to the appropriate authorities in the same manner as with other non-consensual disclosures."

DEFINITIONAL EXCEPTIONS TO EDUCATIONAL RECORDS AND IDEA

Does the "sole possession" exception discussed in Chapter II apply to records relating to a special education student?

Yes. The "sole possession" exception may apply to records relating to a special education student and which are in fact used as a memory aid and shared with no one other than the creator of the record and his/her substitute. However, due to the collaborative nature of special education and the frequent use of teams or groups of educators and parents to make decisions about a child's educational program, the District should be careful to make certain the requirements of this exception have in fact been maintained in each instance.

Is the School required to provide copies of the notes of individual educators, school psychologists, or related service providers (such as the occupational or speech therapist) in response to a FERPA request?

In many cases, the sole possession exception may well apply so that notes created and maintained by an individual acting on behalf of the school, which are not shared with anyone else (including the parent), and which are used as "memory aids," may be excluded from the definition of educational records under FERPA.[19] However, we do caution that the sole possession exception has both a physical and a purposeful dimension—the records at issue must be maintained for the purpose of reminding the note taker (for example, a counselor) as to the contents of their last meeting with a student (in this hypothetical) and so as to facilitate their next meeting with a student. Simply including information, observations or even data about a student within an individual educator's personal notes does not guarantee that these records will fall outside the scope of FERPA.

An Example—Susie School Psychologist brings the case notes from her testing session with Samantha Student to the IEP meeting. At the meeting, Susie is careful not to actually share her notes with anyone else, but she repeatedly refers to her notes and discusses in various parts the contents of her notes with other participants at the meeting. Arguably, Susie's use of her notes and particularly her "disclosure" of the content of her notes with others has eroded the argument that these may be sole possession records, and has now converted these case notes into educational records which are subject to FERPA's and IDEA's parental access and inspection rights.[20]

What about notes taken at IEP meetings by teachers and other school officials—are these considered education records?

While it is possible that these notes could be collected and maintained by the District in such a manner as to fall within the *Owasso* definition of an educational record, in most cases this is not done and such notes either fall within the sole possession exception (discussed in Chapter II), or simply do not constitute educational records at all. For instance, in *Owasso* the Court described educational records as being stored or retained in a single, central file or database—and the partial, incomplete, or handwritten notes taken by individuals in attendance at an IEP meeting typically are not maintained in any such fashion.

Sometimes the District receives or requests medical records in connection with determining the appropriateness of accommodations for the student's disability—are these considered educational records under FERPA?

Yes, these records fall under FERPA, as they are excluded from the HIPPA privacy rule and do not fall within the treatment records exclusion under FERPA itself.[21] Furthermore, their disclosure within the District should be carefully coordinated with the District's definition of school officials with legitimate educational interest in accessing such records, and the confidential nature of the information contained therein emphasized to all such school personnel.

FERPA NON-CONSENSUAL DISCLOSURE PROVISIONS AND SPECIAL EDUCATION RECORDS

Do the FERPA rules discussed in Chapters IV and VI regarding the disclosure of personally identifiable information without consent also apply to the records of disabled students?

Yes. It has been the Department's "longstanding position that consent is required . . . unless the information contained in education records and the disclosure is allowed without parental consent under 34 C.F.R. part 99," (FERPA) in which case consent is not required.[22] This means that any non-consensual disclosures permitted under the FERPA exceptions discussed in Chapters IV and VI are also permissible in the case of students with disabilities and their educational records.

An Example—Mad Max is a troubled, emotionally and behaviorally disordered student at City High, who also happens to have been diagnosed with schizophrenia. Max is 6 feet and 6 ½ inches tall, weighs approximately 300 lbs and was recently dismissed from the football team following repeated instances of unnecessary roughness in practice as well as the game. One day at City High, Max grabs a freshman, pulls him into restroom and claims that voices in his head are telling him to "go medieval on this boy" unless the football coach agrees to let him back on the team and guarantee him a starting position at defensive tackle. When the police respond to City High School's 911 call, the School may share information from Max's latest psychological and functional behavior assessment in order to address this health and safety emergency—one of the permitted exceptions discussed in Chapter VI.

Does either IDEA or FERPA require parental consent before a District in which the student was formerly enrolled may send copies of the student's educational records to a District where the student is currently enrolled?

No, and in fact under both FERPA and IDEA regulations it is specifically permissible for the student's former District to forward copies of the student's educational records to any District in which the student is actually enrolled or in which they seek to enroll.[23]

An Example—After accumulating 12 disciplinary referrals by the end of September, EBD Eddie transfers from County Schools (where he resided with his mother) to Big City Schools, where he will live with his Aunt Amy. When enrolling her nephew in Big City Schools, Aunt Amy refuses to sign a "consent" provided by the school in the enrollment packet for the purpose of having Eddie's educational records forwarded from County Schools. In a common misunderstanding, she assumes the records cannot be forwarded without her consent; however, FERPA and IDEA specifically recognize as appropriate the non-consensual disclosure of educational records from one District to another where the student is actually (or seeks to become) enrolled. The consent of a parent, guardian, or the eligible student is not required prior to the transfer of Eddie's records (including his special education records) from County Schools. Unfortunately for Amy, Eddie's school records (including his disciplinary reports) will soon be arriving in Big City Schools.

When is it appropriate for other school personnel to have access to a child's special education file?

FERPA certainly recognizes that, for a variety of reasons, school personnel may require access to a child's education and/or special education file. For the most part, FERPA seeks to address this reality by recognizing "other school officials with a legitimate educational interest" as one of the basic exceptions to the consent requirement—individuals falling within the scope of this exception may inspect a child's records without notice or consent to the parent. For example, it might be appropriate that a teacher of whom classroom accommodations have been requested be permitted to review the student's medical records underlying this request so as to more accurately understand the frequency and nature of the accommodations to be provided the student.[24] It is very important, however, that the District appropriately define and notify parents annually as to the definition of "other school officials with legitimate educational interest," as this is the basis for permitting the exception.

Practice Pointer—Under IDEA, the District is required to maintain a record of access to a student's educational records in all cases except the inspection and review of the records by parents and "authorized employees of the participating agency."[25] The record of access provision here in connection with special education records is more comprehensive than FERPA generally, which contains several additional exceptions to the requirement that a record of access be maintained, and which is not duplicated within IDEA.[26]

If a child's disability is related to behavioral concerns, how much information from the child's IEP may be shared with other school officials and when is it appropriate to do so?

Though necessarily a case-by-case determination, and always one involving the examination of the District's definition of legitimate educational interest, we believe it is generally appropriate to share information about a child's behavior, such as their behavior intervention plan, with any school personnel who have supervisory responsibility for the student. Typically this will include classroom teachers, but this may also (again, depending upon the nature of the behavior and the settings in which issues have arisen) include, for example, the driver of a student's bus or a coach of the extracurricular activity involving the student. Of course, it is also important to emphasize the confidential nature of the information (in this case, the student's BIP), especially when individuals beyond the traditional classroom setting are involved in the delivery of services and accommodations set forth in the student's IEP.

Practice Pointer—It is a common occurrence that school employees outside the traditional setting of the school building (such as the school bus), and sometimes even regular school employees who happen to also work with students outside the classroom (such as coaches and aides in extra-curricular activities) adopt a more casual approach in their interactions with students. However, there is no relaxed standard of confidentiality under either FERPA or IDEA simply because the student is not in the classroom at that particular time. In our view, this is one area where frequent training and reminders of the duty of confidentiality and standards of ethical conduct can be time and money very well invested in avoiding future claims of inappropriate behavior by staff.

Is consent required before the District shares personally identifiable information with other agencies carrying out the requirements of IDEA?

Generally no, as the IDEA regulatory language specifically states that parental consent is not required in these instances.[27] There are, however, two key exceptions to this general rule. One exception relates to the prohibition on the disclosure of information to a public school District outside the District of residence when the student enrolls in a private school in the second District (discussed further above). The other exception (where consent is required) relates to the release of personally identifiable information to agencies "providing or paying for transition services" under IDEA, such as Vocational Rehabilitation Services.[28]

An Example—VR Vicki has been invited to an I.E.P. meeting for Mad Max (see above), where City High School will be attempting to develop a transition plan for Max. However, in order to invite Vicki to the meeting and share information from his special education records to develop Max's transition plan, City High School will have to obtain the consent of Max's mother, Maureen.

What is the reason for requiring consent before disclosing information to those officials or agencies providing transition services?

Though not entirely clear, it appears that in crafting this rule the Department was primarily concerned with the fact that officials from these outside agencies are often invited to participate in IEP meetings of children to discuss and plan for a child's transition services, where they may have access to a child's entire special education file, and when it is still somewhat uncertain or speculative as to whether and how they may actually be involved in providing these services. In these instances, the Department believes that "important privacy concerns" justify the requirement that consent be obtained for this disclosure.[29]

Practice Pointer—In 2008, the Department determined that the parental consent to share confidential information with an agency representative at an IEP meeting where a student's transition goals or plan will be discussed must be obtained for each individual IEP meeting. The Department's reasoning on this point was as follows—"since the conversations at each IEP Team meeting are not the same, and since confidential information about the child is always discussed, we believe that consent must be obtained prior to each IEP Team meeting if a public agency proposes to invite a representative of any participating agency that is likely to be responsible for providing or paying for transition services . . . one annual consent would not be sufficient if there is more than one IEP team meeting conducted during a 12-month period."[30]

What about sharing information with private employers or companies who permit disabled students to learn skills or work in their settings—is the District permitted to share any information about students with these private entities?

In general, there does not appear to be any non-consensual disclosure provision under FERPA that would permit the District to openly discuss some or all of the special education files of a disabled student who, as a part of their IEP plan, is working several days or hours a week in a commercial business. In some specific and limited instances, the health or safety emergency provision might apply. (See Chapter VI for a further discussion of the health and safety emergency provision.) However, we believe that in almost every case the District would be required to obtain the consent of the parent or eligible student to disclose information from the student's educational records to such a private employer. Of course, there may be many cases in which there is no necessity to consider such disclosure, or when doing so might be counterproductive even with parental consent.

Is the District required to obtain parental consent before sharing educational records with outside consultants in connection with the education of a child with a disability?

Generally no, as the Department's long-standing position has been that the District "may disclose FERPA protected information, without consent, to contractors and other agents who have been retained to perform administrative and other professional services so long as the disclosure would be proper if made to a school official performing the same service."[31]

Practice Pointer—It is vitally important that the District properly designate the criteria that will be used to properly identify school officials with a legitimate educational interest in order to make use of this provision. In one recent case, a District was determined to have violated FERPA when it shared student information with a private behavior consultant. When the parents complained, the District attempted to rely upon the FERPA exception for disclosure of information to school officials with a legitimate educational interest. However, the court found that since the District had not properly given annual notice of the criteria used to determine school officials, the District had violated FERPA by sharing information from the student's educational records with the private, outside behavior consultant.[32]

Further Practice Pointer—In some cases, seeking and obtaining parental consent prior to involving an outside consultant in a child's education (especially when this involves the classroom observation of the student by the consultant) may be a part of building and maintaining a cooperative, trustful relationship between the School and the parent. This may often be the case even when such consent is not technically required. However, school officials should be aware that once a parent believes their consent is necessary to involve an outside consultant, the District will have a difficult time acting without such consent if the parent later becomes dissatisfied with or objects to that particular (or a subsequent) consultant.

Does that mean the District is not required to obtain parental consent prior to the evaluation of a student by an outside expert or service provider?

No. FERPA merely deals with access to and inspection of the student's educational records, and the fact that the District may permit such access by an outside consultant is completely distinct from the requirements under IDEA that the District seek and obtain parental consent prior to the evaluation of a student.

May the District share information with agencies conducting research about areas of disability and treatments for students with disabilities?

There are two provisions under FERPA most relevant to this issue. One is the long-standing "study" exception which permits the disclosure of personally identifiable information to the authorized representatives of "organizations conducting studies for, or on behalf of, educational agencies or institutions."[33] However, FPCO has recently taken a more restrictive view of who may qualify as such a representative. In particular, the authorized representative must be an employee, official, or contractor under the direct control of the LEA or SEA.[34] FPCO has also interpreted the study exception to apply only to research the District or school has authorized, and not to research conducted by an outside entity on its own initiative, even if the study may benefit the District.[35] In most cases, the research entities that have historically sought access to personally identifiable information do not fall under the direct control of the LEA/SEA. Of course, this would not prohibit the LEA or SEA from sharing information with parental consent, or sharing information in the aggregate or non-personally identifiable form.[36] The second likely source of authority for such a disclosure is the new regulatory sections addressing the release of de-identified, student level data (discussed further below in Chapter VI).[37]

Practice Pointer—In the past, many States and Districts have entered into agreements with health departments or other local entities to gather information about students with autism. A common practice at that time was to execute and rely upon a "Memorandum of Understanding" or MOU as authority to designate the health department or other entity as a "school official" for purposes of sharing personally identifiable information about individual students with autism. However, the Department's current position on this makes it highly unlikely that a District would be able to successfully rely on either the "authorized representative" or "study" provision under FERPA to disclose personally identifiable student records.

What steps would the District be required to undertake in order to make certain that any student-level data is not personally identifiable?

The District would have to remove the student's name and any identification number, along with any other "personal characteristics" or "other information that would make the student's identity easily traceable."[38] The latter would include items such as any physical description of the student (race, sex, appearance, etc.), place and date of birth, national origin, religion, participation in activities, clubs or sports, academic performance, employment, criminal proceedings or disciplinary information, etc. Please see Chapter VI for a further discussion of the new rules relating to the release of de-identified student level data.

Does either FERPA or HIPPA require the District to obtain consent when submitting personally identifiable information about a student while seeking Medicaid reimbursement for special education services?

Yes. FERPA itself has been interpreted by the Department to require the District to obtain consent in connection with the disclosure of personally identifiable information while submitting Medicaid reimbursement requests.[39]

Do lead agencies under Part C of the IDEA have to obtain parental consent before disclosing personally identifying information about a child to the State or an LEA who may serve the child under Part B?

No. OSEP has concluded that FERPA would permit this disclosure, at least in those states where the lead agency has been included in the State's child find activities. In two opinion letters, OSEP has relied upon the provision in FERPA which permits such disclosure as necessary to enforce federal statutory requirements of IDEA.[40]

PARENTAL INSPECTION RIGHTS UNDER IDEA

Is there any difference in the timeline the School has to respond to requests to inspect the special education records of disabled students by their parents?

In addition to the FERPA requirement that educational records be made available for inspection no later than 45 days after they have been requested, IDEA also says that such records should be produced "without unnecessary delay" and prior to any IEP meeting, due process hearing, or resolution session convened to address a dispute about the IEP of a child with a disability.[41] In some cases, this can require that records be produced within just a few days, for instance, when parents request to inspect records in advance of an upcoming IEP meeting.[42]

Practice Pointer—One of the rights related to a child's educational records under IDEA that is not present under FERPA is the requirement that the District must (upon request) provide parents with a list of the "types and locations of education records collected, maintained, or used by the agency."[43] As a practical matter, this requirement tends to place an increased burden upon the Special Education Department to have and maintain an accurate and complete understanding of the nature and location of all student records maintained by the District. In addition, IDEA also requires the District to "maintain, for public inspection, a current listing of the names and positions of those employees within the agency who have access to personally identifiable information."[44]

Do the parents of disabled students enjoy the right to have a representative inspect and review their child's educational records?

Yes. IDEA (unlike FERPA) specifically confers upon parents this added right.[45] Also, as under FERPA, there is no provision of IDEA that prohibits the District from assigning a representative to be and remain present throughout the inspection of the records by the parent and/or their representative.

May the District charge the parents of disabled students a fee for copies of their child's educational records?

Yes, the District may charge parents for copies of their child's educational records—this provision is the same under IDEA as under FERPA generally, and so long as the fee "does not effectively prevent the parents from exercising their right to inspect and review those records," a copy fee is permissible. Just as in the case of regular education students, the District may not charge a search or retrieval fee for the educational records.[46]

An Example—In one case where the court interpreted FERPA, IDEA, and State rules that largely mirrored FERPA and IDEA, the hearing officer found no violation where the District had refused to provide free copies of a student's educational records to his father. The father subsequently admitted that he could have paid the $61 which the District quoted as the cost to copy the records at issue. In this case, the hearing officer further limited the District to charging ten cents per page "if it could not document that its costs were higher."[47]

Are there certain education records which must be provided to parents of disabled students at no charge?

Absolutely. For instance, under IDEA the District must provide parents a copy of the child's IEP itself as well as the eligibility report and documentation of the eligibility determination at no cost.[48] In addition, parents are entitled to a free copy of the decision, findings of fact, and written or electronic record in a due process hearing.[49]

Is it permissible for the District to charge only parents of students with disabilities for copies of educational records, or to only charge certain parents of disabled students, when parents of non-disabled students are not charged a copy fee?

While the generally expansive nature of special education student files might lead some school officials to seek reimbursement for the added burden associated with their photocopying, a practice of charging for copies only in the case of a student with disabilities would be prohibited discrimination under both Section 504 and the ADA. In addition, the practice of charging only certain parents of disabled students could be perceived as retaliating against those parents for exercising their rights to inspect the educational records of their children, also prohibited under IDEA, Section 504, and the ADA.[50]

May a District adopt of a general practice of permitting parents of disabled students the right to inspect their child's educational records, but generally refusing to make copies of these same records?

Yes, subject to the limitation discussed above that copies must be provided when the failure to do so effectively prevents a parent's right to inspect educational records, and except for those specific records which IDEA requires be provided to parents at no cost. In one case, a federal district court upheld the general practice of a school district which refused to provide copies of educational records to parents of a disabled student, and which instead permitted parents to inspect these records in the offices of the District. In that case, the parent claimed that copies were necessary for their independent expert and their attorney to effectively review their case; however, the court was unconvinced that the District's refusal to provide copies in either of these instances genuinely frustrated the parent's ability to inspect their child's educational records. [51]

What about when parents or their attorneys repeatedly request the same or overlapping educational records, or request multiple copies, of a student's special education file—does the District have to keep making multiple copies of the same information?

As mentioned in Chapter III, the parent who believes that certain records have not been produced has the burden to identify those records and tailor their request accordingly. Furthermore, FERPA does not require the District to make copies of a special education student's file "upon request" unless and in the rare instance that refusing to do so would effectively prevent parents from inspecting and reviewing the file. In the authors' view, the District may make the file available for further inspection and review, or may elect to copy (and charge for) any materials which have been placed in the file since the file was previously copied, but neither FERPA nor IDEA would require the District to repeatedly copy the entire special education file of the student merely because the parents, their attorney, or advocate consistently request the District to do so. And as discussed above, the District may charge for copies actually provided.

Does IDEA give parents of disabled students access rights to a wider array of "educational records" than the parents of regular education students?

After the Supreme Court's decision in *Owasso*, the answer to this question is not entirely clear and may depend, for instance, upon the records which the District actually maintains as to a particular student and with whom those records have been shared. Remember that under *Owasso*, much of a student's daily and weekly work is not considered to be an education record at all, and as a general rule, no parents would have FERPA access rights to inspect such documents. However, in the case of some special education students, daily work may be included as a sample of the student's current level of performance and is, in fact, "maintained" in a central location by the custodian of special education records. When this occurs, documents related to a particular student that may not have initially qualified as educational records under the language of *Owasso* have now arguably become FERPA records by virtue of the District's treatment of this particular student's records.

An Example—Thelma Third Grader moves into the City School System in mid-October. Thelma has an IEP from her previous school district which includes, among other services, intensive intervention, and frequent one-to-one work with a reading specialist throughout the school year. Over the Summer, Thelma receives extended school year services and works with a reading specialist. During her fourth grade year, Thelma's mother (Teresa) becomes very unhappy with the progress (or lack of progress, in her view) that Thelma is making in reading. Teresa hires her own reading specialists, as well as an attorney, and demands to see all of Thelma's work samples from the third grade and over the Summer, which she contends are all education records under FERPA. Is Teresa correct? Not according to one federal court, which rejected claims by a parent that hundreds of pages of student work samples fell within *Owasso*'s concept of an education record.[52]

Is it possible for State special education rules and regulations to expand the rights of parents to access educational records relating to their children?

Absolutely, and some state special education rules specifically do convey upon parents the right to inspect any records which, for example, are used to make educational decisions about their children. Again, even if these particular records do not fall within the definition of a record after *Owasso*, state rules and regulations may (within the State) expand the list of documents falling within this definition.

Do both parents of a disabled student enjoy the same access rights under IDEA and FERPA?

As a general rule, both natural parents continue to enjoy FERPA and IDEA rights of access to their child's educational records unless and until a court has removed or modified these rights in some way. Furthermore, even the Office of Civil Rights has recognized that the District does not violate Section 504 when it declines to provide access to a student's educational records on the basis of a valid court order to this effect.[53]

Practice Pointer—School officials must be cautious to distinguish between a court order which 'only' removes one parent's right to make educational decisions about their child, and an order which also (or in addition to) takes away a parent's right to inspect their child's educational records. In one case, the Court of Appeals reversed a lower court's dismissal of a parent's complaint alleging denial of access to her child's educational records, even though the custody decree in her divorce proceeding had removed her rights to make educational decisions, since the decree did not address the termination of her parental rights of access to the child's education records.[54]

Does either FERPA or IDEA require that the school produce email communications between staff members concerning a particular student in response to a request for education records?

Under *Owasso*, the authors believe that the determination as to whether email communications between school staff about an individual student are educational records is still very much unsettled. In one particular case, the hearing officer found that "there is certainly no reason why these records would not be education records relating to the Student and thus available to the parents and their attorney . . . in response to a request by a parent for all e-mail communications related to the student."[55] However, notwithstanding the debate as to whether or not such communications are educational records which a parent would be entitled to inspect upon request under FERPA, there is little doubt that the vast majority of these records would be subject to a subpoena in a due process or other judicial proceeding.[56] For a further discussion of electronic records, please see Chapter VII.

Practice Pointer—There is a distinction, we believe, to be drawn between draft reports or documents which might be shared electronically (for example, a draft of an amended BIP being prepared by school personnel), and email communications between staff about a student. In the event that copies of the former are actually maintained in accordance with FERPA, we believe it much more likely that such draft documents will be considered and treated as educational records.[57]

Do the parents of disabled students have a right to access test protocols used to evaluate a student?

The Department's position on this appears to be that "completed test instruments that identify a student are 'education records under FERPA . . . [while] a test protocol or question booklet that is separate from the sheet on which a student records answers and that is not personally identifiable to the student is not considered the student's 'education record' under FERPA.'"[58] As to the latter, therefore, FERPA inspection rights would not attach. It should also be noted that parents have the right to request an "explanation and interpretation" of their child's educational record and this explanation "could involve showing the parent the test question booklet."[59]

Practice Pointer—This is often a point of huge contention between school psychologists and some parents, and for school officials who feel strongly about shielding the protocols themselves from the inspection of parents and others. In at least one case, a court considered and rejected the further argument by the District that copyright law prevented the District from allowing the parent to inspect the test protocols themselves.[60]

Do parents of a disabled student continue to hold FERPA access rights, even after a student with a disability turns 18 years of age?

The Department has stated that in the absence of a guardianship, "it would be reasonable to presume that the parents of such a student are the persons who are in the best position to act on behalf of the student."[61] Of course, any presumption is subject to being rebutted, and in close cases, we suspect that State or local procedures for determining the competency of disabled adults would be the arena in which such a dispute is settled. Furthermore, IDEA requires that parents continue to receive notice of certain special education activities under IDEA in respect to a child who has reached the age of majority, even when FERPA rights have otherwise been transferred to the now eligible child.[62]

HEARINGS UNDER FERPA, DUE PROCESS HEARINGS, AND COMPLAINTS

Do the parents of special education students have a right to challenge the content of educational records of their child?

Yes, the parents of a disabled student may challenge the content of any educational record if they believe the record is "inaccurate, misleading, or otherwise in violation of the privacy or other rights of the child."[63] At this point, parents of both regular and special education students enjoy the same right to contest the substance of an educational record.

If the District disagrees with the parent's contention as to the accuracy, misleading nature, or alleged violation of privacy, what happens next?

The District must inform the parents of their right to a hearing to challenge the content of the records on the alleged basis. IDEA specifically requires that this hearing be conducted under FERPA, so if as a result of the hearing the District determines that the parent's claims are justified, the record(s) must be amended accordingly and the parents must be so informed in writing.[64] However, if the District continues to believe that the records are correct and rejects the parent's position at the hearing, the District must inform the parents of their right to place a statement with their child's educational records, which statement may comment upon the records or explain their basis for contending the records is inaccurate.[65] Please see Chapter III for a further explanation of the rules associated with these hearings.

Are there any rules regarding where and how long the District must maintain a copy of the parent's statement in this instance?

Yes, the District is required to keep a copy of the parent's statement "as long as the record or contested portion is maintained," and the statement must be disclosed to any party to whom the records or contested portion of the record is disclosed.[66]

What is the relationship between this FERPA hearing and the due process hearings which are often requested in special education?

The FERPA hearing discussed above is limited to the issue of whether some information in the child's educational records is "inaccurate, misleading, or an invasion of the privacy or other rights of the child." A FERPA hearing is generally NOT concerned with reviewing the substantive determinations of education officials, but rather, the clerical correctness or accuracy of the records as they exist. Furthermore, the relief parents may be awarded in such a hearing is limited to the amendment of the contested records, if in fact they are determined to be inaccurate. In contrast, the special education due process hearing may be about any aspect of eligibility or delivery of a free, appropriate public education to a student with a disability.

What is the relationship between a complaint with FPCO about an alleged FERPA violation, the FERPA hearing process described above, and a complaint filed with a State educational agency alleging a breach of confidentiality under IDEA?

The FERPA hearing discussed above is specifically limited to whether information contained within the educational records of a student are "inaccurate, misleading, or an invasion of privacy." One the other hand, a complaint may be filed with FPCO alleging any FERPA violation, including the failure to provide parent's access to the educational records of student, or the failure to maintain the confidentiality of information contained within those records. In addition or in the alternative, the parent of a student with a disability may also file a complaint with the State educational agency alleging any violation of IDEA, and which may also include in whole or in part a complaint about the alleged failure of a District to comply with any of the educational records rules specifically set forth or incorporated within IDEA. The FPCO has recently stated that in the event a parent filed both a complaint with the State and a complaint with FPCO (alleging an overlapping violation), "FPCO's policy is to hold the FERPA complaint in abeyance until and pending a decision by the SEA."[67]

May District officials publicly comment upon a due process complaint or hearing filed by parents?

Generally no, unless one of the Act's non-consensual disclosure provisions happen to apply (which is unlikely). In fact, the Department has found that merely disclosing (or confirming) that a student has an I.E.P. (and is therefore a student with a disability) by a Superintendent after the student's parents publicly complained at a Board of Education meeting constituted a violation of FERPA.[68] For a further discussion of the "implied waiver" doctrine, please see Chapter VI.

Practice Pointer—The presentation of confidential information about a student during the course of a due process hearing is certainly permissible. However, the District should present these educational records or the information contained within the records "within the course of a due process hearing during the presentation of evidence." The practice, for instance, of simply and immediately forwarding a student's entire special education file to the appointed due process hearing officer has been specifically rejected by the Department.[69]

Are States required to make due process hearing decisions publicly available?

Yes, IDEA 2004 requires these hearing decisions be publicly available after all personally identifiable information is redacted.[70]

How does the State decide which information must be redacted from due process hearing results?

This determination must be made on a case-by-case basis and a review of the contents in each hearing decision so as to avoid the disclosure of information which would make it reasonably possible to identify a child or make the identity of the student easily traceable.[71]

Are there any particular factors which should be considered when reviewing what information should be redacted from the record of a hearing decision?

Generally, this review should include (but certainly is not limited to) consideration of "the size of the District, school, and grade, the prevalence and knowledge of the child's personal characteristics and other information (e.g., disability, initials, parent's advocacy work) within the school community and the community at large."[72]

What if the parents have chosen to allow the due process hearing to be held and conducted as a public hearing?

While IDEA does give parents of disabled students this option, the records maintained by either the District or the State, and which qualify as educational records of the student, remain subject to FERPA. This means that these records may not be disclosed without the parent's specific, signed, and written consent, even if these records were created or introduced into evidence in a public hearing.[73]

Is it sufficient for the State to simply redact the name of the student from the final decision?

Not necessarily. In response to a request for guidance by a State which routinely published the first and last initials of the parent and student, along with the name of the District, campus, and grade to which the student was assigned, and the student's disability area, the Office of Special Programs has stated that "in a small school district, school, or grade or for a child who has a low-incidence disability, [this practice] could result in the identification of the child with reasonable certainty or make the student's identity easily traceable."[74] In each case, OSEP stressed, the analysis as to which information must be redacted is individualized.

Practice Pointer—In some states, the State has adopted the practice of simply referring to each case as "X.X." versus the District, and abandoned the previous practice of using the student's initials to identify the case.

In a due process hearing, may parents of a disabled student obtain access to personally identifiable information about other students?

According to FPCO, the answer to this question is no. In a 2003 letter, parents of a disabled student involved in a due process hearing sought the names of other students who had accused their son of criminal misconduct. FPCO strongly advised the District and the hearing officer that the due process rights of disabled students "do not override any of the privacy rights of FERPA or IDEA."[75]

DESTRUCTION AND RETENTION OF SPECIAL EDUCATION RECORDS

What special rules govern the destruction of special education records?

Under IDEA, the District is required to inform parents when personally identifiable information is no longer needed to provide services to their child, and this information must be destroyed if so requested by the parents. When parents request that their child's special education file be destroyed, the only elements of personally identifiable information the District is permitted to maintain permanently are the "student's name, address, phone number, grades, attendance record and classes attended, grade level completed, and year completed."[76] Also, remember that in the case of regular education students, FERPA does not require that parents or eligible students be notified prior to the destruction of education records.

How may the District go about notifying parents that special education records of their children are no longer needed?

In some circumstances, the District may be able to address the handling of the files of many graduating students at the last IEP meeting by personally providing parents and eligible students with notice of this information. In the case of recent graduates, contact information may be sufficiently current to allow for direct mail contact with parents or eligible students. In the case of records for students who graduated or left the District a long time ago, a legal advertisement in the City or County paper may be used to advise former students that certain records are no longer needed, presumably no longer required to be maintained under record retention schedules, and will be destroyed unless retrieved prior to a date certain.

An Example—City Schools has finally run out of warehouse space to store the records of the Special Education Department. Upon inspection, the City Schools Records Custodian realizes that in the vast majority of cases, the Department simply boxed up the entire special education file of the student and stacked them in the warehouse. After separating the permanent records from all other documents, a tremendous amount of material remains to be disposed of by the District. Once a week for four weeks, City Schools runs a legal advertisement in the City News—"Attention all students who attended City Schools between 1960–2000 and who may have received any special education services—all non-permanent records are no longer necessary and will be destroyed by (date certain). If any eligible student wishes to retrieve any of their records prior to destruction, please contact City Schools Records Custodian at (number) no later than (date)."[77]

What if the parents or the eligible student do not respond to this notice at all—is the District permitted to destroy those records, or must they be maintained for any period of time?

If the parents ask that the records be destroyed, the District must destroy the records. If the parents do not respond or express any preference for the disposition of the records, the District may treat those records in accordance with the District's general record management policies and practices. If under the District's general record retention policies this means, for instance, that all records beyond the permanent file are destroyed at this point, then the District is permitted to treat the special education records in the same way as other educational records at this point.

After the District has indicated it no longer needs the educational records, are parents or eligible students entitled to retrieve their original records from the District in lieu of the District simply destroying those records?

Neither IDEA nor FERPA conveys upon parents or eligible students the right to receive original educational records. Under IDEA, the only option permitted of parents appears to be to elect that the District destroy those records which do not fall within the concept of permanent records discussed below.[78]

What about students who were examined but found ineligible for special education, or who were identified as eligible for special education but who, for whatever reason (their parents did not consent for services or who withdrew the student and/or moved before services were ever delivered), were never actually served in special education?

The regulatory language under IDEA specifically uses the term to "provide educational services," which in the view of the authors, only includes those students actually served in special education. Consequently, records of students who were examined or even identified as students with a disability, but who were never actually served in special education, are covered by FERPA (and perhaps state or local rules) generally and are not subject to the special rules under IDEA.[79]

Does this apply to records created during the District's implementation of Response to Intervention, such as biweekly progress monitoring reports?

Yes. Educational records created by the District while a student is the subject of various interventions and progress monitoring in response to those interventions should be treated as educational records under FERPA, but not as special education records subject to the special rules discussed in this chapter.[80] Of course, the RTI process itself (and the IDEA 2006 regulations) further requires that parents be provided with documentation of the assessments provided to the student during the RTI process.[81]

What if there is a conflict between the District's policy or practice in terms of the information retained in student's "permanent record" and the information which the District is permitted to retain even if the parents have requested destruction of records?

Each District must examine its own state or local requirements in terms of the information which is permitted or required to be maintained in a student's permanent record. However, when the parents of a disabled student have requested the destruction of their child's educational records, and in the event of a conflict between state or local requirements and the "permanent file" as recognized by IDEA, the District is required to adhere to IDEA's requirements in terms of any information that is permanently maintained about that student.

What about records created in connection with the identification and accommodation of students under Section 504—is there any guidance as to how long these records should be maintained?

The Office of Civil Rights has taken the position that Section 504 requires the District to maintain student records "until at least three years after the student's permanent departure from the district, whether by graduation or withdrawal."[82] Once this three year period has passed, the District may adhere to State or local record retention schedules both as to individual records which are maintained for more than three years (but which may be destroyed at some point) as well as the permanent record.

ENDNOTES

1. It is important to seek legal advice and consider the special education rules in each individual state when addressing issues relating to the handling of special education records. It is frequently the case that during the rule-making process, and not necessarily always intentionally, state special education rules extend additional access rights to parents and/or place added duties of confidentiality upon Districts in the State.
2. 34 C.F.R. § 300.611(b).
3. 34 C.F.R. § 300.622(a)(3).
4. Id. See also Federal Register Vol. 71, No. 156 46736 (August 14, 2006) and 34 C.F.R. § 300.141.
5. In re: Report Cards and Transcripts for Students with Disabilities, Office of Civil Rights (October 17, 2008) 51 IDELR 50. The OCR does conclude that a transcript may indicate that a student took classes with "modified or alternate education curriculum," but may not indicate that the student received accommodations in any class. The OCR letter provides no discussion and indeed appears oblivious to the exception under FERPA for the non-consensual disclosure of information to an agency or institution in which the students seeks to (or actually does enroll). Indeed, 34 C.F.R. 99.31(a)(2) specifically contemplates the non-consensual disclosure of educational records to "institutions of post-secondary education where the student seeks or intends to enroll." Nor does the OCR letter appear to contemplate special education services for behavioral as opposed to academic reasons If this letter is to be taken seriously and not rescinded, it will undoubtedly create confusion anew as to what information a public high school may share with a student's college or university about that student's emotional and behavioral problems and concerns.
6. Id.
7. Franklin City School District, Complaint 15-06-1076 Office of Civil Rights, Midwestern Division Cleveland (Ohio)(June 1, 2006). This complaint is somewhat indicative of the difficulties encountered with 504 and IEP plan implementation at the high school level, where teachers with many students sometimes struggle or resist numerous, individualized accommodations, or modifications. Also, in this case

the student was so humiliated and embarrassed that she withdrew from the class, a harm compounded by the fact that her 504 plan specifically notified teachers that the student was extremely sensitive about her disability, and encouraged teachers to use caution to prevent other students from becoming aware of her condition.

8. We recognize some tension within the idea that the District's choices regarding the degree of parental presence in the classroom generally also have, to some extent, a direct impact upon the scope of privacy and confidentiality interests of individual parents and students.

9. See *Frasca v. Andrews*, 463 F.Supp. 1043, 1050 (D.C.N.Y. 1979)(Congress could not have Constitutionally prohibited comment on, or discussion of, facts about a student which were learned independently of his school records); *Daniel S. v. Board of Education of York Community High School,* 152 F.Supp.2d 949 (N.D. Ill. 2001)(Gym teacher who disclosed to the class that students had been kicked off cross-country team and out of gym class did not violate FERPA, as this information would be "known by the school community").

10. Douglas County School District RE-1, Complaint 2004-502, 41 IDELR 258 Colorado State Educational Agency (June 2, 2004). It is interesting that the complaint officer in this case also distinguishes the *Jensen* case (discussed in Chapter II above) in that the disclosure in the present case was to other parents and not to parents of the student "victim" in the case.

11. Certainly, we recognize that this explanation will be completely satisfactory to all parents in all instances, though we respectfully suggest that such a result is not unique.

12. *Loch v. Board of Education of Edwardsville Community School District,* Case No. 3:06-CV-17-MJR, 49 IDELR 131 (January 7, 2008). In this brief opinion, the court also approved the District's proposal to give information about other students when identifying students by number, as opposed to by their name.

13. Of course, harassment of students by other students on the basis of their disability is actionable even in the absence of a preceding and related breach of confidentiality by school officials.

14. *Scott v. Minneapolis Public Schools*, Special Dist. No. 1, 2006 WL 997721(Minn.App. 2006)(State Data Practices Act authorized jury verdict and award of damages and fees in excess of $180,000 to parents of student whose special education assessment was inadvertently disclosed to other students).

15. In the case of any so-called "invisible" or non-obvious condition, we believe this to be the case. However, this is not always true in the case of a student with an apparent disability (i.e. a student who presents in a wheelchair), though again, the underlying medical cause or reason for the student's current physical condition may continue to be confidential.

16. 34 C.F.R. § 300.535(b)(1).

17. 34 C.F.R. § 300.535(b)(2).

18. Northside Independent School District, Case No. 106-SE-1297 (Texas 1998) 28 IDELR 1118.

19. See Mount Diablo Unified School District (December 24, 1997) 28 IDELR 883 for conclusion that teacher's personal notes were not part of the student's education file to which the parent was entitled.

20. See *The Answer Book on Special Education Law* by Susan Gorn (LRP 1996) p. 7:26.

21. Letter to Mr. David Cope (November 2, 2004).

22. Federal Register Vol. 71, No. 156 46736.

23. 34 C.F.R. § 300.323(g); 34 C.F.R. § 300.622(a) & Federal Register Vol. 71, No. 156 46736 (August 14, 2006); 34 C.F.R. §99.31(a)(2).

24. Letter to Mr. David Cope (November 2, 2004). This opinion letter is concerned with the university setting and an apparent request for accommodations. In the case of a student served under IDEA (which is inapplicable in the post-secondary setting), an IEP team would first consider the need and extent of any accommodations served under special education. While it certainly would be appropriate for any teacher of the student to serve on the IEP team, in the case of a teacher not included on the IEP team but who is expected to make accommodations based upon the decisions of the IEP team, we recognize a potential distinction in the K–12 setting. In some instances, it is also possible that an appropriate understanding of accommodations determined necessary for a student does not require the examination of the medical information serving as the basis for the team's decision.

25. 34 C.F.R. § 300.614. Some confusion may arise by virtue of the Department's use of the language (employees of the participating agency), as opposed to what appears to be the corresponding language in FERPA itself—school officials with a legitimate educational interest. See 34 C.F.R. § 99.31(a)(1).

26. See 34 C.F.R. § 99.32(d), including by way of example, the provisions relating to subpoenas when the issuing court has ordered the subpoena is not to be disclosed. 34 C.F.R. § 99.31(a)(9).

27. 34 C.F.R. § 300.622(a).

28. 34 C.F.R. § 300.622.

29. See Federal Register Vol. 71, No. 156 46736, where the Department refers to these agencies as "likely to provide or pay for transition services," and that they "may be providing or paying for transition services," where this terminology (likely, may) are not contained in the regulations themselves. In the comments, the Department also states that "we do not believe that the representatives of these agencies should have access to all the child's records unless the parent…gives consent."

30. Letter to Gray (March 17, 2008) 50 IDELR 198.

31. Letter to Jerome H. Sullivan (August 27, 2004); Letter to Parent (September 7, 2004). In the second letter, the Department stated that "one exception permits institutions to disclose education records without consent to parties such as outside legal counsel, psychologists, or collection agents because they are providing the types of services that would allow them to obtain access to education records without consent as if they were in fact 'other school officials under FERPA.'" In other words, the Department said, "we believe that FERPA was not intended to prevent schools from seeking outside assistance in performing certain tasks that it would otherwise have to provide itself."

32. *Caledonia Independent School District v. Minnesota State Educational Agency,* 51 IDELR 25 (May 29, 2008).

33. 34 C.F.R. 99.31(a)(6).

34. Letter to Dr. Allan M. Lloyd-Jones (February 18, 2004); Letter to Amy Foerster (February 25, 2004). The position taken in these 2004 letters and further reflected in guidance issued by the Department indicates a changed, more restrictive interpretation of "authorized representative."

35. This reflects FPCO's interpretation of the language "for or on behalf of" the agency in connection with such a study. Letter Dr. Allan M. Lloyd-Jones (February 18, 2004). Also note that such studies must have as their intended purpose the development, validation, or administration of predictive tests; the administration of student aid programs; or the improvement of instruction. See Chapter VII for a further discussion of the study provision.

36. Letter to Amy Forester (February 25, 2004).

37. 34 C.F.R. 99.31(b)(1).

38. Id. In this letter, FPCO also specifically cautions that the release of information about small numbers of students may mean that other information makes the student's identify easily traceable, and any such information must also be removed from records provided in this manner.

39. Letter to Mr. Dann Stephens (October 12, 2005).

40. Letter to Elder, OSEP 41 IDELR 270 (February 11, 2004) & Letter to Anonymous OSEP (February 12, 2004). Also related to this point is the Department's interestingly contrary position as to personally identifiable information about a child who transfers from one LEA to a private school in another LEA, and where the Department has concluded that parental consent is required prior to the disclosure of the child's identification as a child with a disability by the first LEA to the second LEA.

41. 34 C.F.R. § 300.613(a).

42. Absent a crisis or other deadline in the conduct of the IEP meeting, it is also an option for the District to delay for a short period of time an IEP meeting if there simply is insufficient notice by the parent in order to organize and permit an orderly inspection of a child's records prior to the IEP meeting.

43. 34 C.F.R. § 300.616.

44. 34 C.F.R. § 300.623(d).

45. 34 C.F.R. § 300.613(b)(3).

46. 34 C.F.R. § 300.617.

47. Board of Education of the Springville-Griffith Institute Central School District, New York SEA No. 01-063 (May 21, 2002) 37 IDELR 54. The issue with the .10 per page limitation appears to be a product of local policy language which indicated that the costs charged would be the "actual cost" of duplication, and the District had not conducted any study to justify a higher rate. We question whether most or many courts in other states would entertain a limitation or distinction between .10 or .25 per page copy charges.

48. 34 C.F.R. § 300.322(f); Federal Register Vol. 71, No. 156 46645 (August 14, 2006).

49. 34 C.F.R. § 300.512(c)(3).

50. We do not mean to suggest that it would be completely indefensible for a District to adopt a neutral rule in respect to the provision of records (ex. One free

copy per year, charges apply thereafter), though whether the rule may have disparate impact upon students with disabilities and their parents, and whether such an effect is impermissible or not, has not yet been decided.

51. In this case, there was no showing that the parent's expert or attorney were in any way unable to accompany the parent to school to inspect the records in lieu of copies being provided to them. It is also worth noting that in a subsequent reincarnation of this case, the court did hold that once the parent filed for due process, their attorney was entitled to copies of the educational records. *Bevis v. Jefferson County Board of Education*, 2:06-CV-0853-RDP, 48 IDELR 100 (January 31, 2007). Of course, parents and/or their attorneys do have a right to obtain copies of records when a due process hearing request is filed, though this is not a right derived from FERPA. See Jefferson County Board of Education, 06-88, Alabama State Educational Agency, 48 IEDLR 117 (March 1, 2007).

52. *K.C. & A.C. v. Fulton County School District,* Civil Action File No. 1:03-CV-3501-TWT (N.D. Ga. 2006).

53. Lake Villa School District #41, Complaint 05-06-1151, 46 IDELR 292 (OCR, Midwestern Division, Chicago) (April 21, 2006).

54. *Taylor v. Vermont Department of Education,* Case No. 01-7466 (2nd Cir. 2002) 38 IDELR 32. Interestingly, the court in this case rejected Ms. Taylor's access claims under FERPA, but found that since a parent's enforceable access rights under IDEA were not clearly foreclosed from suit under Gonzaga, this part of her claim survived.

55. School District U-46 v. Illinois State Educational Agency (45 IDELR 74, 2005). Even though this case was decided after *Owasso*, the judge does not discuss (or appear to consider) the Supreme Court's language in addressing the definition of educational records. However, we certainly also recognize that given the degree of uncertainty and indeed disagreement as to the very definition of an educational records, even in the wake of *Owasso*, some courts will adopt (we believe incorrectly) a broader definition of the term.

56. The most frequent exception to this will be privileged communications, such as between school personnel and their attorney falling within the attorney-client privilege.

57. The issue of access to drafts of documents can become quite contentious and complex, and while it is often found that the author of a report that is being revised simply writes over previous versions during the process of composing the final version of the document, individuals who receive electronic copies of earlier drafts often do retain these documents in their inbox. On a separate but related note, current and emerging software technology increasingly makes it possible for individuals to trace the development and changes to electronic versions of documents over time—effectively accomplishing much the same goal as inspecting various hard copies of draft documents.

58. Letter to Mr. Gary S. Mathews (September 13, 2005); School District U-46, 45 IDELR 74 (2005). See also *The Answer Book on Special Education Law* by Susan Gorn (LRP 1996) pp. 7:26–27 and the older OSEP letters cited therein.

59. Id.

60. *Newport-Mesa Unified School District v. State of California Department of Education,* 371 F.Supp.2d 1170 (C.D. Cal. 2005). Again, this is a point with which

some school officials may not initially agree. However, if the FERPA right of access does extend to test protocols (as the Department has interpreted it does, at least in some instances), then it would be highly unlikely for a court to find that the District may enter into a contact which abrogates a parent's federal statutory rights.

61. Federal Register Vol. 53, No. 69 11951 (April 11, 1988).

62. 34 C.F.R. § 300.625(c).

63. 34 C.F.R. § 300.618(a).

64. 34 C.F.R. § 300.621.

65. 34 C.F.R. § 300.619; 34 C.F.R. § 300.620.

66. 34 C.F.R. § 300.620(c).

67. Letter to Anderson (March 7, 2008) 50 IDELR 167. On a related note, perhaps one of the most significant distinctions between IDEA and FERPA in this particular respect is that a complaint of a violation of the confidentiality provisions under IDEA may be filed within one year of the alleged violation, while FERPA generally requires a complaint be filed within 180 days. Id.

68. Letter to Dr. Robert Wagoner (March 10, 1999). Of course, the public disclosure of the nature or content of due process proceedings is a completely different matter from disclosure necessary to defend the District within the due process hearing, such as to District counsel, expert witnesses, or the court itself. See again the implied waiver doctrine in Chapter VI.

69. Letter to Ronald Sadler (July 5, 1996) 24 IDELR 973.

70. Section 615(h)(4) and 617(c).

71. OSEP Letter David A. Anderson (October 13, 2006).

72. Id.

73. Letter to Jerome Schad (December 23, 2004). This opinion letter was predicated upon the view of the Department that common law rules relating to privilege and waiver did not apply to non-judicial authorities. Of course, statute or case law in a State may have adopted or applied these common law rules to quasi-judicial proceedings conducted under the auspices of a District. And it should also be pointed out that even FPCO acknowledges this opinion would not apply to records maintained by a court, but only those maintained by a District.

74. Letter to Anderson, Office of Special Programs (October 13, 2006).

75. Letter to Parent (October 31, 2003).

76. 34 C.F.R. § 300.624. For purposes of IDEA, the act of "destruction" is defined as "physical destruction or removal of personal identifiers from information so that the information is no longer personally identifiable." 34 C.F.R. § 300.611(a). Notably, FERPA does not contain a similar definition of destruction allowing for the removal of personal identifies, but otherwise, maintaining the actual physical, electronic, or other format of educational record. Consequently, where FERPA requires the destruction of an educational record (as in the case of the study provision under 99 C.F.R. 31(a)(6)(ii)(C)(4), physical destruction (or return of the records to the institution) would appear to be required. See also Chapter IV.

77. 34 C.F.R. § 300.612(b) provides for notice to parents on the part of the SEA in a newspaper, other media, or both "with circulation adequate to notify parents

throughout the State of the activity" prior to any "major identification, location, or evaluation activity." At the local level, we understand a similar practice has been followed without, to the best of our knowledge, any valid objection or complaint.

78. The idea behind this particular provision appears to be that if records beyond the permanent file are to be maintained, they will be maintained by the District. In the event of parents who obtain a copy of their child's complete education records and then request the District destroy all records outside the permanent file, we recommend the District specifically consult with legal counsel prior to the destruction of any records. It is possible, for instance, that such records may in fact be needed or necessarily maintained for some legitimate purpose after further consideration.

79. We are not aware of any authority directly on this point, and acknowledge that retention of such files in an inactive file within the special education records generally may argue in favor of subject the file to the additional records rules of IDEA.

80. In certain instances, these same records will likely become special education records in the event the student is subsequently found eligible for special education.

81. See 34 C.F.R. § 300.309(b)(2) which requires the eligibility group to consider "data-based documentation of repeated assessments of achievement at reasonable intervals, reflecting formal assessment of student progress during instruction, *which was provided to the child's parents*." (Emphasis added).

82. Frederick County Public Schools, Complaint 03-06-1153, 46 IDELR 230 (OCR, Eastern Division, Philadelphia)(Maryland)(August 31, 2006).

Chapter 9

The Protection of Pupil Rights Amendment

The Protection of Pupil Rights Amendment ("PPRA") was passed by Congress in 1978, and is commonly known as the "Hatch Amendment." The PPRA, while a federal law separate from FERPA, is codified proximately to FERPA in the federal education code, and directly addresses a number of the same topics, including providing parents certain inspection, notice, and consent rights in connection with particular activities in the school setting. The PPRA also places a number of limitations on surveys, analyses, or evaluations funded by the federal Department of Education, as well as surveys, analyses, or evaluations created by third parties but administered or distributed by the school.

Under the PPRA, the District must obtain prior written parental consent before undertaking certain types of student evaluations—specifically, (1) those funded in whole or in part by the United States Department of Education and (2) asking for what might ordinarily be considered "personal" information in eight specific areas (such as political affiliation, religious beliefs, sexual behavior, or attitudes discussed further below)—hereafter referred to as "protected information surveys." Although educators may be less familiar with PPRA than FERPA, issues typically arising under the PPRA touch upon the very core of societal notions of the rights of parents to control their children's upbringing and education—matters invariably and ultimately resolved by the federal court system.[1]

OVERVIEW, BASIC CONCEPTS, AND DEFINITIONS

What is the Protection of Pupil Rights Amendment?

The Protection of Pupil Rights Amendment is a federal law, closely related to FERPA, giving parents the right to inspect certain instructional materials, as well as requiring parental consent before the administration of any survey, analysis, or evaluation funded in whole or in part by the United States Department of Education that would require the students to reveal certain information about the student or the student's family.[2] In the case of surveys which are not funded by the Department of Education, but which also solicit personal information about students or their families, the PPRA requires that parents be notified and given the opportunity to opt their children out of the survey.

What is the purpose of PPRA?

The purpose of PPRA is to prevent schools from asking students for information of a personal nature without the prior notice or consent of the student's parents. The PPRA protects these interests in two (2) ways. First, a school receiving federal education funds must afford parents the opportunity to review certain surveys or instructional materials *used in connection* with surveys or evaluations—should the parents choose to do so. Second—and far more limiting—if the school is conducting an evaluation or survey funded in whole or part by federal education funds and the survey asks about certain types of information (listed below), schools must first request and receive prior written consent from parents.

INSTRUCTIONAL MATERIALS

What kinds of instructional materials do parents have the right to inspect under the PPRA?

The definition of "instructional" materials is very broad, and includes "teacher's manuals, films, tapes, or other supplementary materials which will be used in connection with any survey, analysis, or evaluation." The definition specifically includes "instructional content that is provided to a student, regardless of its format, including printer or representational materials, audio-visual materials, and materials in electronic or digital format."[3]

Does this mean a parent has a right to inspect all instructional materials, or that this right is limited to materials used in connection with surveys, analyses, or evaluations?

The right to inspect instructional materials extends to any such material which is to be used as a part of the educational curriculum, and is much broader than those specific categories of personal information which, when the subject of a survey, analysis, or evaluation, require either parental consent or notice. The language used by the Department in its model PPRA notification to parents expressly suggests schools notify parents of their right to inspect any "[i]nstructional materials used as part of the educational curriculum."[4]

Does the PPRA give parents the right to inspect teacher-prepared test?

No. The PPRA specifically excludes "academic tests or academic assessments" from the definition of instructional materials.[5]

Does the parental right to inspect materials used by the school include the right to copy such materials?

The PPRA itself contains no such right to obtain a copy of the materials, only permitting (in these circumstances) a parental right of inspection. While the lack of an express right to copy these documents under PPRA should, in most events, resolve the issue in the institution's favor, parents might attempt to avail themselves of other laws to access these materials, including:

(1) Parents may seek to apply FERPA's provision allowing for copies in the relatively narrow instance that a parent's right of meaningful inspection would be frustrated in the absence of copies (see Chapter III), and/or
(2) State "Sunshine" or open records laws may apply to some of the materials to be inspected and sometimes do include an affirmative right to obtain copies.[6]

Does the PPRA require schools to obtain parental consent before using instructional materials which parents or students may find objectionable on a political or religious basis?

No. The PPRA only grants parents the right to inspect such materials. Moreover, parents who attempt to use PPRA to require schools to obtain prior parental consent appear to be acting *directly contrary* to PPRA's purposes. In enacting regulations for PPRA, the Department of Education specifically noted: "It is not the purpose of [PPRA] to resolve complaints which are focused on academic subject areas selected by the school district."[7]

Does the PPRA apply to the teaching of evolution?

Under the PPRA, parents have the basic right to inspect the instructional materials used in or in connection with the science curriculum. However, as noted elsewhere, the PPRA is not intended to resolve disputes between parents and schools over academic subject areas selected by the school. Theoretically, PPRA consent requirements might apply to very specific, limited activities associated with the teaching of evolution. For example, a survey of students who agree or disagree with the theory of evolution may arguably elicit information about the religious beliefs of some students and therefore be covered by PPRA. If the survey were funded by the Department of Education, then parental consent would be required before student participation in this particular activity. We suspect, however, that the vast majority of educators who instruct students in some or all aspects of evolutionary theory do so (or can do so) without finding it necessary to solicit the personal, religious beliefs of students.

Does the PPRA limit or govern a school's instruction on matters such as diversity and tolerance of other religious or cultural groups? What about sexual education programs, including birth control, family planning, or homosexuality?

The answer depends on what is intended by the term "instruction." If "instruction" includes the administration of a survey funded in whole or part by the United States Department of Education and the survey inquires as to—for example—a student's family's position on homosexuality or religious affiliation, then PPRA would require prior parent consent. If, however, no federally-funded survey was administered, then PPRA should not affect instruction other than the right of parents to inspect the instructional materials themselves.

What should an educator do if he or she receives a form letter declaring that the school does not have permission to subject the student to any educational activities involving areas covered under the PPRA?

First, it is important to identify the educational activities which are actually planned or to be implemented. As stated above, the PPRA does not give parents any general right to exempt their child from educational lessons or activities due to the parent (or child's) political, religious, or philosophical disagreement with those materials. However, if the upcoming classroom activities do involve a "survey, analysis, or evaluation," then the parental consent requirements of the PPRA *may* be implicated. In order to determine whether the PPRA actually applies in this instance, the school will have to make a determination as to whether the "survey, analysis, or evaluation" falls within the scope mandatory survey consent subjects of PPRA, and—importantly—whether the instructional activity is related to a federally-funded survey or evaluation.

Does PPRA give parents any right to object to or block the use of instructional materials they may find objectionable?

No. The PPRA only conveys upon parents the right to inspect such materials. Presumably, parents who have concerns about such materials after inspecting them may seek to participate in the state or local governance processes of the school district to influence these curricular decisions.

An Example—Parents in County School District protest the decision of County High School to include several literary texts from ancient Greece and Rome addressing sexuality and homosexuality. The parents believe these are unsuitable for immature students and file a complaint under PPRA. They are informed that because the teaching was not in conjunction with the administration of a survey or evaluation, they have no case under the PPRA. Instead, they pursue a political route by filing a complaint with the local Board of Education. After some consideration, the board agrees that the particular texts at issue are too explicit for many of the students, and agrees to remove them from the curriculum. When other parents file suit claiming that the board "censored" the texts, the court determines that making these types of curricular determinations are within the authority of the school board. [8]

Does the parental right to inspect materials under the PPRA apply to materials in a school library or media center?

To the extent that such materials are included *as part of the educational curriculum,* parents would have the right to *inspect* these items. However, many items in the typical school library may be of educational value—but not necessarily specifically adopted as a part of the educational curriculum—and therefore are not strictly subject to "inspection" rights under PPRA.[9]

Sidebar. However, we caution that even if the PPRA does not specifically convey a right to parents to instruct certain materials in the school library, it may be problematic for a school to take and defend the position that school library holdings, purchased with public tax dollars and widely available to the student body, are somehow secret or confidential as to the parents of the students in the school. Furthermore, school district policy may even encourage (and State "Sunshine" laws may entitle) parents to inspect and make recommendations regarding school library holdings.

SURVEYS, EVALUATIONS, AND ANALYSES

What is a survey for purposes of the PPRA?

The definition of a survey under the PPRA is rather limited, stating only that "the term survey includes an evaluation."[10] While the PPRA states that it is inapplicable to "physical exams or screenings" administered in accordance with IDEA, the Department of Education has also stated that the PPRA is inapplicable to any survey administered to a student in accordance with the Individuals with Disabilities Education Act.[11]

What are the definitions of analysis and evaluation?

Unfortunately, the PPRA does not contain a definition of either term. The precise scope of both of these terms is further confused by the subsequent definition of "survey" to include an evaluation—if the evaluation was already included within the concept of a survey, one must wonder what purpose Congress intended by separately including this term in the list of covered activities under section (b). There is no discussion in the statute of any definition of the term "analysis."

For what surveys or evaluations is prior written parental consent required?

The PPRA does not require schools to obtain prior written consent before administration of all surveys to students. Rather, PPRA's requirements for prior parental consent (as opposed to parental opt out rights in connection with third party surveys) apply solely to the administration of surveys, analyses, or evaluations that are funded by the United States Department of Education, *and* which address any one of the following eight types of protected information:

(1) Inquire as to the political affiliations or beliefs of the student or student's parents;
(2) Inquire as to mental or psychological problems of the student or student's family;
(3) Inquire as to the student's behaviors or attitudes about sex;
(4) Illegal, anti-social, self-incriminating, or demeaning behavior;
(5) Request the student conduct "critical appraisals" of others with whom the student has a close family relationship;
(6) Inquire about legally recognized "privileged" relationship, such as that between an attorney and his client, a doctor and her patient, or a minister and her parishioner.
(7) Inquire about religious practices, affiliations, or beliefs of the student or his or her parents; and
(8) Inquire about family or student income, save to the extent required by law to determine program eligibility.[12]

Does the PPRA require parental consent before a student meets with a school counselor to discuss matters which may fall within any of the protected areas discussed above?

Generally, no. The PPRA is concerned with a survey, analysis, or evaluation which has the "primary purpose" of revealing such protected information. Further, even though the definitions of survey, analysis, and evaluation contained in PPRA are not especially helpful, we do not believe they can reasonably be interpreted to include the oral, voluntary exchange and discussion of information initiated by the student. Of course, if during the course of meeting with an individual student, a counselor determines that it would be useful to administer a particular federally funded survey, analysis, or evaluation instrument for the primary purpose of gathering information in an area falling within one or more protected categories, then the appropriate PPRA consent requirements would apply.[13]

Which surveys, analyses, and evaluations specifically require prior consent before administration under PPRA?

As noted above, the PPRA requires that any survey, analysis, or evaluation which reveals information concerning (1) the political beliefs or affiliations of the student or their parent; (2) psychological or mental problems of the student or their family; (3) sex attitudes or behavior; (4) demeaning, self-incriminating, anti-social, or illegal behavior; (5) critical appraisals of other individuals with whom respondents have close family relationships; (6) legal recognized privileges or analogous relationships, such as those of ministers, physicians or lawyers; (7) religious beliefs, affiliations or practices of the student or their parents; or (8) income (except as may be required to determine program eligibility or financial assistance) shall not be required without the prior consent of the student or their parents.

Are psychological examinations or questions included, such as a school psychologist asking students about sexual behaviors as part of a federally-funded survey?

Yes. The PPRA provides that "no student shall be required to submit without prior consent to psychiatric examination, testing, or treatment, or psychological examination, testing, or treatment, in which the primary purpose is to reveal information concerning" any of the covered areas listed above.[14]

Who is required to give consent prior to the administration of any federally funded survey, analysis, or evaluation inquiring about subjects addressed under PPRA?

When the PPRA requires consent, consent must be provided by the parent or the student, if the student is an adult or an emancipated minor.[15] Interestingly, parental consent on behalf of a minor student must be in writing, while consent on the part of the emancipated minor or adult student is not specifically required to be given in written form. Of course, obtaining such consent in writing should greatly diminish the likelihood of a question about the existence of consent at any future point, and it is recommended that the school at the least document the receipt of consent, and preferred that the consent be in writing itself.

Who is considered a parent for purposes of the PPRA?

A parent is defined as "a legal guardian or other person standing in loco parentis (such as a grandparent or stepparent with whom the child lives, or a person who is legally responsible for the welfare of the child)."[16]

Is there a difference between the definition of a parent for purposes of FERPA and for purposes of the PPRA?

While the definition of parent under FERPA certainly includes the legal guardian or person standing *in loco parentis* to the child (as well the natural parents, of course), there is also a requirement under FERPA that individuals other than parents or guardians must specifically be acting "in the absence of a parent or guardian." This limiting condition is not present in the PPRA parent definition, and consequently the class of individuals who may qualify as parents under the PPRA may be larger and broader than under FERPA.

What would be an example of an individual who would be a parent under the PPRA, but who might not be a parent for purposes of FERPA?

Under the PPRA, a grandparent living in the household with one natural parent and the child could qualify as a parent under the PPRA, but since this individual (the grandparent) is not acting "in the absence of a parent or guardian," (the parent in this example is distinctly present) they would not typically qualify as a parent under FERPA. Of course, the natural parent in such cases can and often does consent to the grandparent's access to educational records of the child.

What type of evidence is relevant in determining whether a survey, analysis, or evaluation is truly voluntary?

In one disputed case, the court looked at evidence as to the actual administration of a survey on the particular day, including the testimony of students as to the instructions they received from their teachers, announcements given over the loudspeakers, the completion rate of the surveys, the absence of any consent forms or opt-out instructions to parents, and the setting in which the survey was administered (during a class period when students were required to remain at their desks throughout) in finding that the entire administration of the survey so much resembled the administration of mandatory, standardized tests as to support a conclusion that the survey "as administered" was involuntary.[17] The sheer numbers of individuals who may be involved in the administration of a school-wide survey make it especially important that schools comprehensively train all involved staff and document those facts supporting the conclusion that the test was truly voluntary on the part of the students.

Did No Child Left Behind Act expand parental rights under the PPRA in any way?

Yes. The Tiarht Amendment to NCLB specifically amended the original PPRA to expand the category of surveys requiring prior parental consent or notification to include surveys, analyses, or evaluations revealing information about the "religious practices, affiliations, or beliefs of a student or student's parents."[18] Additionally, NCLB expanded PPRA's coverage to include surveys created by third parties (any party other than the Department of Education), as well as conveyed additional rights upon parents in connection with physical examinations or screenings administered by a school and the collection of personal information from students for purposes of marketing or resale of that information. In respect to each of these three areas, the Amendment requires institutions to develop policies in consultation with parents.[19]

Did NCLB make any other changes to the original limitations on Department of Education funded surveys, analyses, or evaluations?

Yes. NCLB added a reference to the political "beliefs of the student or the student's parent" to the list of limitations included above, and deleted a prior reference to "potentially embarrassing" as a part of the limitation as to mental and psychological problems of the student or the student's family.[20]

Does the PPRA apply only to those surveys, analyses, and evaluations that are funded by the federal Department of Education?

Prior to NCLB, the answer to this question was generally yes. However, another aspect of the Tiarht Amendment was to create a parental notice requirement that extends the PPRA to all surveys (even those created by non-Department of Education funded parties, hereafter referred to as third party surveys) covering any of the eight substantive areas listed above and which are conducted by a local educational agency that receives any federal funds.[21] Thus, this provision effectively extends the PPRA to all covered surveys conducted by any public elementary and secondary schools.

Is there any difference between the original coverage of the PPRA, and the expanded coverage of NCLB as related to surveys, analyses, and evaluations?

Absolutely. The original PPRA section (b) limitations applied (and continue to apply) to all federally funded surveys, analyses, and evaluations, while the PPRA amendments contained in NCLB apply only to "third party surveys." Moreover, while NCLB requires that parents be notified of covered surveys, and that parents (and adult or emancipated students) be given notice and the opportunity annually to opt out of participation in all such surveys, NCLB does not require prior consent as is the case in all surveys, analyses, or evaluations under section (b) of the PPRA.

Does PPRA give parents the right to inspect their child's responses to any such surveys?

No. The PPRA itself does not specifically convey any such right, nor does it require the school to maintain survey responses in a manner traceable to the individual student. Of course, most surveys seek student data only in aggregate form. It is often the case that the structure of the survey instrument itself will require anonymity. However, in the unlikely event that the school did maintain individually identifiable student responses to such surveys, we recognize there is certainly a reasonable argument that these response records are educational records subject to a parent's right of access under FERPA.

Under PPRA, do parents have the right to inspect any third party survey prior to its administration, or only those surveys that solicit information under any of the eight covered areas under the PPRA?

The PPRA's right to *inspect* third party surveys (as opposed to opting their child out of participation) is not statutorily limited to only those surveys which cover one of the eight types of protected information addressed above.[22] Consequently, there is a reasonable interpretation of the Act that parental inspection rights as to third party surveys are more expansive than either the specific consent or opt-out provisions discussed previously, and is more analogous to the rights of parents under the Act to inspect any instructional materials.

What about the right to "opt out" of surveys—does this extend to all third party surveys regardless of the subject-matter or topic, or is this limited to surveys soliciting only "protected information"?

In contrast with a parents right to inspect any third party survey, the PPRA's "opt out" rights are specifically limited to those third party surveys seeking protected information (the eight categories of information listed above). In reference to surveys seeking protected student information, recall that any such Department-funded survey requires specific consent, rather than merely the opportunity to opt out.

Does the Tiarht Amendment require parental consent prior to the administration of third party surveys of adolescent sexual behavior, or drug/alcohol use?

In the case of a third party survey, the Tiarht Amendment requires that parents be notified and given the opportunity to opt their children out of any such survey, but not that parents provide specific, individualized consent to each such survey. In this situation, the failure of a parent to opt their child out of the proposed survey after being given notice and the opportunity to do so takes place in lieu of a particular requirement that the parent affirmatively provide consent. As a general rule, however, a State or LEA could always choose not to conduct any covered surveys unless parents have specifically consented to their child's participation.

Practice Pointer—While this can certainly be confusing, it is important to remember the distinction between federally funded surveys and third party surveys—if the survey described above was funded by the U.S. Department of Education, parental consent (as opposed to notice and the opportunity to opt out) would be required.

So what exactly does the Tiarht Amendment require the District to do in connection with third party surveys, analyses, or evaluations?

The Tiarht Amendment requires that parents be notified annually at the beginning of the school year of the approximate dates during the year when any covered survey may be administered, allow parents the right to inspect the survey prior to its administration, require the District to arrange to protect the privacy of students in connection with the survey, and give parents the right to choose to opt their child out of the survey.

An Example—City High School's student handbook provides notice of only the following information in respect to possible student surveys (none of which are federally funded, for purposes of this analysis):

> Occasionally, the School administers needs assessments, Youth Risk Behavior Surveys, PRIDE, and locally developed instruments to determine attitudes and practices regarding substance abuse. Copies of these surveys are on file and may be viewed upon request. If you do not wish your child to participate in these activities, please contact Ms. Jones (the counselor), no later than September 1st.

If the school provides no further information or opportunity to "opt out" to, this is probably insufficient under PPRA. For instance, this notice does not give parents any idea as to when the assessments or surveys may be administered during the year (the law requires such notice to include "the specific or approximate dates during the school year when activities . . . are scheduled, or expected to be scheduled"), nor does this notice provide specific contact information regarding Ms. Jones. [23]

Other than the PPRA, do parents have a fundamental right to "protect" their children from administration of surveys (or analyses/evaluations) which may ask their children about sensitive subjects such as sexual attitudes, thoughts about suicide, etc?

Courts that have addressed this issue have tended to find that once parents enroll their children in public school, they do not have a fundamental federal right to prohibit the introduction of controversial ideas to students through the administration of student surveys. In one case concerning a survey administered to elementary school students, the court held that "there is no fundamental right of parents to be the exclusive provider of information regarding sexual matters to their children."[24] Of course, this is a very controversial subject, and we recognize that some judges may disagree with the existing case law on this topic. In addition, some school administrators may choose to accommodate parental concerns in this area even though the current federal law does not require them to do so.

In the event a particular survey does not fall within the PPRA, are there any other sources of Federal law which may be relevant in the event that some parents express concern or complain about the survey instrument?

Depending upon the particular survey involved, it is always possible that another Constitutional interest may be implicated. Perhaps most importantly, the federal courts have recognized a constitutionally protected "zone of privacy" which can be involved, for example, when questioning students about their own sexual activities, drug or alcohol use, or relationships with their parents. However, federal privacy cases often involve a very factually specific balancing test, and consequently, it is always possible that an actual intrusion upon the privacy interests of the individual will be justified by the public interest.[25] In short, each contested case must be examined individually and with the assistance of counsel knowledgeable in this area of the law.

Sidebar. We recognize the foregoing may be confusing, especially to the non-lawyer audience. Briefly, there is a great deal of difference between a "fundamental right" on the part of parents to conclusively control their child's education in the public school setting, and the recognition of a privacy interest that is subject to balancing by the court in selected controversies between school and parents. For instance, the belief in a fundamental right in this area can involve a much wider array of educational issues than a legally recognized privacy interest. For example, objections to a social studies class which views the documentary "An Inconvenient Truth" by former Vice President Al Gore may be based in a parent's sense of a right to control the political information to which their children are exposed, and historically has not been well received by the courts. On the other hand, classroom activities in a middle school health course which require students to disclose information about their personal sexual experiences are more likely to at least implicate legally recognized privacy concerns, which may then be subject to a balancing test as against the teacher or school's articulated reason for conducting the activity in the first instance.

Can parents choose to opt their children out of only individually selected, covered surveys included in the District's annual notice, or must they choose to remove their child from all covered activities?

The language of the PPRA states that parents must be offered an opportunity "to opt the student out of participation in *an* activity" (emphasis added) covered by the Tiarht Amendment, which we believe best supports the interpretation that parents may not be required to make an all or nothing selection in reference to the opt-out provision.[26] We would further caution school officials to at least carefully consider the parental perception or reaction to a more aggressive, all or nothing approach, in that such a position taken by the school may be perceived as punitive or inflexible. Even though the Act is styled the protection of "Pupil" rights amendment, in reality the Act is very much a parental rights law.

Does the PPRA contain any specific requirements for local policies developed regarding third party surveys?

Yes. The PPRA requires local school districts to develop policies governing the administration of third-party surveys. These policies must be developed in consultation with parents and must address the right of parents to inspect third party surveys prior to their administration (within a reasonable period of time after a request to do so), and protect student privacy in connection with third party surveys that cover any one of the eight (8) types of protected information surveys addressed in the PPRA.

MARKETING ISSUES AND STUDENT INFORMATION

What does the PPRA require in terms of a school district's policy regarding personal information collected from students and used for purposes of marketing or resale?

The PPRA requires that the District "develop and adopt policies, in consultation with parents" that address the collection, disclosure or use of personal information collected from students, make arrangements to protect student privacy, and permit parents to inspect any instrument used to collect this information before the instrument is distributed or administered.[27]

Practice Pointer—The PPRA does not require the District to develop such new policies if either the State or the LEA already had policies in place on January 2, 2002 that satisfied this requirement. In this event, the District must "provide reasonable notice to parents and guardians of students" of these policies. In fact, this procedural safe harbor applies to all the local policy requirements under the PPRA, including the use of third party surveys, parental inspection of instructional material and the administration of physical examinations or screenings.[28]

What is considered personal information about a student under PPRA?

The PPRA states that personal information "means individually identifiable information including a student or parent's first and last name, home or other physical address, telephone number, or social security number."[29] Interestingly, the definition of personal information under the PPRA is not identical to the concept of personally identifiable information under FERPA. To the extent that the PPRA authorizes the collection of information about students for marketing purposes, there is no authorization under the PPRA to collect personally identifiable information under FERPA (subject to the curious case of social security numbers discussed below).

Are there any exceptions to these limitations on the use of student information for marketing purposes under PPRA?

Yes. The restrictions on the gathering and release of information for marketing purposes do not apply to the following activities:

- College, post-secondary education, or military recruitment
- Book clubs, magazines, and low-cost literacy products
- Curriculum and instructional materials used by elementary and secondary schools
- Certain tests and assessments used by elementary and secondary schools
- Sale by students of services and products for education or school-related, fundraising activities, and
- Student recognition programs.[30]

An Example—Coach Carl is the only male educator at City Elementary School, and Carl decides that it would be a good idea for the students to see him as more than "just a coach." Carl decides to start and lead a Junior Great Books Club at the school, and as part of his efforts to publicize the club, Carl requests that the school provide him with the mailing address of all students at the school so he can send them a brochure advertising the book club. Since the activity for which Carl requests this information falls within one of the exceptions to the rules (notice to parents and the opportunity to opt out of participation), the school is not limited by the PPRA when responding to Carl's request. This means the school's policy governing the use of personal information for marketing purposes does not apply, and that parents do not have a PPRA right to inspect the "mail out form" used to collect this information. Of course, we suspect in most instances the prudent school administrator would have no objection to sharing this form with any curious parent.

If the marketing information collected by the school overlaps with the information included within the school's directory information policy, may a parent opt out of the former when they opt out their child out of the directory information policy at the beginning of the year?

Yes, the Department has taken the position that so long as the "personal information" which is the subject of the commercial use is the same as, or included within, the District's definition and scope of directory information, the "school may meet PPRA notice requirements for specific marketing activities that involve only designated directory information by allowing parents to opt out of directory information at the beginning of each school year."[31] Of course, the District wishing to make use of this provision must be certain that the directory information policy does in fact include any and all information collected for commercial purposes.

Does the PPRA limit an institution's ability to disclose directory information under FERPA when requested by a commercial vendor for marketing or retail purposes?

This is an interesting question, and one to which the answer is not entirely clear. On the one hand, FERPA's directory information provisions permit (but do not require) an institution to disclose directory information. State Sunshine laws may or may not recognize any distinction based upon either the identity of the requesting party (news media as compared to a commercial vendor) or the purpose for which the information is requested (i.e. marketing purposes). However, the PPRA marketing limitations (which address only that personal information discussed above) are the most recent statutory expression of Congressional intent in this area, and the law does specifically address the "collection, disclosure, *or use* of personal information collected from students for the purpose of marketing or for selling that information *(or otherwise providing that information to others for that purpose)*." Arguably, providing personal information about students to other entities, including commercial vendors pursuant a State Sunshine law request and for marketing purposes, is covered by the PPRA even when the institution has not collected any information for this purpose and is only responding to a request for information already identified as directory.

Practice Pointer—As noted previously, PPRA requires that parents be given notice and the opportunity to opt out of such marketing activities. However, once a parent has been provided (and failed to avail themselves of) the opportunity to opt out of the school's directory information policy, neither the PPRA nor FERPA would require that parents be provided any further notice prior to a disclosure of such information required by State law.[32]

Does this mean that if the school notifies parents and gives them the opportunity to opt out of information collected for marketing purposes, and parents fail to opt out of this activity, that the school may sell a list of student Social Security Numbers to a commercial vendor?

While a literal reading of PPRA might support such a view, we strongly disagree with any such interpretation. The Department itself has stated that in reference to Social Security Numbers, the school may not rely on opt-out provisions to disclose such information, but must instead obtain specific consent.[33] Furthermore, the underlying purposes of both PPRA and FERPA are to protect student privacy and limit dissemination of personally identifiable information regarding students for educational purposes. Consequently, an interpretation of the PPRA which would permit the school to sell student social security numbers for marketing purposes (even after parents have been given the opportunity to opt out of any such procedure) is extremely suspect in our view. Since the school retains complete discretion as to whether a student's social security number could ever be designated for such a commercial purpose, we strongly suggest that any school seriously considering such a step seek competent legal advice. In general, we believe this practice should be avoided.

PHYSICAL EXAMINATIONS OF STUDENTS

What is a non-emergency, invasive physical examination for purposes of the PPRA?

The PPRA defines this as "any medical examination that involves the exposure of private body parts, or any act during such examination that includes incision, insertion, or injection into the body."[34] The implication of the use of the term "invasive" is important, as some kinds of medical examinations do not fall within the definition of "non-emergency, invasive physical examination" since they do not happen to require the exposure of private body parts or any "incision, insertion or injection" into the student's body.

An Example—On November 22–24, the City Health Department will administer swine (H1N1) flu shots (types A and B) to all children at City Elementary in grades 1–6. If you do not wish your child to participate in this activity, please notify Ms. Smith (contact phone, email, and address) by (deadline).[35] Since the flu shots are injected or inserted, this activity would generally fall within the PPRA definition of a non-emergency, invasive physical examination. Of course, it is also possible that the prevalence and severity of any particular flu strain might rise to the level of an emergency and thus outside the parameters of the PPRA.

Does the definition of non-emergency, invasive physical examinations include routine screenings provided by schools, such as for student vision, hearing, or scoliosis?

No, the statutory definition of the term "non-emergency, invasive physical examination" specifically excludes "hearing, vision, or scoliosis screening."[36]

Are all non-emergency, invasive physical examinations or screenings covered by the PPRA?

No, only those examinations or screenings that are (1) required as a condition of attendance, (2) scheduled by the school in advance and administered by the school, and (3) unnecessary to protect the immediate health or safety of the student or of other students.[37] Again it is important to note how the language of the statute further narrows the actual number and type of examinations or screenings which are subject to the PPRA's requirements.

An Example—County High School requires that any student who wishes to play football receive a basic medical checkup and clearance from the County Health Department or their family doctor. Last season, a young offensive lineman playing for City Schools suffered heart failure on the 1st day of practice. As a result, County High School instituted the additional requirement that any students who wish to play football must also to be screened for abnormal heart conditions. Since these medical examinations and screenings are not a required condition of school attendance, but only related to participation in an elective, extra-curricular activity, the PPRA does not apply to these procedures.

In the event an examination or screening is covered by the PPRA, what does the PPRA require the school to do?

The PPRA requires that parents (or eligible students) be notified and afforded the opportunity to opt out of participation in the examination or screening. The PPRA itself does not require parental or student consent, though it is possible that State law or local policy may create or recognize such a requirement.

What if State law already permits certain examinations or screening without parental notification?

The PPRA specifically allows that neither the parental notice nor opt out provisions discussed above apply to "any physical examination or screening that is permitted or required by an applicable State law, including physical examinations or screenings that are permitted without parental notification."[38] Notably, this provision is not simply a "grandfather" clause exempting a State law requirement already in existence at the time the PPRA was enacted—this provision would recognize an exception under the Act in the case of any subsequently ratified State law.

Would the PPRA apply if a District decided to administer a medical screening that is not specifically authorized by State law, but is required under a local board policy?

Yes, the PPRA notice and opt out provisions would apply, since the exception for physical or examinations or screenings is specifically based on State law, as opposed to a District policy or decision. However, if a screening were administered by a City or County Health Department, this would arguably fall outside the scope of the PPRA since the District itself would not be administering the examination.[39] Of course, school officials should be sensitive to any perception that they are intentionally misleading or withholding information from parents by an interpretation of the Act which may well appear to be technical or self-serving.

Is a mental health examination or screening considered a "physical examination or screening"?

This point is unclear. The current statutory language of the Amendment does not specifically cover mental health evaluations, though there is language excluding surveys (and by extension, evaluations) administered under I.D.E.A. Additionally, the federal regulations still include "psychiatric examination" and "psychological examination" as among the activities which may only be undertaken with prior parental consent when they are federally funded, not directly related to academic instruction, and designed to elicit certain information about attitudes, habits, traits, opinions, or feelings.[40] Although the federal rules in this area are outdated and not entirely consistent, a cautious approach to legal compliance on this point would suggest obtaining parental consent prior to administration of such mental health examinations, regardless of the funding source. This approach may also constitute best practice in terms of building and/or maintaining healthy school-parent relationships.

What is the definition of a psychiatric or psychological examination or test for purposes of the PPRA?

In the regulations, this is defined as "a method of obtaining information, including a group activity, that is not directly related to academic instruction and that is designed to elicit information about attitudes, habits, traits, opinions, or feelings."[41]

What is the definition of psychiatric or psychological treatment under the PPRA?

This is defined as "an activity involving the planned, systematic use of methods or techniques that are not directly related to academic instruction and that is designed to affect behavioral, emotional, or attitudinal characteristics of an individual or group."[42]

Do the PPRA regulations address all federally funded psychiatric or psychological examinations or treatments?

No. The PPRA regulations (which again have not been updated) address only those psychiatric or psychological examinations or treatments which are not related to academic instruction and in which the primary purpose is to reveal information concerning one or more of the following:

- Political affiliations;
- Mental and psychological problems potentially embarrassing to the student or his or her family;

- Sex behavior and attitudes;
- Illegal, anti-social, self-incriminating, and demeaning behavior;
- Critical appraisals of other individuals with whom the student has close family relationships;
- Legally recognized privileged and analogous relationships, such as those of lawyers, physicians, and ministers; or
- Income, other than that required by law to determine eligibility for participation in a program or for receiving financial assistance under a program.[43]

Again, however, we suggest that the School or District carefully consider whether State law, local policy, or best practice suggest or require that parental consent be obtained prior to the administration of any psychiatric or psychological examinations or treatments of students.

If a District is considering adoption of a random drug testing policy for student athletes, or for students who engage in any extracurricular activities, does the PPRA apply?

The PPRA should not apply in this instance for at least two reasons. First, these drug tests are not required as a condition of attendance in school but only as a condition of participation in elective, extra-curricular activities. However, the issue might be decided differently in the case of a school which has implemented a mandatory, random drug testing policy for all students enrolled at the high school or middle school grade level.[44] The second reason we doubt the PPRA would apply to student drug testing is that while there are a variety of drug testing methodologies available, most would probably not qualify as an invasive physical examination under the PPRA.[45] Recall that part of the definition of an invasive physical examination was "any medical examination that involves the exposure of private body parts." Even if one concedes that a urinalysis is a medical examination (a point which we believe is debatable), almost all public school districts that have implemented such testing measures have used "unviewed" sample collection that does not involve the exposure of private body parts.

Practice Pointer—A related question sometimes arises concerning the confidentiality (or not) of the results of random student drug tests. In general, the rules relating to permissible or mandatory disclosure of random student drug testing results are established in the policy or program governing the administration of the drug tests themselves. To the extent that the District anticipates instances in which it may wish to retain the discretion to disclose results, or anticipates a conflict with State laws arguably requiring the reporting of test results in certain instances, we strongly suggest the District work with an attorney familiar with the laws of the State to create a random testing program that will incorporate parental agreement and consent into the desired/required scheme for the disclosure of test results.

Does the PPRA require that a school's policy address medical examinations or screenings?

Yes. The PPRA requires that the school policy address the administration of physical examinations or screenings the school may administer to a student. This is in addition to the Act's requirements that the District's PPRA policy address the following five, additional areas:

- The right of parents to inspect third party surveys generally;
- Arrangements to protect the privacy of students in connection with any survey of covered, personal information;
- Parental right to inspect instructional materials which are a part of the curriculum;
- The collection, use, or disclosure of personal information for marketing purposes;
- The right to inspect any instrument used in connection with collecting student personal information for marketing purposes.[46]

When must a school notify parents of its PPRA policy?

PPRA requires that parents be notified "at least annually, at the beginning of the school year, and within a reasonable period of time after any substantive change in such policies."[47]

Are there certain specific events about which Districts must provide parents additional notice under the PPRA?

Yes, the PPRA requires that the District notify parents "of the specific or approximate dates during the school year" whenever activities "involving (1) the collection, disclosure, or use of personal information collected from students for the purpose of marketing or selling that information" are scheduled or expected to occur, (2) whenever any survey containing any of the items listed above is administered, and (3) of certain non-emergency, invasive physical examinations or screening.[48] Notice of any of these three specific, triggering events could be provided in connection with the annual PPRA policy notice, if the District is in fact able to specify the approximate date on which any of these three events is scheduled to take place.

An Example—The school includes a copy of its PPRA policy in the student handbook and on the school Web site. At the time the handbook is prepared for printing (often in May or June prior to the beginning of school), the school is not aware of any dates on which one of the three specific, trigging events may be scheduled to occur. After the beginning of school, the counseling department receives notice from the Central Office that an evaluation of student attitudes toward premarital sex will be conducted in light of the soaring teenage pregnancy rate in the District. The school sends written notice home with each student to be surveyed and posts updated information about the specific covered event on the school Web site.

FILING A COMPLAINT UNDER THE PPRA

If a parent believes the school has violated their rights under the PPRA, what is the process for filing and resolving such a complaint?

As under FERPA itself, a parent who believes that the School has violated their rights under the PPRA may file a complaint with the Family Policy Compliance Office. The Complaint should contain "specific allegations of a fact giving reasonable cause to believe" a violation has occurred, include "evidence of attempted resolution of the complaint at the local level (and at the State level if a State complaint resolution process exists), including the names of local and State officials contacted and significant dates in the attempted resolution process."[49]

Who may file a complaint alleging a violation of the PPRA?

According to the Department, "only a student or parent or guardian of a student directly affected by a violation . . . may file a complaint."[50] This provision was specifically added to the regulations in 1984 in response to the concerns expressed by some school officials that interest groups might file frivolous complaints under the PPRA in an effort to challenge local curricula decisions.

If the Department finds a District in violation of the PPRA, what are the penalties the Department may enforce?

As under FERPA, the Department may terminate certain federal funding. However, the funding subject to termination is limited to funds issued under specific provisions of the federal rules.[51]

ENDNOTES

1. Seminal cases dealing with this amalgam of issues include *Meyer v. Nebraska*, 262 U.S. 390, 43 S.Ct. 625, 67 L.Ed. 1042 (1923); *Pierce v. Society of Sisters*, 268 U.S. 510, 45 S.Ct. 571, 69 L.Ed. 1070 (1925) and *Wisconsin v. Yoder*, 406 U.S. 205, 92 S.Ct. 1526, 32 L.Ed.2d 15 (1972).
2. 20 U.S.C. 1232(h)(a) & (b).
3. 20 U.S.C. 1232(h)(c)(6)(A). The Grassley Amendment removed the requirement that such instructional materials be intended for use in connection with a research or experimentation program.

4. United States Department of Education "Model Notification of Rights" (2004), downloaded from http://www.ed.gov/policy/gen/guid/fpco/ppra/modelnotification .html on December 21, 2008.

5. Id.

6. Further support for the view that the PPRA itself does include a general right to obtain copies of instructional materials can be found in the Department's comments to proposed revisions to the regulation. See Federal Register Vol. 60 No. 166 44695 (August 28, 1995).

7. Federal Register Vol. 49 No. 174 35319 (September 6, 1984).

8. *Virgil v. School Board of Columbia County*, 862 F.2d 1517 (11th Cir. 1989).

9. Parents and schools involved in disputes about the appropriate nature of school library materials should consult the Supreme Court's decision in *Island Trees v. Pico* 457 U.S. 853 (1982)(Supreme Court limits the authority of local school boards to remove library materials), as well the progeny of this seminal case.

10. 20 U.S.C. 1232(h)(c)(6)(G).

11. 20 U.S.C. 1232(h)(c)(5)(A)(ii); See also "Recent Changes Affecting FERPA & PPRA" (April 2002), retrieved from www.ed.gov/policy/gen/guid/fpco/hottopics/ ht10-28-02.html on May 21, 2008.

12. 20 U.S.C. 1232(h)(b); 34 C.F.R. § 99.8.

13. We also note that the issue of parental notice or consent in connection with students who meet with counselors provided by the school, especially to address personal or family issues, may also be governed by State law, local policy, or practice.

14. 34 C.F.R. § 98.4(a). It is important to be aware that the PPRA regulations have not been updated to reflect recent statutory changes to the Amendment.

15. 20 U.S.C. 1232(b). It is interesting to note that the PPRA recognizes the authority of emancipated minors to provide legal consent, while FERPA generally does not recognize the concept of the emancipated minor for purposes of transferring FERPA rights. One justification for this may well be that while parental consent under FERPA is a sufficient basis to disclose personally identifiable information to third parties, the PPRA for the most part (with one notable exception related to marketing surveys) does not involve the disclosure of individual student information to parties outside the school setting. Consequently, the perception of risk associated with the decision of the emancipated minor may well be less under the PPRA than under FERPA.

16. 20 U.S.C. 1232(h)(c)(6)(D).

17. *C.N. v. Ridgewood Board of Education,* 430 F.3d 159 (3rd. Cir. 2005). In *Ridgewood*, there is a noticeable 'concern' on the part of the court that school officials were in fact very much interested in fostering the maximum amount of student participation they could possibly achieve (the survey completion rate, for instance, was 100 percent) so that the identification of individual instances in which the voluntariness of the survey was addressed seemed to be treated as almost perfunctory by the court.

18. 20 U.S.C. 1232(h)(b)(7).

19. 20 U.S.C. 1232(h)(c)(1).

20. 20 U.S.C. 1232(h)(b).

21. 20 U.S.C. 1232(h)(c).
22. 20 U.S.C. 1232(h)(c)(1)(A)(i)
23. 20 U.S.C. 1232(h)(c)(2)(B).
24. *Fields v. Palmdale School District*, 427 F.3d 1197 (9th Cir. 2005). As a general rule, however, we would caution school officials to be make comprehensive efforts to ensure that parents are truly placed on notice prior to the administration of surveys concerning the sexual behavior of elementary age students, and thereby to the extent possible permit the potential plaintiffs to either decline to provide their consent or opt their children out of any such survey (depending upon whether the survey is federally funded or not), thereby decreasing the risk of legal action.
25. See again *C.N. v. Ridgewood Board of Education*, *supra*; *United States v. Westinghouse Electric Corp*. 638 F.2d 570 (3rd 1980); *Whalen v. Roe*, 429 U.S. 589, 97 S.Ct. 869, 51 L.Ed.2d 64 (1977). In addition, State law may recognize privacy interests which encompass surveys, analyses, or evaluations not specifically addressed under the PPRA.
26. 20 U.S.C. 1232(h)(c)(2)(A)(ii). This view is also consistent with the Department's position under FERPA that parents may opt out of some or part of the list of directory information designated by the District.
27. 20 U.S.C. 1232(h)(c)(1); (c)(1)(E) &)(c)(F)(i).
28. 20 U.S.C. 1232(h)(c)(3).
29. 20 U.S.C. 1232(h)(c)(6)(E). Interestingly, the statute here does not include expansive language such as "including but not limited to," or "similar to" when setting forth the list of personal information under the PPRA. Therefore, we do not believe the LEA has discretion to "collect, disclose or use" additional information for marketing purposes beyond that specifically listed in the statute.
30. 20 U.S.C. 1232(h)(c)(4).
31. See PPRA Model Notice and Consent/Opt-Out for Specific Activities "Note to Schools" retrieved from www.ed.gov/policy/gen/guid/fpco/hottopics/ht10-28-02.html on May 21, 2008.
32. See PPRA Model Notice and Consent/Opt-Out for Specific Activities "Note to Schools" retrieved from www.ed.gov/policy/gen/guid/fpco/hottopics/ht10-28-02.html on May 21, 2008, especially the Note on page 2.
33. Initially, we struggle mightily to understand the policy rationale for a District to collect social security numbers for marketing purposes, and would generally counsel against any such practice. Any yet inexplicably, the Department's Model Notice and Consent/Opt Out includes an example of precisely this, though the Department does caution that specific parent consent should be obtained. We do not believe it is clearly established that parental consent to the disclosure of a minor's social security number entirely absolves the District from responsibility and/or liability in the event that information is subsequently misused, particularly when the District received a financial benefit in exchange for this disclosure. In short, just a darn bad idea all around.
34. 20 U.S.C. 1232(h)(c)(6)(b).
35. Adapted from the Department's PPRA Model Notice and Consent/Opt Out for Specific Activities.

36. Id.

37. Id.

38. 20 U.S.C. 1232(h)(c)(4)(B)(ii).

39. In both 20 U.S.C. 1232(h)(c)(1)(D) and (c)(2)(C), the statute specifically refers only to examinations or screenings "that the school or agency may administer to a student" or that is "administered by the school and scheduled by the school in advance." Therefore, the plain language of the PPRA does not apply to examinations or screenings administered by other entities. Of course, we recognize that some courts may be sympathetic to the argument that any entity with which the school cooperates in this regard is acting as the agent of the school, and a question may arise as to whether such a non-school entity is subject to the same limitations.

40. 34 C.F.R. § 98.4)(a).

41. 34 C.F.R. § 98.4(c)(1).

42. 34 C.F.R. § 98.4(c)(2).

43. 34 C.F.R. § 98.4(a).

44. Few school districts have sought to require random drug testing as a condition of attendance at school for all students, and we have serious reservations of the Constitutionality of such an approach. One notable and unsuccessful attempt to do so occurred in the case of *Tannahill v. Lockney Independent School District*, 133 F.Supp.2d 919 (N.D. Tex. 2001).

45. The obvious exception to the later point would be the collection and testing for drugs by use of blood samples, but this is not a common practice even among the school districts which have adopted random student drug testing policies. Urinalysis testing is the much more common, and less invasive, method of drug testing among the student population, and increasingly schools are moving toward even less invasive methods of testing, such as saliva or hair sample testing.

46. 20 U.S.C. 1232(h)(c)(2)(A).

47. 20 U.S.C. 1232(h)(c)(2)(A)(i).

48. 20 U.S.C. 1232(h)(c)(2)(C)(iii).

49. 34 C.F.R. § 98.7.

50. Id.; Federal Register Vol. 49, No. 174 35320 (September 6, 1984).

51. 34 C.F.R. § 98.10. The funding which may be terminated or withheld is that pursuant to 34 C.F.R. §§ 78.21, 200.94(b), or 298.45(b).

Chapter 10

Self Audit

In this Chapter, we have attempted to pull together many of the most important and/or frequent compliance issues or concerns addressed previously in the book, and which we have also seen in our experience working primarily with public school districts. In some ways, the points raised below serve as a summary of the major issues addressed at greater length in one or more places above. While a review the points raised below is in no way a substitute for the information discussed previously, this chapter is intended to provide a roadmap to a school or school district official who is attempting to identify whether or not major compliance problems exist. In addition to a thorough knowledge of FERPA and IDEA, the true self audit of any individual agency or institution must also include a minimum reference to State Sunshine (Open Records) laws, individual privacy Acts, or case law within the State which may create expectations of confidentiality beyond FERPA, and State ethics rules for certificated educators in the P-12 setting. In the case of special education departments or records, State rules and regulations should also be consulted in addition to the opinions and interpretations of the Office of Civil Rights and the Office of Special Education Programs within the federal Department of Education.

DISTRICT-LEVEL COMPLIANCE ISSUES

At the District or Institutional level, we suggest inclusion of the following points or concerns in connection with the self audit:

- Has the District adopted a directory information policy, and if so, have parents and eligible students been properly notified and given the opportunity to opt out of the directory information policy?

- In designating directory information, has the District considered each item of information as to whether it is desirable or beneficial to declare this particular information as directory (as opposed to simply copying the list of potential directory information from the Department of Education)?
- If any information beyond that specifically listed in the federal regulations is included as directory at a school, has the District specifically consulted with legal counsel as to the propriety of that designation?
- Has the District also provided parents and eligible students with notice of their FERPA rights and responsibilities (recalling that this notice of rights is required even if the District does not adopt any directory information policy)?
- Has the District provided parents with notice of their rights under the Protection of Pupil Rights Amendment?
- Has the school translated the annual FERPA notice of rights and responsibilities, Directory Information Policy (if there is one), and notice of rights under the PPRA into any foreign languages as may be required under Title VI?
- Has the District thoughtfully defined the scope of school officials with a legitimate educational interest in the annual notice of FERPA rights?
- Review definition of school officials with legitimate educational interest to make certain outside consultants, experts, or service providers who may be necessary to evaluate or serve disable student are included.
- If the District has a law enforcement unit, has this unit been properly identified and designated as a "school official" for purposes of sharing information under FERPA?
- Do law enforcement unit members and school principals understand when records they handle or maintain are properly considered law enforcement unit records (exempt from FERPA), and when these records become educational records subject to FERPA?
- Are individuals who create and maintain personnel files aware of the extent to which FERPA may (or may not) apply to documents submitted by applicants or current employees?
- Does the District have its own consent form to document the consent of parents or eligible students to any disclosure requiring such consent?
- If the District does not have its own consent form, does the District have a checklist to make certain that any consent supplied by a 3rd party includes all the required elements of a valid consent under FERPA?
- Are all student transcripts purged of any reference to a student's disability or special education status, including a disability under Section 504?
- If the District currently has any contract, agreement, memorandum of understanding, or other arrangement which governs the sharing of student level data with outside entities for research purposes, have these contracts, etc. been reviewed for compliance with the current FERPA regulations?

- When otherwise disclosing de-identified student level information, are school officials following the most recent and current guidance from the Department of Education?
- Does the District have any current student record retention and destruction policies? If so, are these policies consistent with IDEA and the guidelines from the Office of Civil Rights?
- Review all instances in which the District is recording or intends to record video images of students (school bus, hallways, parking lots, classrooms) and consider the purpose, actual potential use, and State law; determine whether some, all or none of these videos will be educational records under FERPA or public records under State law.
- Specifically consult State special education rules to determine whether parents or eligible students have been granted (perhaps unintentionally) any additional rights?
- Specifically consult State special education rules to determine whether schools or LEAs have been assigned any additional duties or responsibilities.
- Make certain that central office administrative and support staff responsible for handling special records receive annual training in the access and confidentiality provisions of FERPA and IDEA.
- Consider the District's policy of providing copies to parents or eligible students of educational records upon request, or whether to provide for inspection generally and to copy records only when this is necessary.
- If copies of educational records are routinely provided to parents, consider whether and how much to charge parents or students for these copies, and make certain that this practice is uniformly applied to all parents at all schools in the District.
- Review any use or collection of student social security numbers, and make certain that these SSNs are redacted from any records disclosed to anyone other than a parent or pursuant to one of the non-consensual disclosure provisions.
- Review any Web sites for individual schools to make certain that personally identifiable information about students is not inadvertently disclosed on the Internet (unless a proper parental consent form has been obtained).
- If the District has a student records policy, has this policy been reviewed and updated in accordance with the 2008 regulatory changes, and have school administrators and other school officials been trained as to the changes in the updated policy?
- If the District has a records retention policy, has this policy been reviewed recently and is this policy consistent with actual practice in the District?
- Is each individual school in the District following the records retention policy, especially as related to how long particular student records are maintained and when certain records can be and are being destroyed?

SCHOOL-LEVEL COMPLIANCE ISSUES

In the P-12 setting especially, the collection, handling, and maintenance of student educational records frequently takes place at a number of locations throughout the District. This physical reality itself raises a number of compliance issues which are less likely to be of a policy or system-wide nature per se, but which do place a premium on the level of information and training provided to many different members at the individual school level. Even when parents do not move during the course of their child's education, the natural matriculation of a child from school to school as well as the redrawing of attendance zones in some Districts will often result in parents interacting with a number of schools within the District. When access, confidentiality, or record security (or other issues under FERPA) are handled differently from one school to another within the same District, this can greatly undermine the confidence of parents in the degree of attention and competency of school personnel. In our view, the following points should be included in an audit of school-level FERPA compliance in the District.

- Have all school-level personnel been trained or instructed as to when they may properly (as well as when they may not) access student records under the District's definition of legitimate educational interest?
- To the extent that school volunteers are included within the definition of school officials with a legitimate educational interest, have these volunteers been instructed in the confidentiality aspects of FERPA?
- Are those staff persons most likely and able to exercise supervision of volunteers properly equipped in their own level of understanding to monitor volunteers for FERPA compliance?
- Do all certified or licensed staff understand the FERPA confidentiality issues and requirements, in addition to any unique State ethical rules and regulations related to the maintenance of their certification or license?
- Do all non-certified staff also understand the FERPA confidentiality requirements, and do they appreciate the seriousness of any breach of confidentiality for school-parent relationships?
- Do all school personnel (certified and non-certified) understand that FERPA also governs the oral or verbal disclosure of information contained in an education record, and is not limited to simply sharing copies or providing physical access to student education records?
- When forwarding educational records to another school or school district in which a student is currently enrolled (or is attempting to enroll), do school-level officials understand that consent of the parent or eligible student is NOT required?

- Are school-level officials aware of the provisions under NCLB and IDEA which require certain educational records to be forwarded to a student's new school?
- When intentionally sharing educational records (for example, mailing out report cards) does the School have some process in place to verify the accuracy of the address to which records are sent?
- When individuals visit a school and request access to a student's educational records, are all school office workers (including student workers and substitutes) aware of the protocol of verifying the identity of the individual?
- Are all school level officials aware of the District's protocol for addressing claims by one parent that another parent should not be granted access to a student's educational records?
- Are school-level officials and office workers aware of the basic rights of parents and eligible students to inspect and obtain copies and receive an explanation or interpretation of student records?
- At the school-level, is a list of parents and students who have opted out of directory information policy properly maintained and up to date?
- Do school personnel provide a copy of the directory information policy (if one exists) to parents and eligible students who transfer into the school during the school year, and are any opt out decisions by these persons documented?
- Do school officials know and remember to consult the list of parents and students who have opted out of the directory information policy whenever sharing directory information with outside parties?
- Have the parents of high school juniors and seniors been notified of their option to opt their children out of the NCLB requirement that military recruiters have access to the student's contact information?
- Make certain all IEP team leaders are aware of the requirements for specific parental consent to share information with transition agencies at each meeting to discuss or plan transition services.
- Review the sole possession exception with IEP Team leaders and members so that all school personnel understand when this exception may apply (and when it will not apply).
- Review physical security of student records in general and special education records in particular to make reasonably certain that unauthorized personnel do not have access to educational records about other students.
- Make certain that individuals who handle special education records do receive annual training required under IDEA.
- Do all school-level administrators understand the importance of consistency in handling student records issues in a similar fashion at all schools in the District?

- In connection with the PPRA, has the school identified any covered survey, analysis, or evaluation which will require that parents be notified and given the opportunity to opt out of this event?
- Also in connection with the PPRA, has the school identified any covered survey, analysis, or evaluation which will require that parents specifically consent to their administration?

Conclusion. The Family Educational Rights and Privacy Act is one of the most sweeping federal education statutes enacted, and arguably has more impact on how school officials must conduct themselves on a daily basis than any other federal law. Unlike other statutes which deal only with certain, identified students, FERPA touches upon the conduct of every classroom teacher, teacher's aide, or paraprofessional every single day of the school year. Moreover, the confidentiality provisions of the Act continue to govern the behavior of school officials away from their work, even when school is no longer in session. Parents and students have also internalized a very general expectation of privacy of student information, and while their public perception may not always appreciate the nuances of which records are specifically covered by FERPA, or when a specific, non-consensual disclosure provision may apply, the public expectation of privacy in this regard is such that even an arguable breach of confidentiality can cause long-term damage or loss of confidence in a school or school officials. In some cases, we have even seen this breach of confidentiality serve as the trigger for litigation against the District or school officials personally—even when the primary legal claims eventually filed are not primarily based in FERPA. We sincerely and deeply hope that this work has been and will continue to be of some assistance to the conscientious school official engaged in this very formidable endeavor.

Index of Questions

CHAPTER I INTRODUCTION AND OVERVIEW

CHAPTER II EDUCATIONAL RECORDS: IDENTIFICATION, MAINTENANCE, AND DISCLOSURE

What is the definition of a record under FERPA?

What is the definition of an educational record under FERPA?

Who is a student for purposes of FERPA?

Does FERPA's definition of an educational record mean that any record that includes a student's name falls within FERPA?

What about video records, such as the tapes from school bus or school hallway surveillance cameras, and which include the images of students—are these educational records under FERPA?

What about video tape records of a classroom—are these educational records, and if so, who may be permitted to inspect them?

Are there specific records that are excluded from the definition of educational records under FERPA?

What exactly is a sole possession record?

What is the purpose of the sole possession record exception?

Does this mean that any record about a student which is created and used by one person, and never shared with anyone else, automatically qualifies under this exception?

Do sole possession records lose their status if they are shared with anyone other than a "temporary substitute for the maker"?

May sole possession records be subpoenaed by parents or other parties involved in litigation?

What is a law enforcement unit (or "LEU")?

CHAPTER III RIGHTS OF PARENTS AND (ELIGIBLE) STUDENTS

CHAPTER IV INTERNAL DISCLOSURES WITHOUT CONSENT

CHAPTER V DIRECTORY INFORMATION

CHAPTER VI DISCLOSURE TO OUTSIDE PARTIES WITHOUT CONSENT

Are there specific record-keeping requirements uniquely associated with the use and determination of the health or safety emergency exception?

Under what conditions may an educational entity report suspected abuse or neglect to a state agency tasked with investigating the same?

What about requests for information about a child who has previously been referred to protective services—is an institution permitted to continue to make these disclosures under FERPA?

What about reports relating not to the physical or sexual abuse of a child, but reports or referrals that a child may be neglected by their parent or guardian—do these fall within the scope of FERPA health or safety emergency exception?

May educational records be disclosed to a student's parent(s) after he or she reaches the age of 18 or enrolls in post-secondary education?

Does the fact that a parent pays all or part of student's tuition and other expenses while the student is enrolled in a post-secondary institution entitle them to inspect their child's education records?

May a post-secondary institution require students who are not dependents to execute a release of their educational records to their parents?

In the case of parents who are separated or divorced, does that mean that only the parent who claims the students as a dependent on their tax return that year may receive information from their child's education record?

What information may the college or university disclose to parents of a dependent student?

Do parents of dependent student continue to hold additional FERPA rights, such as the right to seek a hearing regarding the accuracy of information contained within such records?

Does FERPA give parents of dependent students the right to discuss their child's education with the faculty or staff of a post-secondary institution?

Is there any information contained with a student's educational records which the post-secondary institution is prohibited from sharing with the parent of a dependent student?

Does this mean that parents of dependent students have a FERPA right of access to this information?

Are there any other instances (beyond the tax dependent eligible student) where information may be disclosed to parents of a student 18 years old or older?

CHAPTER VII ELECTRONIC RECORDS

CHAPTER VIII SPECIAL EDUCATION RECORDS

CHAPTER IX PROTECTION OF PUPIL RIGHTS AMENDMENT

About the Authors

Daniel R. Murphy is a partner in the education law firm of McLocklin & Murphy in Winder, Georgia, where he serves as General Counsel to the Georgia Association of School Business Officials and the Georgia School Finance Association. In addition to his law practice, Dan is also the president and founder of the Center for School Law & Policy (www.cslap.org). Murphey is a frequent and requested presenter across the southeastern United States on all manner of education law issues, as well as the American Association of School Personnel Administrators (AASPA) at numerous national conferences. He is the co-author of the *The Fair Labor Standards Act in American Public Schools* and the *American Association of School Personnel Administrator's Family & Medical Leave Act Compliance Manual*, the author of the *2009 AASPA FMLA Supplement*, and the forthcoming *Discipline and the Disabled Student* (Rowman & Littlefield Education, 2010).

Mike L. Dishman is an attorney whose practice has centered upon the representation of public schools for more than a decade. Concurrently an associate professor of educational leadership at Kennesaw State University and of counsel to Brock, Clay, Calhoun & Rogers, L.L.C., Dishman writes on law, leadership and policy in education. He is the co-author of multiple books and articles, the most recent of which is *Leading Schools During Crisis* (Rowman & Littlefield Education, 2009). He holds a J.D. from the University of Mississippi (1996) and an Ed.D. in Leadership and Policy from Vanderbilt University (2007). He serves on the editorial board of the *Peabody Journal of Education* and the publications review board of the American Association of School Administrators.